She was cred<br>
of them destroyers.

Her captain, Sam Dealey, devoted son and loving husband and father, was a product of peace.

Sam Dealey, deadly torpedo marksman and destroyer killer, was a product of war.

Aboard the *Harder* there was no time for gloating over her victories. Dealey himself never gloated. As we have said, his attack manners were calm. He indulged in no shouting, no fanfare of destruction. After his torpedoes hit, he went about the business of bringing his ship into a postion of safety as rapidly as possible. He did not linger to rejoice at the sight of an enemy going down. In his veins ran the milk of human kindness, in his heart was a feeling of humility and humanity that could not find pleasure in the destruction of a beautiful ship and a hundred odd human beings—deadly enemies though they were.

Perhaps he remembered the worlds of Captain Philip of the old battleship *Texas* at the Battle of Santiago, who called to his cheering crew as their Spanish adversary sank: "Don't cheer, boys; those poor devils are dying." While Dealey never said so, in so many words, one could conclude that he hated the job of killing but knew it had to be done and did his best to carry out his duty.

# THROUGH HELL AND DEEP WATER

Charles A. Lockwood,
Vice Admiral, USN, ret.
and
Hans Christian Adamson,
Colonel, USAF, ret.

BANTAM BOOKS
NEW YORK · TORONTO · LONDON · SYDNEY · AUCKLAND

*This edition contains the complete text
of the original hardcover edition.*
NOT ONE WORD HAS BEEN OMITTED.

THROUGH HELL AND DEEP WATER

*A Bantam Falcon Book / published by arrangement with
Greenburg Publisher*

*PRINTING HISTORY*
*Greenburg edition published 1956*

*Bantam edition / September 1991*

*FALCON and the portrayal of a boxed "f" are trademarks of
Bantam Books, a division of Bantam Doubleday Dell Publishing Group, Inc.*

*All rights reserved.*
*Copyright © 1991 by Charles A. Lockwood and Hans Christian Adamson.*
*Cover art copyright © by Paul Sample: 'Cruise Quarters Aboard
Pacific Submarine,' 1943 Courtesy of Defense Audio Visual Agency.*
*No part of this book may be reproduced or transmitted
in any form or by any means, electronic or mechanical,
including photocopying, recording, or by any information
storage and retrieval system, without permission in
writing from the publisher.*
*For information address: Bantam Books.*

ISBN 0-553-29178-5

*Published simultaneously in the United States and Canada*

*Bantam Books are published by Bantam Books, a division of Bantam
Doubleday Dell Publishing Group, Inc. Its trademark, consisting of the
words "Bantam Books" and the portrayal of a rooster, is Registered in
U.S. Patent and Trademark Office and in other countries. Marca
Registrada. Bantam Books, 666 Fifth Avenue, New York, New York 10103.*

PRINTED IN THE UNITED STATES OF AMERICA

OPM    0  9  8  7  6  5  4  3  2  1

## Dedication

To All Men
Of All Ranks and Ratings
Who Served aboard the
United States Submarine
HARDER
May This Book
Pass the Word
Which Our Nation Has Passed:
"WELL DONE"

★★★★★★★★★★★★★★★★★★★★★★★★★★★★★★★★★★★★★★★★★★★★★★★★

# Acknowledgments

The authors proudly acknowledge, in the preparation of this volume, the invaluable assistance of the United States Navy and of dozens of officers and enlisted men—Regulars and Reserves—who served in World War II. The first-hand accounts and personal anecdotes of men "who were there" have made the difference between a mass of statistics and what is, we hope, an alive, human document. The eagerness to assist and the spirit of comradeship which they have displayed are typical and worthy of that service in which we all have the greatest pride.

The contributions of Sam Dealey's mother, Mrs. Virgie Dealey, his wife, Edwina Vawter Dealey, his brothers, George William and Jerome K., his sisters, Mrs. Ethel Dealey Jones and Mrs. Margaret Dealey Royal, with other immediate relatives, have been open-handed and open-hearted. Priceless mementos, photographs, documents, and personal letters have been made available without reserve. This also has been true with respect to next of kin and former shipmates of the *Harder's* complement.

Mr. Fletcher Pratt and the Naval Institute kindly gave us permission to reprint portions of an article called "Two Little Ships" (Copyright 1947 by the U.S. Naval Institute).

Permission to use some inspiring lines of "Annapolis"— author unknown—was granted by The Trident Literary Society, U.S. Naval Academy (Copyrighted 1936).

We appreciate, also, permission from Joseph F. Jones,

ex-submarine *BASHAW*, now Chief Yeoman in the *Orion*, to use two excellent verses from his poem "Submarine."

Last but not least, our thanks are given to Major Bill Jinkins, A.I.F., for his keen interest, for many photographs, and for his stirring account of the Borneo coastwatcher pick-up.

In the preparation of a volume of this nature—research for which has covered many months—reams of correspondence have been exchanged with men and women who gave generously of their time and recollections. It is impossible to acknowledge each individually, but to all go our thanks. We only hope that we have done justice to the material supplied—and to the *Harder*.

Charles A. Lockwood
Hans Christian Adamson

★★★★★★★★★★★★★★★★★★★★★★★★★★★★★★★★★★★★★★★★★★★★★★★★

# Contents

# THROUGH HELL
# AND DEEP WATER

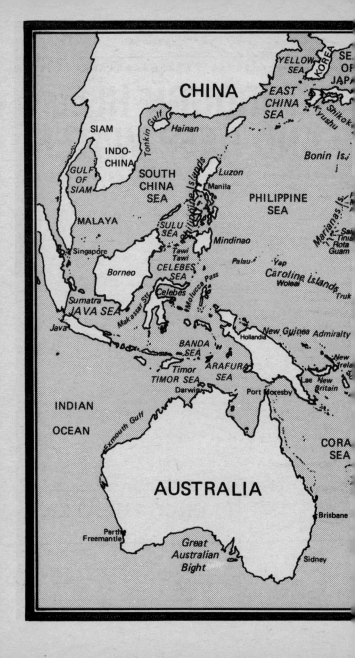

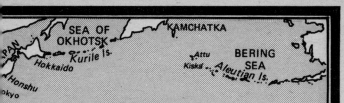

SEA OF
OKHOTSK
KAMCHATKA

JAPAN
Kurile Is.
Hokkaido
Attu
Kiska
Aleutian Is.
BERING
SEA

Honshu
Tokyo

NORTH PACIFIC
OCEAN

Marcus

Midway

Wake

Hawaiian Islands

Eniwetok

Kwajalein

Wotje

Johnston

Marshall Is.
Majuro

Jaluit
Mili

Makin

Tarawa
Apamama

Gilbert Islands

Santa Cruz
Islands

New Hebrides

Loyalty Is.
Fiji Is.

## PACIFIC THEATER

Nautical miles

| 0 | | 600 | | 1200 | | 1800 |

NEW
ZEALAND

In the acrid breath of the engine room
Where the diesels throb all day;
Where you feel the chill of the deep sea gloom
Through the plates so wet and gray;
In the life you crave with a fierce desire
Where your senses are keen and alive;
Where you suddenly feel your pulse beat higher
At the squawk-box command: "Dive, dive!"

★★★★★★★★★★★★★★★★★★★★★★★★★★★★★★★★★★★★★★★★★★★★ 1

# Men at Work

"Contact! Radar contact, sir. Range one eight thousand; bearing three five zero. Looks like five ships—three big ones, two escorts."

"Aye, aye," acknowledged Machinist Carl Finney, the Officer-of-the-Deck. "Call the Captain."

"Captain to the bridge, Captain to the bridge," rasped out the squawk boxes. The raucous call had barely died away when up from the control room into the conning tower came the Captain, Comdr. Samuel David Dealey, of Dallas, Texas. Sam's crew, who swore by him in many things, also swore that he was the fastest man in the U.S. Navy up and down a submarine's vertical steel ladders—a result perhaps of footwork learned during years of amateur boxing at the Naval Academy.

Just where he got the keen, gold-flecked brown eyes with which he now surveyed the situation in the conning tower, they did not know, but each of them had plenty of occasion to thank God for Sam Dealey's sharpshooting eyes and the lightning-fast brain behind them. A rapid glance at the radar screen and then a quiet command in the pleasant Southern drawl his men loved to hear: "All ahead, flank. Bring her left to course two seven zero."

"All ahead, flank, sir; left to course two seven zero," repeated the steersman.

"Station the tracking party," continued Dealey.

"Tracking party to the conning tower," rasped out the squawk boxes.

"Give me the target's approximate course and speed soon as you can, Frank," he directed, as the Executive Officer, Lieut. Comdr. Frank C. "Tiny" Lynch, came scrambling up the ladder from the control room.

"Aye, aye, sir," acknowledged Frank, ducking past the periscopes to the plotting board. Tiny's six-foot three-inch height, with a build to match it, was always a handicap to him in the confined spaces of a submarine but he never let it interfere with his job.

Even the dim red lights of the conning tower could not conceal the excitement in his sun-browned face as Sam turned and disappeared up the ladder to the bridge.

The chase was on. Armed enemy tankers and destroyers were out there in the darkness of the tropical night. Undoubtedly they were headed for the oil docks of Tarakan to obtain vitally needed supplies of fuel for the Japanese fleet. It was the *Harder's* job to stop them. Her torpedoes lay ready in the tubes awaiting the thud of the firing impulse.

At 1930 (7:30 P.M.) of 6 June 1944, Comdr. Dealey with his United States Submarine *Harder* had been headed for Sibutu Passage—the narrow strait which separates the northeast corner of Borneo from Tawi Tawi, the southernmost group of the Philippine Archipelago. His ship, commissioned in December of 1942, was already a veteran on her fifth war patrol. Most of her officers and enlisted men had been with her since the beginning of her career. One of her missions—highly secret—was to rescue a group of desperate British and Australian coast watchers from the jungles of North Borneo—a mission which two other submarines had failed to complete. One had narrowly escaped losing her landing party.

That mission would have to wait. Damage to the enemy takes precedence.

The moon was full, brilliant, and climbing higher toward the zenith as the approach proceeded. True, there were intermittent, low cumulus clouds but this attack would have to be run very, very carefully to avoid detection. Radar depth at first (submerged to about 42 feet where the radar antenna would still be above water) and then full periscope depth might do the trick.

Dealey planned to dive ahead of the target group and bore in to a position halfway between the port flank escort and the column of tankers. The enemy's base course, at first, plotted as 180 true with 30 degree zigs right and left at a speed of 14–15 knots, but as soon as he cleared Sibutu Passage the base course was changed to 240 true—straight for the entrance of Tarakan harbor, some 130 nautical miles ahead.

Dealey worked his speed up to 19 knots in a desperate attempt to pull ahead and still keep out of the range of observation of enemy lookouts.

Alas, for the best laid plans, at 2125 the moon broke through and flood-lighted the submarine. The nearest escort destroyer, some 12,000 yards away, sighted the *Harder*.

"It was immediately apparent," reads Dealey's log, "that he was headed hell-bent for the *Harder*, smoking heavily and showing a prominent bow wave. We turned tail toward the destroyer, made flank speed, and hoped that the Jap would get discouraged and return to his convoy, but he had other intentions (none of the friendly variety). His speed increased to 24 knots and the range was gradually whittled down to 9000 yards as he followed down our wake. (At 19 knots we left a wake that looked like a broad avenue for five miles astern.)

"It was painfully evident that our business with the convoy would have to wait until the destroyer was taken care of."

As the range to the pursuing destroyer shortened, Sam, expecting every moment to see the deadly orange flashes of gunfire erupt from her forward guns, quietly said to the O.O.D., (Officer of the Deck), "Sound battle stations. Stand by to dive. Lookouts below."

Hardly had the musical, blood stirring bong, bong, bong of the general alarm died away when he gave the order:

"Clear the bridge. Sound the diving alarm. Take her to periscope depth."

As the bridge personnel scrambled below, the O.O.D. jammed the handle of the diving alarm twice against its stop and shouted, "Dive, dive. Take her to periscope depth," into the 1 MC—the bridge microphone.

The raucous, demanding "Ahgoowa, ahgoowa" of the diving klaxon rasped through the compartments; ship control men, already at their stations, deftly opened flood and vent valves; set the bow and stern planes to take her down fast. Vents spouted like a school of whales, the ship pointed sharply downward and the rushing seas rose over the hull. Meanwhile, with swift practiced movements, the engine and maneuvering room crews secured the diesel engines and shifted propulsion to full speed on the electric motors.

Comdr. Dealey, the last man to leave the bridge, yanked down on the wire lanyard to latch the conning tower hatch. As it slammed shut on its seat, the quartermaster was instantly beside him and spun the hand wheel which dogged it shut.

"Hatch secured," he reported.

The entire operation, which required perhaps one minute, had been without hitch or confusion. Whatever may have been the thoughts or blood pressure of these eight or ten men in the conning tower, no sign, except perhaps brightened eyes and a touch of excitement in whispered words, indicated any difference between this and a hundred other dives they had made in months gone by.

"Left full rudder," ordered the Skipper. "Course zero nine zero. All ahead one third. Make ready all tubes."

"Make ready all tubes," repeated the ship's Talker into his microphone. Tall, stalwart pharmacist's Mate Angelo Locoscio, in undershirt and dungaree trousers, had been chosen for the job of Talker because of his good speaking voice and quick-thinking ability. Too, the demands for his medical services during combat were not likely to be heavy. In submarine warfare, all hands usually come back with whole skins—or they don't come back at all. Tonight, it could be the latter. Destroyers are not recommended targets for submarines. Their high speed and maneuverability make them difficult to hit and, in the event of a miss, vengeance from their 600-pound depth charges could be swift and final. Despite this dread possibility, officers and men went about their duties without fumbling or nervousness. Skill and assurance marked every action. Here and there possibly a wide-eyed newcomer gazed at the faces of the old-timers as though searching for a panacea to quiet the butterflies in his stomach. But, all in all, the atmosphere of the ship was one of confidence—confidence radiating from the Skipper. All hands knew they were watching an expert at work. This was a situation made to order for Sam Dealey and his crew.

"All tubes are ready, sir," reported the TDC (Torpedo Data Computer) officer, Lieut. Tom Buckner.

"Up periscope," ordered Sam; "stand by after tubes."

For the first time that night a look of grim determination came into his face. He had slowed the submarine's speed to 3 knots in order to allow the pursuer to catch up and also to reduce the telltale periscope "feather" to a minimum. Now, as he watched through the periscope with cautious 5- or 6-second exposures, he saw his enemy coming right down the *Harder's* old course at 23 knots, presenting a very easy fire control problem.

At 2159, with a range of 1050 yards, torpedoes set to run at 6-foot depth and with gyros on zero, the skipper gave the order: "Fire!"

The quartermaster at the firing panel slammed the silver-dollar-sized firing button for Tube Number 7; waited 8 seconds by the stop watch held in the palm of his left hand; slammed Tube Number 8; waited 8 seconds more; slammed Tube Number 9. Then he checked fire. Dealey figured three would be enough.

Meanwhile the Talker repeated back the reports from the after torpedo room: "Number Seven fired; Number Eight fired," and so on.

The sonarman, ear phones clamped to his head, also had reports to make as he crouched before his 'scope: "Seven running, sir; Eight running; Nine running. Hot, straight, and normal!"—music to any torpedoman's ears.

The torpedoes, each with a 750-pound load of Torpex, our latest high explosive, in its warhead, sped on with their freight of death and destruction.

Sam, eye glued to the periscope, saw the first torpedo hit just forward of the MOT (middle of the target). The second hit farther aft, and the run of the third was not observed. The target was immediately enveloped in flames and smoke, the tail rose straight in the air and half a dozen of his depth charges started going off.

"2203—Surfaced 1000 yards away," records the *Harder's* patrol log, "watched the destroyer go under, and headed back toward the spot where it had been. A lone life buoy burned over a large oil slick—but there was no ship and there were no survivors to be seen."

The last moments of the Jap DD were observed through the periscope or from the bridge by the Skipper, most of the fire control party, the bridge lookouts, and Capt. Murray J. "Tich" Tichenor. The last named was Operations Officer for Comsub's Seventh Fleet, commanded by Rear Admiral Ralph W. Christie, and was aboard the *Harder* just for the ride.

There could be no doubt about it, one enemy destroyer and her crew of perhaps 150 souls had gone to Davy Jones' Locker. As Sam and Murray Tichenor stood at the bridge rail watching the lonesome buoy light, Dealey said very little save to give orders to resume the chase. He was not exultant about his victory. Evidently the thought of having destroyed fellow human beings saddened him even though it was his life against theirs. Or was he thinking of Tex Edwards, his ideal throughout his early years, who had gone down in the same way in the Atlantic with his ship, the four-stack destroyer *Reuben James*.

But there was little time for introspection. Those three tankers were still on their way to the oil docks. All four of the *Harder's* main engines were put on the line at full speed. Because of the loss of time incident to sinking the Jap DD, it was now an even more desperate race to see who would reach Tarakan first.

As the diesels roared into action, Sam turned to Frank

U.S.S. Reuben James

Lynch. "Secure from battle stations, Frank," he drawled. "Let the off duty hands get some sleep."

Fate and the Imperial Japanese Navy, however, decreed otherwise. Just two minutes later, at 2217, the radar operator picked up another ship contact at 14,000 yards, evidently a destroyer moving at high speed and headed directly for the *Harder*.

Again the bong, bong, bong of "Battle Stations" was followed by "Dive, dive," and the submarine slid down to radar depth so as to track her opponent more accurately. If this DD was looking for trouble, Dealey was in the mood to give it and, instead of turning away, he headed for the destroyer.

When the range had closed to 8000 yards, Sam increased submergence to periscope depth. However, he had difficulty in obtaining good periscope ranges because the intermittent moonlight did not illuminate the target well enough.

"At 2242," reads the *Harder's* log, "with an estimated range of 1250 yards, with 80 degrees port track angle and target speed of 12 knots, fired 6 bow tube shots with torpedoes set at 6 feet and diverging spread.

"Both range and estimated target speed are believed to have been in error, though 'sound' reported the first two shots running erratic. All torpedoes missed as target made a figure S while combing their tracks. The destroyer turned and headed for the *Harder*. Rigged for silent running, depth charging, and went to 300 feet. Five depth charges exploded as we reached depth."

The enemy's counterattack was not too severe, but a personnel casualty—one caused by an error of a new stern planesman—nearly brought a tragic ending to the *Harder's* triumph. This youngster, whom Dealey with characteristic consideration does not name, observing the plane indicator inoperative—the interior communication (I.C.) circuit had been cut out for silent running—thought he had lost power on the planes and made a quick shift to hand operation. Then he wrongly put the planes on dive instead of rise as the submarine passed 300 feet. Controlling the planes by hand is slow and before the Diving Officer realized the lad's mistake, the ship took a 15-degree down angle and went to a dangerous depth, well beyond that for which she was designed. All available men were rushed from forward to aft to right the ship. The pandemonium which resulted can well be imagined. The rushing of alarmed men through the control room, the crashing of loose gear, and the noise of hard-soled shoes clattering on the steel decks might have shaken the nerve and stampeded the thinking of the most rugged submariners—but not Sam Dealey and the Diving Officer, Sam Logan. They did not stampede easily and their quick thinking and quick orders undoubtedly saved the *Harder* from sharing the watery grave of the Japanese destroyer she had just sunk.

Before the men could be gotten forward again, the *Harder* took a 15-degree up angle and shot up to 250 feet.

Suddenly, over the ship's intercom came a frightened voice: "Hot run in Number 9 Tube."

Frank Lynch and Tom Buckner took off like broken field runners for the after torpedo room. A hot run in a tube can be extremely dangerous.

When the *Harder* took this sudden rise angle, her tail was flung sharply down and the stop bolt in Number 9 tube had carried away. This permitted its torpedo to slide downward past the tripping latch, thus starting the electric propelling motor. Fortunately, this was a Mark 18 electric "fish," a missile that runs at a lower rate of speed than the so-called steam torpedo. The latter high-speed type creates terrific heat which might fuse the steel shell of the torpedo to the inside of the tube. The truly terrifying thing about such a casualty is the haunting fear that the warhead might be detonated. So far as is known, that tragedy has never happened.

The *Harder's* torpedo eventually ran its batteries down, but the piercing scream of its racing propellers sent plenty of chills up and down the spines of the after torpedo room personnel.

"This whole incident," wrote Sam in his log, "was a personnel casualty which never should have occurred but, considering the noise and concussion of the depth charging at the moment, the Commanding Officer considers that the officers and crew—consisting in part of 20 men on their first cruise—acted with admirable courage and calmness. It is described in detail in the hope that it may help some other sub to avoid a similar experience."

Depth charging continued until midnight and evasive maneuvers opened the submarine out from her attacker. Welcome negative gradients were found on the bathythermograph at 150 feet and 280 feet and these were utilized to lose the destroyer.

Negative gradients are layers of colder water which give good protection to a submarine because they deflect the echo-ranging pings of the pursuing destroyers. Dealey's standard procedure for shaking off a DD was to "keep the guy astern, go deep, and be patient," as he expressed it. This plan had much to recommend it, for, by keeping the stern of the *Harder* toward her pursuer, the smallest target was presented and the "pings" of the searching

U.S.S. Harder

vessel might be rendered inaccurate by the disturbed water of the submarine's wake current.

When the *Harder* finally surfaced at 0036 of 7 June there was no hope of beating the tankers to Tarakan, so Sam again set a course for Sibutu Passage and his secret mission.

At 0528, with day breaking and enemy airfields too close for comfort, the *Harder* submerged but had a slight misadventure with a reef and was forced to blow ballast tanks, surface, and back clear. Miraculously, none of her delicate sound heads and depth-finding gear were damaged. Fortunately, too, no planes were about, and Navigator Frank Lynch was able to obtain a navigational fix which showed the sub to be far to southwestward of its dead-reckoning position. The 2- to 4-knot current—its

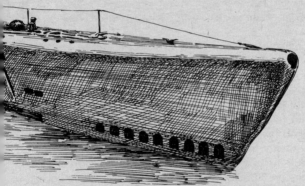

direction governed by the flood and ebb tides—which sweeps through Sibutu probably accounted for that.

The *Harder's* adventures for the day were only just beginning, however. She attempted to make use of a rain squall to cover her surface run northward in order to gain more distance toward her objective. This attempt was thwarted in mid-morning by a plane which chased her down but dropped no bombs.

After that she remained submerged and bucked the heavy current with a paltry 5 knots.

"At 1134," continues the log, "the periscope watch sighted a Fubuki type destroyer at a range of 4000 yards, angle on the bow 20 port. (It might have been summoned by the plane or it might have been sent out to avenge the loss of a sister ship the night before.) Sounded battle stations and headed for target."

There was nothing hesitant about the way Sam Dealey handled the situation. Only two months before, in April, Cominch (Commander-in-Chief U.S. Fleet) Fleet Adm. E. J. King had raised the priority of destroyers as torpedo targets to a position above cargo ships. Prior to that time, because of the scarcity of torpedoes, the doctrine had been to avoid enemy destroyers. Now that torpedoes were more plentiful—and fleet engagements imminent—Cominch was eager to cripple the enemy fleet. The torpedoes of Japanese destroyers were very formidable, long-range weapons which had wrought havoc among our ships in the Solomons Campaign. Adm. King wanted that menace removed.

To Sam Dealey this expressed desire was an order—one which he was glad to obey. He remembered the *Reuben James*.

"At 3000 yards," wrote Dealey, "the destroyer headed directly at us. (He may have sighted our periscope.) Stood by with four tubes ready forward, to fire down his throat. Angle on bow changed from zero to 10 degrees starboard, then quickly back to 15 degrees port. He was using a fast constant helm (a type of zigzag). At 650 yards, with 20 degrees port track, gyros on zero and a torpedo spread of 1/4 a degree, commenced firing just as target started swinging back. Fired one- two- three in rapid succession (about 5 seconds interval). Number Four wasn't necessary! Fifteen seconds after the first shot was fired, it struck the destroyer squarely amidships. Number Two hit just aft. Number Three missed ahead. Ordered right full rudder and ahead full to get clear of the destroyer. At range of 300 yards we were rocked by a terrific explosion believed to have been the destroyer's magazine. Less than one minute after the first hit, and nine minutes after it was sighted, the destroyer sank tail first, observed by the Commanding Officer, the Executive Officer, and Captain Tichenor."

As Murray Tichenor, eye glued to the periscope was

saying, "Scratch destroyer number two," the sonar man sang out: "Contact, Captain. Fast screws. Bearing zero nine zero."

Tichenor jumped back from the periscope. Dealey seized the training handles and swung it to starboard, took a quick look and then: "Down 'scope. All ahead full. Take her down fast. Three hundred feet. Rig for depth charge. Rig for silent running."

The Talker relayed the orders via the squawk boxes and the sound of closing watertight doors and ventilation flappers could be heard throughout the ship. Ventilation motors and all others not vitally needed were stopped. Some men wearing hard-soled shoes removed them. Some shifted into sneakers. Unconsciously the pitch of voices dropped.

The *Harder*, slanting sharply downward, had almost reached her depth. Dealey turned to the Exec. "Frank," he said, "slow to creeping speed and bring that destroyer astern. Secure from battle stations. I'm going to catch forty winks."

"Aye, aye, sir," said Lynch, but before Dealey could reach his cabin, a pattern of five depth charges landed above them. The noise and concussion were terrific. The submarine was thrown about like a toy boat on the waves. Cork rained from the overhead; locker doors flew open; light bulbs popped; loose gear was flung everywhere.

There would be no "forty winks" for Dealey.

"All compartments report damage," called Lynch into the mike. And to Sam Logan, the Diving Officer: "Bring her back to 300 feet."

The terrific pressure had driven the ship down about 100 feet.

One by one, from forward to aft, the compartments reported no serious damage. The damage control detail was called to effect various repairs while the spare hands were attempting to bring order out of the shambles of the control room, when its forward watertight door opened and in stepped a tall Australian officer in short-sleeved shirt and khaki shorts. His uniform was immaculate, his high peaked cap sat his head at a jaunty angle; from mustache to shiny boots he might have stepped right out of Sandhurst. In him you saw the pukka British officer who led his troops across No Man's Land in World War I, swinging his walking stick and looking bored at Death.

"I say, Captain," said he in a perfect Piccadilly accent, "what's all the shooting about?"

"Oh," drawled Sam, "it's just some of your Jap friends, Major, having a bit of sport. They evidently don't want us to pick up your gang of saboteurs in North Borneo."

"Damned rude of them," muttered the Aussie, tugging at his mustache.

Thus did Major William L. "Bill" Jinkins, Australian Imperial Forces, cloak and dagger man par excellence, get his first real baptism of depth charges.

"Well, don't be discouraged," said Sam, "with luck we should get through this damned strait tonight."

The enemy counterattack lasted for two hours, during which seventeen depth charges and a number of lesser charges—probably ahead-thrown projectiles similar to our "mouse traps"—were dropped. Only superficial damage was done and nerves a bit jangled.

The *Harder* slipped away southward under a protective "layer" at 300 feet and at 1550 was able to return to periscope depth. Immediately two Fubuki-type destroyers were sighted and warhorse Dealey promptly sounded battle stations, submerged, and commenced an approach on them. However, at a range of 4000 yards the destroyers reversed course and disappeared.

Things were looking more and more ominous for the *Harder*. Echo-ranging was heard from several different bearings. The destroyers were obviously looking for her. First, two were sighted, then three. One of the latter detachment was equipped with a "bedspring"-type radar on her foremast, so that even night surface running was going to be hazardous. And maybe they had radar-equipped night flying planes. Two medium bombers had been sighted during the afternoon and one of them had dropped two bombs, although not very close. Despite all her crawling to northward, the *Harder* was still about where she had started some twelve hours before.

And the plight of Major Jinkins' coast-watcher saboteurs was desperate.

At 1725 Dealey again sounded battle stations as he began an approach upon the group of three destroyers which were apparently patrolling in the area of his last attack. However, these too reversed course and the opportunity was lost.

Nevertheless, in spite of all these signs of a concentration designed to end the *Harder's* career, when, at 1840 six DD's in line of bearing were sighted heading for her position, it required all of the persuasive powers of Frank Lynch to convince Sam that discretion would be the better part of valor. Dealey evidently depended upon the judgment of his man-mountain Exec. to restrain the vein of recklessness which he undoubtedly knew ran through his body.

Of this incident Sam wrote in his patrol log: "Looks as though the *Harder* has worn out its welcome here. We felt as if we had a monopoly on the whole Pacific War this date. (Such popularity must be preserved.)

"Made a quick review of the whole picture and decided that discretion here was definitely the better part of valor. The battery was low, air in the boat was none too good, the crew was fatigued, and our navigational position in a narrow strait, with strong and variable currents, was not well known. I really believe that we might have gotten one or two more of the enemy ships, but under the above listed conditions, a persistent and already humiliated enemy (after two sinkings within 24 hours and just off a fleet base) would probably have developed an attack from which the *Harder* might not have pulled through. No apologies are made for my withdrawal. The gamble would have been made at too great a risk.

"Commenced evading to the northward in an effort to lose the destroyers and get on with our assigned task."

Well after the tropic night had fallen, the *Harder* surfaced with the destroyer patrol some ten miles to southward of her, and headed north with two of her four diesels on propulsion and the other two "jamming juice" into the depleted storage battery, or "can," as it was generally called.

The ship's radar screen was purposely kept trained away from the destroyers lest they have the recently developed German radar detector which would warn them of the submarine's position. All lookouts were utilized to watch for night fliers. The moon was full and brilliant.

Suddenly at 2206, radar contact was made on a small object dead ahead at 1500 yards. "It was immediately sighted from the bridge," records the *Harder's* log, "and at first believed to be a small boat. At 1200 yards it was discovered to be a low pinnacle sticking straight up out of the sea, with white foam breaking around it. Ordered full right rudder and came within 400 yards of grounding on this pinnacle as we reversed course. Special credit is due to Wilbur Lee Clark, RT2c, USNR, for his alert watchstanding which undoubtedly prevented a grounding which might well have been disastrous. Headed to the eastward while navigator again took star sights and checked our position.

**Fabuki-type Destroyer**

"Radar now made contact on Sibutu Island light and correct position was established."

Captain Murray Tichenor also was credited with an assist in picking up this pinnacle that was part of the same reef on which the *Harder* had grounded at 0730 this same day. In fourteen and a half hours she had advanced exactly zero miles toward her rendezvous with Major Jinkins' cloak and dagger boys.

However, the thought of two enemy destroyers in their bag—two Rising Sun flags to be added to the rainbow they would fly on returning to port—served as some compensation for loss of sleep and wear and tear on nerves to which those aboard the *Harder* had been subjected for the last twenty-four hours.

The next morning, through the periscope, they sighted the northeast tip of Borneo slowly slipping by. They had won the Battle of Sibutu Passage. The rendezvous could be reached by nightfall.

# *Harder* Beats the Mangrove Bushes

The situation into which, on June 8, the *Harder* was projecting herself was one fraught with great danger and difficulty. Other submarines had failed in this same mission, and now the lives of six hunted allied agents were at stake.

In the Southwest Pacific Area, probably the most rugged and daring type of mission in World War II was called coast-watching. It sounds very innocuous and might bring to mind visions of gay beach umbrellas, white sands, foaming surf, and pretty girls, Bikini-clad. However, as the term was employed in Australia, coast-watching referred to spotting the movements of enemy ships and forces and reporting them to headquarters in Melbourne or to Allied submarines in adjacent waters.

The players in this dangerous game were usually Australians—with a sprinkling of British, Americans, and natives of the South Pacific or East Indian islands. Scores of these men—frequently former residents of the areas to be watched—after intensive training in the Intelligence Schools of the Australian Imperial Forces, were landed from submarines with utmost secrecy in the dead of night, via rubber boats, on the beaches of enemy-held territory—usually islands but sometimes the mainland of Asia.

There, equipped with a portable, two-way radio, they

set up shop. They were on their own from the moment they landed, unable to trust anyone, vulnerable to exposure by disloyal or traitorous natives who were tempted by the price set upon the heads of these white men. Hunted by the enemy with planes, bloodhounds, and native trackers, many left their bones in tropical swamps and jungles— victims of disease and undernourishment. Others finished the war in prison camps, but most of those captured felt the bite of the executioner's sword. Miraculously, some of these unsung heroes of the Allied intelligence services survived their assignments and rendered superlative assistance to their comrades in arms and to their homelands.

Coast-watching was not a job for the faint-hearted or those too greatly dependent upon creature comforts. It was a job which, as our Marines would say, separates the men from the boys.*

In May, 1943, it was decided by the Australian G.H.Q. to put a party of coast-watchers into the British North Borneo Area for the purpose of contacting local natives and securing intelligence regarding enemy activities, installations, and movements; and preparing the ground work for a campaign of sabotage and underground resistance when the time became opportune.

Major F. G. L. "Gort" Chester, who had been a resident in British North Borneo for twenty years prior to the war and had an extensive knowledge of the country, and who was known personally to many of the leading natives and Chinese, was selected as leader of the party. He was instructed to draw up plans for this operation and to select personnel.

After an extended course of training in Brisbane, the party, consisting of four officers and two sergeants, was flown to Western Australia and embarked in U.S. Submarine *Kingfish*, Comdr. V. L. "Rebel" Lowrance, of Catawba,

---

*For the full story of these gallant men read THE COAST WATCHERS by Commander Eric A. Feldt, R.A.N. Another volume in the Bantam War Book Series.

North Carolina. They carried stores sufficient to make them self-supporting for four months. On 6 October 1943, without incident, the *Kingfish* landed them on the swampy east coast of Borneo in the vicinity of Labian Point. Their hand-powered radio set was established in a hilly area back from the beach and made contact with Australia on 7 October. Their station was quickly put into business and supplied valuable information by reporting ship movements in Sibutu Passage for a considerable period.

In December, 1943, it was decided to reinforce the party, and six more agents, with Major W. L. "Bill" Jinkins, Australian Imperial Forces, in charge, were landed, with stores, from the submarine *Tinosa*, Comdr. D. F. Weiss, a Massachusetts lad, on 20 January 1944.

The expedition achieved some success in the matter of sabotage and in making contact with a resistance force of Chinese operating on the west coast of Borneo. However, sickness and Japanese counter measures soon took their toll.

On March 5, three officers, including Major Jinkins, were evacuated to Australia by the submarine *Narwhal*, Comdr. F. D. Latta of Burlington, Iowa.

As enemy counter-intelligence operations increased, those remaining in North Borneo under command of Major "Gort" Chester were sore beset. Their camp had to be moved several times; Sergeant W. Brandis, as it was later learned, had been betrayed by a local native headman and handed over to the Japs, while Lieut. A. J. Rudwick and Sgt. D. G. McKenzie were captured in an ambush. Soon it became obvious that these agents were too harried and harassed to perform any useful service; hence it was decided to evacuate the whole party. This was easier said than done. The first attempt, made in April, 1944, was unsuccessful; contact was not established.

The next attempt, made on 22 April by the *Redfin*, Comdr. M. H. "Cy" Austin of Aetus, Oklahoma, nearly ended in disaster when the submarine's landing party was ambushed.

Such was the unpromising prospect with which Sam

Dealey and the *Harder* were confronted on the morning of 8 June. Security with regard to this side show had been closely preserved. Before the *Harder* left Fremantle, Australia, on 26 May 1944, to begin her fifth war patrol, only her Captain had any inkling of what special mission was in store for her. And he, as they would say in Australia, took a poor view of the whole idea. The *Harder* was an expert torpedo shooting boat. Dealey preferred to stick to that department of his trade and keep out of shallow waters. Nevertheless, he had his sealed orders in the ship's safe and so far as he was concerned, that was that.

The night before the *Harder's* departure from Fremantle, an Aussie Army lorry pulled up on the dock and delivered to the submarine a consignment of special equipment which set speculation and the never-absent scuttlebutt rumors chasing each other through the compartments.

"What's this, Chief?" asked a bearded torpedoman as a couple of collapsible kayaks called folboats were carried into the forward torpedo room. "Who's going to play Eskimo?"

"Aw," explained another, "we're going to paddle into Tokyo Bay and bring Tokyo Rose back alive."

"Stow it, son," said Chief Torpedoman Mays, the Chief of the Boat, "these gadgets are all top secret. You haven't even seen them."

Other items aroused even more speculation: Army walkie-talkies, submachine guns, powerful long-beamed flashlights ("torches," to the British), two boxes of hand grenades, two one-quarter-horsepower outboard motors, and a dozen businesslike-looking limpet bombs. When the receipt of this equipment was reported to the Skipper, he merely acknowledged the report and ordered one walkie-talkie delivered to the Commanding Officer of the *Redfin* which was moored alongside. She would be sailing northward with the *Harder* on the morrow. Sam offered no further comment. However, it was obvious somebody was going to hit the beach.

Good-looking Lieut. Tom Buckner, the Torpedo Officer, from the deep South, always ready for a frolic or a

U.S.S. Tinosa

fight, drawled to the Exec.: "Yes, suh, Mista Lynch, I sure hope you'll save me a seat in one of those kayaks. I'd like to look over some of this romantic tropic scenery."

Next day, half an hour before sailing time, Rear Adm. Christie's two-starred car rolled down the dock. Out of it stepped Commander Subs, 7th Fleet, himself, followed by a major and a sergeant, both in Australian uniforms. The trio strode rapidly across the intervening submarine tender, *Orion,* and, as they came aboard the *Harder,* all hands on deck came to attention and saluted the Admiral. Comdr. Dealey shook hands with Adm. Christie and with the major and his sergeant. Then without introducing the Army men to anyone, he sent them below with an escort. Minutes later, after the Admiral departed, on the dot of 1300, the *Harder* took in her mooring lines and backed away from her mother ship out into the harbor. Her momentous fifth war patrol had begun. The *Redfin* followed her to sea.

An hour or so after the submarine cleared Fremantle breakwater, the skipper ordered a "trim dive"—a dive always made after a stay in port, especially after taking on stores and fuel—to insure that the ship had been properly "compensated" (ballasted) and was ready to make a crash dive at any moment.

When the state of trim reached the perfection which Sam Dealey always demanded in the *Harder*, he called Chief Torpedoman Elmo B. Mays of Kentucky to the conning tower.

"Mays," he drawled, "I'm having a conference of all officers in the wardroom. Take charge. Run at 150 feet until we have finished."

Mays was young for his important rating and not impressive in stature, but the expression in his face and the determination in his eyes left no doubt as to his competence. A wide grin lit up his sunbrowned countenance.

"Aye, aye, Captain," he said and stepped to the periscope for a final look around.

"Pass the word," said Sam. "All officers to the wardroom."

"All officers to the wardroom," rasped out the loud speakers.

When the ship's officers were assembled, Dealey introduced Major Jinkins and his non-com, Sergeant Stanley W. Dodds, both of the Australian Imperial Forces. Major Jinkins was faultlessly turned out. There was not a crease in his hand-tailored, short-sleeved khaki shirt and shorts that did not belong there. It was difficult to picture him in one of those kayaks paddling ashore to some God-forsaken island until you forgot his sartorial perfection and looked at his attractive, clean-cut features and his steel-gray eyes. There you found the stamp of spirit, daring, and determination to cope with whatever the occasion might demand. Sergeant Dodds was of a powerful build, with wavy brown hair and alert blue eyes. He also looked fully competent for hazardous missions.

Comdr. Dealey, seated at the head of the tiny wardroom table, broke the seal of an official envelope, studied its contents for a minute or so, and then looked up at his officers. "Gentlemen," he said, "in brief, our special mission is to evacuate six Allied Intelligence Bureau agents from the northeast coast of Borneo. Major Jinkins and Sergeant Dodds are prepared to go ashore in those kayaks we have stowed aboard and ferry them out to us. The time of rendezvous is between June 6 and 12. If not successful on the first attempt, I am directed to make further attempts as deemed feasible by me. Therefore, I suggest that we leave no stone unturned to make the first try a success. I don't like hanging around in shallow water any longer than necessary." Turning to Jinkins, Dealey said: "Major, will you take over now and give us the pitch?"

Major Jinkins' remarks were brief and to the point. In his pleasant, modulated voice he explained that his two-man mission had been placed aboard the *Harder* to rescue a group of secret agents which had been smuggled into Borneo the preceding October to promote disloyalty among the natives toward the Japanese and to wreck oil-producing plants and other installations where possible. To this end they had taken along a large amount of money and quite a few implements for sabotage.

Jinkins went on to report as much information as he had on the six survivors and on the two previous attempts to rescue them.

Dealey interrupted at this point to say that he had a copy of the *Redfin's* report on their adventure and would go over it, in detail, with Captain Austin when the two ships topped off with fuel at Exmouth Gulf.

Jinkins went on to say that these agents had been hunted by the Japs by the use of traitors, bloodhounds, airplanes, and native trackers. Big rewards had been placed on their heads but, through some miracle, they had survived.

A few weeks previously word had come out of Borneo that the men, long given up as dead or captured, were still alive and free. Plans were therefore immediately set up for their rescue at a given spot on the northeast coast of Borneo.

The plan, as finally approved, called for the *Harder* to steal as close in to the rendezvous as the depth of water would permit; then, on one of the designated nights, between certain specified hours, to exchange flashlight recognition signals with the agents. To avoid the danger of having these signals seen over too wide an arc and thus alert the Japs, it would be necessary to send the boats close inshore.

The challenge and replies were to be made with the shore party by light flashes followed by voice-recognition tests. But what these code letters or words would be was not disclosed by Jinkins until just three days before the pickup. He suspected a leak back in Australia and, since his own life and the lives of seven others—and possibly the safety of the *Harder*—depended upon the security of the recognition signals, he was understandably close-mouthed. However, the cloak and dagger man knew the frequency of the shore party's radio set; hence direct two-way communication without relay through Australia could be—and later was—achieved.

The possibility that the Japs might have the Aussies' special code could not be overlooked. Jinkins, as he expressed it, kept his last and final recognition signal "up the spout" and did not divulge it to anyone. However, the place of rendezvous was given to the shore party because they were back in the hills and had about a six-day hike before them to reach the chosen spot.

Once recognition was established, the folboats would paddle in and bring the men out. Each could carry 800 pounds—1000 in a pinch. The Aussie expressed himself as fully satisfied with his equipment—his 17-foot rubber and canvas, flat-bottomed folboats were sturdy and could hardly be detected in the dark at ten paces, and he had infra-red signal lamps with which to communicate with the sub.

He also had complete confidence in his partner, Sgt. Dodds, who had been a platoon sergeant with Jinkins. As Bill wrote some time later: "I had a partner whom I could rely upon to do anything I myself was game to try, and do many things probably better. He did not lack guts, which is the main requirement."

"This is the last try," concluded Jinkins. "If this one

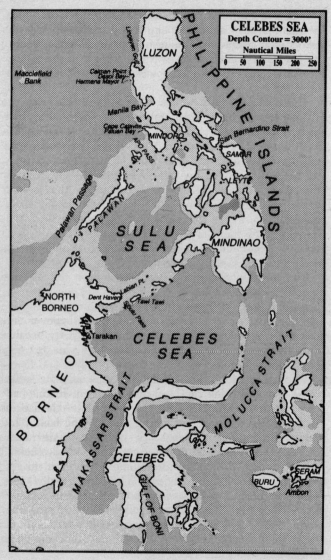

Celebes Sea

fails, Headquarters say they will have to write Gort Chester and his boys off the books. I am personally deeply interested in this venture. Chester I have known for years, Warrant Officer Alex Chew was my batman in the Army. We were captured—and escaped—together. You may be sure that if we can't get those boys out, nobody can. But we've got to have a lot of help."

As Jinkins finished, Sam asked his officers if they had any questions or saw any fatal weakness in this operation. There were no questions or comments. Each man was busy with his own thoughts—thoughts of those six men waiting there in Borneo. As Jinkins talked, a wave of enthusiasm—so strong that it was almost physical—had swept through the wardroom for the support of this cloak and dagger man and his mates ashore. The sympathy and imagination of our submarine lads were fired by the picture presented of the spine-tingling dangers and never-ending hardships endured by these hunted fellowmen in reeking jungles. This rescue must be made. The *Harder* had done one similar job during her fourth war patrol—and under fire. She could do it again.

If Sam personally had entertained any doubts about undertaking this assignment, they were swept away by the earnestness and personality of Bill Jinkins and his partner. Their job, as they expressed it, was to "kill Japs and more bloody Japs." They entertained no illusions as to what would happen to them if they were captured. Jinkins had been a prisoner of war on Ambon Island after the fall of Singapore but had escaped via a native fishing boat. The information he had brought back as the first Australian officer to return from a Jap P.O.W. camp was very useful. The Japs knew of this and Jinkins could not afford to get caught a second time. He now carried, carefully concealed, a "long sleep pill" which he would use to rob any future captor of inhuman sport with his body. On the present job he would also carry a limpet mine which could not only eliminate himself but also take some enemies with him.

Immediate plans were made for dry runs and dress

rehearsals at Exmouth Gulf, where both the *Harder* and the *Redfin* would top off their fuel tanks. Walkie-talkie tests were arranged with the *Redfin*. From the status of a questionable sideshow, the *Harder's* rescue mission had rapidly risen to a heartily endorsed major undertaking.

All hands left the wardroom in an inspired, a fighting, mood. The ship's officers returned to their duties while the Skipper, Jinkins, and Dodds went to the control room. There Sam stepped to the microphone and spoke to all hands. He introduced the two Australians and restated the highlights of the mission. When, at the conclusion, he asked his crew how they felt about this mission, he was answered by hearty cheers from bow to stern.

"Okay, men," he said with a smile, "if any of you have ideas on how the plan can be improved, let me have them."

During the course of night experiments with the ship's radar in tracking the folboats, Frank Lynch developed a metal target to be carried in the boats. This gave a better pip on the radar screen and permitted the kayaks to be tracked out to several thousand yards, a much greater distance than would otherwise be possible.

While the two submarines were moored alongside the fuel barge in Exmouth Gulf, Sam Dealey and Cy Austin held a short powwow in the *Harder's* wardroom. Frank Lynch, Ray Levin, Major Jinkins, and Sergeant Dodds sat in with them. Coffee was by "Alabama" Moore, the smiling Negro wardroom steward and an ordained minister who played his silvery trumpet, not like Gabriel, but in the heart throb manner of Louis Armstrong. Alabama was one of the ship's favorite characters.

Sam asked for amplification of some parts of the *Redfin's* secret report on her attempted recovery of these same intelligence agents whom the *Harder* was now ordered to rescue.

"For instance," asked Sam, "how come you used such a simple identification signal?"

"Well, Sam," replied Austin, "we were in Makassar Strait on 21 April—just over one month ago—en route to

Fremantle, Western Australia, having completed *Redfin's* second war patrol, when we received orders to pick up a party of about six Australians on the Island of Borneo, position Lat. 5°–13–10N and Long. 119°–16–10E. There is the spot marked on my track chart. The security signals were to be a white sheet shown from dawn until 0800 and from 1600 to 1800, also a single flash of light every fifteen minutes between the hours of 1800 and 1900. The challenge was Victor for Victor—that is, the Morse code letter V; to be answered by the same letter. We were to start 22 April and try for three days to make the pickup. There had been previous attempts and we were to watch for traps. We were to advise if mission could not be attempted. We arrived off the pickup point at 0507 on 22 April and spent the day submerged, looking the place over.

"There just wasn't any time to make other arrangements or recognition signals, although I realized *Victor* answered by the same letter was poor and that flashing a light every fifteen minutes from a mile off the beach was liable to be picked up by the Japs. However, at that time, I believed the agents had a boat and would be able to elude enemy patrols and launch their craft when the coast was clear. I was wrong about that."

"Did you have any dope," asked Dealey, "about the locations of Jap forces ashore?"

"Yes, the Japs were supposed to have some 8-inch guns mounted at Labian Point and just north of Dent Haven. They must be well camouflaged. I did not see any signs of them."

"How about the currents," asked Sam, "in close to the beach?"

"Well," replied Cy, "we lay off there submerged all that day and found a strong northerly set. You will be around on the northeast coast and shouldn't have so much current. . . . But to go on with the story. You will see most of the details in my report. We saw a steam launch towing a small boat in the afternoon, right near the pickup point. It hung around for some time and then disappeared around Labian Point. I had a hope it might be a friendly native

M1 Carbine

craft leaving a boat for our coast-watchers. I learned later they were actually Japs searching for our men.

"Just before sunset, I sighted a white sheet spread over some rocks at the rendezvous. So, at 1822, I surfaced and exchanged *Victors* with the party. Then we waited for their arrival but kept a sharp lookout for any surprise attack. Two hours later I got a dispatch from Comsubs 7th Fleet, saying the agents were in position but had no boat. This was a blow, but we broke out our four-man rubber boat."

The landing party consisted of Ens. E. R. Helz, Yeoman K. G. Harrington, Gunners Mate G. E. Carinder, and Radioman R. E. Kahler. In addition to one Browning automatic rifle, one Springfield, and two carbines, they carried four hard-hitting .45-caliber automatic pistols in the holsters of their web belts, plus various emergency flares and survival equipment.

"I could see several lights in Dent Haven," continued Austin, "so I instructed Ens. Helz to head straight in for the beach. And to keep away from Dent Harbor, as it was probably full of Japs.

"To myself, I said a little prayer for the good Lord's help. As things turned out, they were to need it—and, indeed, receive it."

Soon after the boat slipped away, it became obvious that it was being swept northward, off its course, by the strong current. Despite all his efforts, Austin's frantic signals to recall his men were unsuccessful.

An hour went by. Two hours. Midnight. Nothing happened as the *Redfin* rested on the surface, the nerves of all aboard her taut and alert for trouble rising out of the dark. If the Japs had radar, their heavy guns could make short shrift of the *Redfin*.

At 0131, all hell broke loose in Dent Harbor. First the flashes of cannon fire and the long evil lines of tracers— then the crack, crack, crack of small arms. Now groups of flares, isolated or in strings, sprung into being. To Austin it was obvious that the Japs were trying to light up the harbor.

Cy Austin faced that frantic and heart-crushing situation that comes to any commanding officer when he cannot go to the rescue of his own men. But for him to have entered Dent Harbor on a pitch-black night without navigational aids would have been wanton recklessness. Tough as the truth was, he realized that he could not risk the loss of the *Redfin* and her crew in an attempt to rescue four men who might, by that time, already be dead.

"I never felt more downhearted in my life," said Austin.

"About an hour later," he went on, "I picked up a small boat on the radar and tracked it right into the beach at Dent Haven. This meant to me that our party was captured and probably kiled immediately. However, we did not give up hope.

"At 0340 I was searching the area carefully with my glasses when I sighted a very small signal light. The shooting had stopped. The signal light was definitely identified as our boat.

"At 0413, just at first light, I flooded down and started

into this treacherous harbor ready to fight it out in order to get our men back. An hour later we picked up our entire party. No one had been hurt, but they were completely exhausted, so much so that they could not even get out of the rubber boat. I immediately headed out of the harbor and was able to clear and dive without further fireworks. It was very tempting to fire just a few rounds into the Jap camp which we could see; however, our position among the reefs was too vulnerable to take a chance."

Once again aboard the *Redfin,* battle-weary Ensign Helz reported that the current had swept him north. But since the signals ran as scheduled and he kept receiving a *Victor* for his *Victor,* he presumed the beach party was walking along the shore with him. Actually, it was the Japs answering the very poorly chosen security signal.

When their craft grounded, Helz left Harrington and Kahler at the boat to man the Browning automatic and carbine, and he and Carinder waded in to the beach about thirty feet apart. As they approached the shore, a Jap ran out into the water and attempted to bayonet Carinder. He parried the thrust with his rifle butt. The footing was bad in the soft, gooey mud and both men fell down in the water and lost their guns. Carinder came up first with the Jap's gun but could not fire it. As the Jap ran landward, Harrington killed him with the Browning automatic. The four men momentarily answered the Jap fire, which came from several points along the beach. But, as soon as they could, they re-embarked in the rubber boat and paddled for their lives. In the melee they lost an oar but did bring back the Jap's rifle. They spent the rest of the night dodging mortar shells and trying to stay out of the lighted areas.

Austin was ready to make another attempt but received word to call it off because the coast-watchers had also been detected and were on the run into the hills.

"I feel," said Cy, "that our mission failed because of lack of proper recognition signals and proper equipment."

During Austin's story of the *Redfin's* nearly tragic rescue attempt, a little of Sam's enthusiasm for his special mission had oozed out of his system. But he was not the man to let his spirits remain too long down in his boots. This job was really a challenge—the *Harder* could handle it.

"You surely had a lot of tough breaks, Cy," said he, soberly, "and I'm mighty glad you got your boys back. We are going in better prepared and, with this old fire-eater Jinkins on our team, we ought to make a go of it."

"We'll have a good try at it, in any case," agreed Jinkins, smiling broadly beneath his formidable mustache.

"I wish you luck," said Austin, as he shook hands all round, "and good hunting."

"Thanks, Cy, and good hunting to you."

When the *Harder* arrived off her rendezvous point at 1400 of 8 June, Dealey, with the *Redfin's* experiences fresh in his mind, was fully prepared for the night's project. The thrilling events of the past few days and the sinking of two enemy destroyers had raised the ship's esprit de corps to an unprecedented high level. As they held a final conference that afternoon, Sam looked around the wardroom table with obvious pride, as well he might.

On his right sat his Exec., Lt. Comdr. Frank C. Lynch from the show-me state of Missouri. Cool, calm, intelligent, capable, and indefatigable, he was indeed a tower of strength. Dealey had great respect for his sound judgment.

Next in seniority was Lieut. Samuel M. Logan of Owensboro, Kentucky. Young, brilliant without ostentation, he had graduated Number One in his Naval Academy Class of 1942. That he had a good sense of humor was proved by the scraggly Irish, picture-frame beard, mustache, and goatee with which his face was adorned—if, in fact, the word *adorned* can be used.

Lieut. E. H. "Ray" Levin, a reserve officer from Iron Mountain, Minnesota, came next in line. His job was Communications and Electronics. He was quiet, capable, and excellent in his specialty. His equipment was always in perfect shape.

The Gunnery and Torpedo Officer, Lieut. T. W. "Tom"

Buckner, another reserve officer, was from Nashville, Tennessee. This droll Southern wit was beloved by all. He was a perfect genius as a TDC operator, even though it was a new job for him.

The junior members of the mess, Ensign Dan James, Ensign Philip Sampson, and Ensign Bob Roosevelt, were just fine, good-looking young boys—willing and eager but still slightly bewildered by submarine life. One of the first questions asked them by the Skipper when they reported aboard, shortly before this patrol began, was: "Can you carry a melody?"

James and Roosevelt both had good voices and were welcome additions to the wardroom evening song fests. Phil Sampson, assigned as the Plotting Officer, was to prove himself a wizard at that job.

Last in officer rank, but not least in the esteem of his shipmates, was Warrant Machinist C. W. "Carl" Finney. This lad was the coolest, calmest, and most capable man any skipper could hope to have with him. He was voted by all to be the best OOD in the ship. He had lost a brother in the *Trout* in February, '44, which left him some unfinished business to settle with the Japanese.

Yes, Sam Dealey's team was definitely in the big league and left him in the happy position of being able to delegate most matters to his subordinates—a help to him and a definite boost to them.

Only minor details remained to be settled—except one important point which Jinkins brought up. "Remember, Captain," he said, "this could all be a deadly hoax. Could be the Japs caught our men. Tortured the plan out of them. They may be sitting in there waiting for us. In case you hear shooting, I urgently request you beat a quick retreat. Don't try to do anything for us—we'll take the will for the deed. At any rate it would be too late—for they'll never take us alive. If our bullets don't get them, our limpet bombs will get all of us."

Reluctantly Sam agreed with the logic of Bill's plan. However, it was arranged that if fighting did break out, the *Harder* would remain off the rendezvous and await orders from Australia just on the off chance that someone might escape and get back to the hand-powered radio set.

The afternoon had been spent submerged making a periscope study of the coast line, of prominent hills, and of the tidal currents. From the chart—which, however, might not be too accurate—it appeared that the submarine could get in to a point about three miles from the beach and that there were no outlying dangers such as rocks or shoals in the immediate vicinity. The coast at this point was not unlike the shores of Mississippi delta bayous, where vast stretches of swamplands are cut by streams of open water and where clusters of trees rise in scattered groups out of the reeds and canebrakes. The spot for landing was not hard to find—a wide mangrove area with islands of towering trees to the right and left.

Until early evening the *Harder* kept herself under the wet blanket of the opaque coastal waters. She snatched frequent periscope looks which indicated that all was well so far as the presence of unwanted visitors was concerned.

After a thorough check to see that everything was in readiness, the order was given to surface. Three strident blasts of the diving alarm brought the ship up at 1940 to the accompaniment of high-pressure air rushing into the ballast tanks and the clatter of feet on the control room and conning tower ladders. Dealey kept the ship flooded down to deck level and, with propulsion on the electric motors, slid in toward the coast. The supersonic sounding machine was kept operating constantly to insure sufficient depth of water under the keel.

In deep silence the boats and equipment were carefully brought on deck and assembled. Many volunteers had to be refused permission to help paddle the boats in. They would have crowded the return trip too heavily.

The area had been thoroughly searched by radar and sonar and no intruders had been located. However, later, it was learned that the enemy customarily had two launches in the shallow bay—one to eastward and the other to westward of the spot which had been selected for the rendezvous.

Frank Lynch and Jinkins went over the radar and plot plans. Ray Levin went over the walkie-talkie arrangements and provisions for three separate contingencies: (1) in case the landing party had to go ashore and search for the coast watching party; (2) in case the landing party was interfered with and unable to get back out; (3) in case the *Harder* had to shove off and come back later. Each contingency, carefully outlined on paper, had its own rendezvous and recognition signal.

Finally, with one fathom of water under her keel, and the rendezvous 6500 yards ahead, the *Harder's* headway was killed and the folboats gently lowered over the starboard side.

The cloak and dagger men were ready to embark. There were handshakes and last-minute checkups. The ship's Talker had been moved from the conning tower up to the bridge, where he hung over the rail ready to rush any word or directions to the radar operators, radio men, or other vitally concerned personnel below.

In a low voice Levin was saying to Jinkins, "Our radar man will follow your radar target just as long as he can. If you get off the line of bearing to the landing, I'll coach you back on by walkie-talkie."

"Right-o," said the Major, "I'll be all ears."

"Good luck, Bill," said Dealey, "and successful hunting. We'll be right here waiting for you."

"Thanks, Captain, and God bless," replied Jinkins as they shook hands—a handshake which Jinkins said later "took some of the shake out of my own hand."

Then, at 2140, he and Dodds were in the leading boat with the second boat on a short towline behind them. The compass course to the rendezvous was 158 degrees and the radar-walkie-talkie combination was most successfully used in keeping the boats on their proper heading.

The weather, according to the report Jinkins made to his Headquarters, was ideal for that type of operation: wind very slight; water, smooth; sky, cloudy and overcast; moonrise at approximately 2130 but hidden by overcast; tide, slight westerly set.

Sam Dealey doubled his bridge watch and concentrated all attention upon looking for night fliers and enemy patrol craft. God help the *Harder* if she were caught by either in these shallow waters.

Breaking the tense silence of the anxious group of watchers on the cigarette deck (the after-extension of the bridge deck, a favorite smoking place) came a voice out of the night: "Jinks to Ray, Jinks to Ray. Do you receive me? Over."

Levin replied with relief showing in his voice: "Ray to Jinks, Ray to Jinks. I hear you low and clear. Your course is okay. Keep your set turned on, Bill. That way we'll instantly know if you are in trouble. We are recording everything on our wire recorder."

"Smart fellow," came back from the darkness.

Eventually the radar target faded and was lost in the tangle of trees, brush, and tall grass that framed the picture on the radar screen. The waiting group on the *Harder's* bridge was tense with suspense and apprehension. This was the critical, the deadly dangerous time.

Writing of the pickup twelve years after, Bill Jinkins, now a retired colonel and working as an oil company executive in this same North Borneo area, says: "The trip in was by paddle and in fact so quiet we could hardly hear ourselves—whenever we heard a sound we stopped and were quite scared to talk for fear of the voice carrying across the still water.

"When we grounded on the soft mud, we little realized the danger. The Japs were one and a half miles on either side of us and had been patrolling this bay each day, at least over the pickup period—the only time the land party was there.

"The light signal *V* for *Victor* was flashed shorewards to the spot we had arranged. No answer. I flashed about 400 yards to the left. No answer. Then 400 yards to the right. This time an answer came from the first position—*W* for *William*."

The reason for the delay in answering was that the men ashore had waited three nights and seen nothing. This night, only half an hour before the end of the pickup period, their spirits were pretty low and the man with the only torch had started back through the mangroves for their temporary hideout. When that light flashed from out to seaward, one of the other watchers broke all known speed records to get the torch back. Their joy knew no bounds. They just couldn't believe their eyes. And the relief to Jinkins and Dodds was terrific, too.

"Thank God," breathed Dealey when he heard that the first signal was correctly answered.

The second and third recognition signals were likewise correctly exchanged, but that did not prove too much. A Jap might have been working that torch. Everything now depended on the voice recognition.

"Jinks to Sam, Jinks to Sam," squawked the *Harder's* walkie-talkie. "We've got the right signals. Now we are going in for voice tests. That's the pay-off."

"Okay," replied Sam. "Play it safe, Bill."

"Right you are, Sam," said Bill, "and remember if I say 'Eureka and MacArthur,' all is well. But if I say 'Eureka and General MacArthur,' we have fallen into a trap and you chaps better be on your way."

"Keep your chin up, old man," replied Sam. "We are all behind you. Call for covering fire if you need it. My gunners here could knock a gnat's eye out at this short range."

"Thanks for everything, Sam," said Bill; and then, almost as though talking to himself, came the words: "In a sec the chips will be down. Remember the signal."

"We poled the boats closer in," writes Col. Jinkins in a letter to the authors, "until we stuck in the mud. We were not yet sure the party was free, so I made my first challenge:

" 'Who are you?'

" 'Gort,' came back the reply—certainly the voice of Gort Chester.

"My second challenge was: 'Is Alex with you?'

" 'Yes,' came back the voice of my ex-batman.

"The final clinching identification came when I told Alex to identify the next voice he heard. Knowing that Dodds had been Alex's platoon sergeant for some time, I told Dodds to ask him how he was, confident that he would give some non-committal answer if he were under duress.

"'Hello, Alex, how are you,' called Dodds.

"'Doddsie, you bastard!' came back the completely convincing reply.

"We asked for no more."

It was impossible to walk in the thick mud and the men came crawling out on hands and knees. Major Chester was first to arrive. He was haggard and drawn and literally fell on Jinkins' neck.

The minutes of waiting for news on the *Harder* seemed like hours. Sam Dealey fidgeted and pulled fiercely on his long-dead pipe. Ray Levin, whispering to himself, had his ear glued to the walkie-talkie.

Suddenly came an excited, exultant voice that almost blasted Ray's ear off: "We got 'em! We got 'em!" almost shouted Jinkins, all restraint thrown to the winds, "and, oh, yes, Eureka and MacArthur."

The other members arrived in various stages of exhaustion and undress. Some, half-dead and delirious with malaria, could hardly make it. Warrant Officer Chew, ever mindful of his duty, was almost left behind while burying his rust-covered, useless weapons in the mud.

The boats were dragged out to deeper water and the shore party struggled aboard. It meant three in the cockpit and one lying on the bow of each folboat—dangerous overcrowding in shark-infested waters where a capsizing would bring maiming or cruel death. The outboard motor on one boat was got going and, towing the other canoe astern, Bill headed out for the *Harder*.

"Everyone wanted to talk," remembered Jinkins. "Gort just couldn't seem to stop himself."

The bits of conversation which were picked up and played back on the *Harder's* wire recorder gave a wonderful insight into what is uppermost in the minds of half-dead, delirious men snatched from the jaws of death.

"There was lots of subdued shouting from Sam and about a dozen of his crew," writes Col. Jinkins.

"By this time we noticed a very bad smell. It was the unwashed and unchanged clothes of the boys, now covered with the stinking mud of the mangrove flats. We politely suggested they strip before going below and drop the stinkers overboard. I had brought new clothing for them all. They did so reluctantly. It was quite strange—their desire to hang on to threadbare shirts and trousers.

"Sam immediately headed to sea and we stowed the canoes, after removing the mud. We hoped to use them again on this cruise. We had brought a few sets of limpets and a few other gadgets.

"Chester and the boys meantime were washed up and wolfing steaks and ice cream until they were ill. Several of them were in a very bad way and were just out in time. Their efforts paved the way for the insertion by parachute and M.T.B. of two separate parties, one into the interior and the other to North Borneo, both prior to the Allied invasion by six months. Chester led the party into North Borneo."

In spite of all they had gone through and their half-starved condition, these rugged souls were in good spirits. They really had something to tell their grandchildren. The rescued men were:

Major F. G. L. "Gort" Chester (General List British Army), Lieutenant Lloyd J. Woods (A.I.F.), Warrant Officer A. "Alex" Chew (A.I.F.), Sergeant L. L. "Lew" Cottee (A.I.F.), Sergeant L. L. "Fred" Olsen (A.I.F.), and Sergeant S. "Stan" Neil (A.I.F.).

The intelligence organization these men had established on the east coast of British North Borneo had gathered information on enemy activities, dispositions, movements, and installations. Such information of immediate operational importance which came to hand was reported by radio, and the remaining information was subsequently compiled in a series of reports. Their coast-watching resulted in a total of eighty-eight enemy shipping movements being reported during the whole operation.

The *Harder's* competent Pharmacist's Mate Angelo Locoscio took the men in hand, assisted by Lt. Tom

Buckner, who had worked his way through Vanderbilt University Pre-Med for two years as an orderly in the University Hospital. He was almost as good as a doctor.

When the men were told that they would not be taken directly to Australia, they were not too disappointed. Nor did they show much concern on learning that the *Harder* was headed for combat with enemy men of war. "Nothing can scare us after what we have been through," said one of them.

He and his mates were to swallow those words before they returned to the serene shores of Australian terra firma. In fact before too many hours had passed they received their first real taste of the life of a submarine sailor.

★★★★★★★★★★★★★★★★★★★★★★★★★★★★★★★★★★★★★★★★★★

# *Harder* Stampedes Jap Fleet

Sam Dealey heaved a sigh of relief as the *Harder*, working up to cruising speed, churned out of the murky, shallow waters of North Borneo's coast and headed out for the deeper blue of the hundred-fathom curve. He felt that he had had a great plenty of inshore work. Below, the newly-rescued coast-watchers were being cared for, while among the crewmen ran the quick and colorful scuttlebutt of what had taken place in the night above, and what was coming next. The morale aboard the sub was sky-high. Action was what the men wanted and action they got. Although, like moles, they sensed rather than saw what was going on, the feeling of combat tension was the staff of life to them.

"If they keep giving us rescue missions like this—and the one at Woleai last patrol," Dealey remarked to Frank Lynch, "we had better put in a requisition for a set of wheels." His reference to Woleai meant the rescue on 1 April of Ensign John Galvin, a downed Navy flier, from a beach where he was certain to be captured by the Japs.

"We'll need them or a rubber bottom for bouncing off reefs," agreed the harassed Lynch with an embarrassed grin. After all, as the navigator, it was his job to keep the *Harder* off the rocks and shoals.

Now the *Harder* could get back to the major item of her patrol orders—to reconnoiter the Tawi-Tawi Islands which

U.S.S. Nautilus

lay a scant fifty miles ahead of her plunging bow. Intelligence had reported a considerable concentration of enemy fleet units in the spacious anchorage inside protecting reefs at the southwest end of the main island. This anchorage had figured in U.S. Navy war plans for many years, but when the war broke, the Japanese drove our meager Asiatic Fleet southward to Java and Australia and pre-empted Tawi-Tawi as a base of their own.

Obviously, it would be some considerable time before our Pacific forces could fight their way back to it. But, meanwhile, one of its outlying islands was a regular port of call for a hardy branch of the submarines of the Seventh Fleet, called the "Spyron," which meant the Spy Squadron. This was a flexible group of half a dozen submarines, led by our two huge subs, the 3000-ton *Narwhal* and the *Nautilus*. They transported and supplied guerrillas, landed coast-watchers, and evacuated refugees. When called upon for services of that order, they had the able coordination furnished by that master spy and daredevil from Manila,

Comdr. Charles (Chick) Parsons, also known as Comspyron, whose wonderful and daring work had been of such enormous help to the resistance groups in the Philippines.

It was particularly important, at this period of the war, for Fleet Admiral Nimitz, Commander in Chief Pacific Fleet, and General MacArthur, Supreme Commander, Allied Forces Southwest Pacific Area, to know what forces the enemy had in its well-hidden and well-protected Tawi-Tawi anchorage.

General MacArthur, only 1300 miles away at Hollandia in New Guinea, had completed the conquest of that area in May and was even then gathering strength and preparing for the long-awaited return to the Philippines. Incidentally, Spyron submarines carried thousands and thousands of packages of cigarettes into those beleaguered islands bearing the General's resolute promise: "I shall return." This popular "MacArthur brand" made the Japs not only smoke, but, indeed, also burn with red-hot ire.

Admiral Nimitz' interest in the movements of the Japanese Fleet was even more immediate, for at that very moment Admiral Raymond Spruance, with his tremendous Fifth Fleet and hundreds of transports, landing craft, and auxiliaries, was en route to Saipan. There he was to land General Holland Smith's Marine and Army divisions on June 15 for the conquest of that island.

It was calculated, and rightly so, that this assault on Saipan, regarded by the Japs as one of the chief bastions of their Empire, would trigger off a major operation on the part of the Japanese Fleet—an operation designed to aid their comrades-in-arms in the Marianas Islands. This, Admiral Spruance and Admiral Nimitz fervently desired. Still, the Fifth Fleet must not be caught off balance. Hence, information as to the strength, composition of, location, and movements of the enemy's fleet was vitally important to the campaign.

To help supply that intelligence, the *Harder* had orders to reconnoiter Tawi-Tawi, report enemy strength there, and to patrol waters to the south of the island group. The *Redfin*, companion of the *Harder* during the first days of the patrol, was assigned the northern billet. Other submarines were stationed farther west and north in Palawan Passage to cover the probable line of advance of enemy naval forces reported to be in Singapore.

The *Harder* had not passed within sight of the Tawi-Tawi anchorage on her northward transit of Sibutu Passage. However, the number of big destroyers which she encountered en route to it indicated the presence of a sizeable portion of the enemy fleet. Normally, the Japanese did not use their biggest and newest destroyers for convoy work or for patrol purposes. Just as the U.S. Navy employed destroyer escorts for such jobs, so did the Imperial Navy use older ships and anti-submarine craft for such routine work. However, the destroyers with which the *Harder* had clashed in Sibutu were no second-team players. In fact, the *Hayanami*, which she sank on 7 June, was a new 2100-ton type—the counterpart of our own fleet destroyers.

Definitely Sam Dealey was up against members of Hirohito's first team as he left Borneo behind, and they were out for blood—preferably his. The same thing applied to the air units encountered. They were alert for the subs that had raised such havoc at the start of the month. Their vigilance spelled trouble, and trouble spelled: *Harder*.

As the *Harder*, running at 15 knots on the surface, stood down toward the northern end of Sibutu Passage in the all-too-brilliant tropic moonlight, she felt very naked and awfully uncomfortable. Dealey would have preferred to be submerged, but he had to make time and, if possible, get into the Strait before daylight. That would give him fully charged batteries for propulsive power when he faced the fast and vengeful enemy hunters now on his trail. The *Harder's* radar was kept going continuously and lookouts, hand-picked for sharp-eyed and cool alertness, were constantly searching their sectors through powerful binoculars. In spite of all these precautions, at 0532, while still seventeen miles north of Sibutu, and on the pink fringe of dawn, a float-type plane slipped up in the glow of the rising sun. He was sighted by the submarine's bridge lookout at close range—much too close, and almost too late.

"Clear the bridge!" shouted Tom Buckner, who was Officer of the Deck. "Dive, dive! Flood negative! Take her to 120 feet fast!"

The ensuing scramble to get down through the narrow hatch could have been ludicrous had it not been so serious—so freighted with the imminence of sudden death. Heads were stepped on, shoulders trod upon—and anyone grasping the treads of the ladders risked a handful of broken fingers. Submariners learn early in their careers to slide down the ladders grasping only the vertical members. Eight to ten seconds was the time allowed to get six or seven men off the lofty lookout platforms, off the bridge, and down the hatch to the conning tower—this time limit permitted no dragging of feet. Speed, or lack of it, could make the difference between getting back to base alive or sitting dead in a steel coffin among the coral heads and marine monsters of the dark ocean bottom.

With its hatch tightly locked, the *Harder* bow nosed bottomward at a stomach-gripping angle. Fore, aft, and amidship, loose gear crashed, men leaned aft to compensate for the sharp downward plunge of the bow. The *Harder* reached periscope depth in record breaking time and continued on as though the devil were right on her tail. Even that was not fast enough. At 75 feet on the depth gauge, the ship received a close aerial depth charge whose tooth-rattling detonation threw sleep-seeking crewmen—if any were really asleep at this point—out of their bunks.

Captain Tichenor, eleven years after the event, recreated the dramatic scene: "I can still vividly remember that bomb. I was sleeping in the top one of the two fold-up bunks in the wardroom. I was awakened by the ship apparently trying to stand on her head. Then came the terrific whooom of a bomb on our port side. It flung the ship over to starboard so sharply that I was tossed out of my bunk and landed on the wardroom table."

One of the rescued Aussies, so recently snatched from the dangers and horrors of jungle life, was also thrown out of his bunk. As he picked his skin and bones up off the deck, he complained, "I sye, I'd loike to be back in Borneo. Too bloody much noise around 'ere!"

It was found, when chaos had been reduced to silent running conditions, that a framed picture of Dinah Shore in the forward torpedo room had been torn from the bulkhead by the concussion. Miraculously, the glass was not even cracked—certainly a favorable omen. The good lady probably does not know it, but she was unanimously voted "the Guardian Angel" of the *Harder* during an earlier patrol. Her picture adorned the compartments from stem to stern—in officers' quarters and crew's quarters alike. And whenever the squawk boxes were ringing out with musical entertainment, one could be fairly sure it was the melodic voice of Dinah that he heard. Lieut. Tom Buckner was responsible for obtaining her pictures. As a youngster he had gone to school with Dinah Shore in Nashville, Tennessee.

The sub was thoroughly shaken, as Dealey recorded in his log: "The event resulted in an early and prompt reveille for all hands, but no damage of a serious nature was sustained. Altered course 90 degrees to left and went to 275 feet to check for density layers. Found a gradual negative gradient down to 250 feet, then a sharp, reassuring negative thermocline."

The skipper of the *Harder* hoped that he would not have to waste time hiding beneath this ping-proof layer of colder water. But destroyers from Tawi-Tawi, forty miles away, were expected to arrive by 0900. The smooth, glassy sea, with aircraft overhead, removed chances of successful torpedo attacks by the *Harder* at periscope depth. So it was decided to swing to the northeast and not attempt a southward transit of Sibutu until it could be accomplished under the cover of night. Moreover, Sam felt that the longer the sub remained undetected, the more convinced the Jap aviator, who had staged the sudden dawn attack, would be that his bomb had hit the mark. Such an assumption, Sam admitted to himself, would not be far wrong.

Therefore, the sub ran that day on a northeasterly course at 200 feet.

Just before mess call that noon, "Sound" picked up propeller noises of two destroyers approaching from the westward. Even according to Dealey's daring code, a periscope attack in the glassy sea against alerted destroyers with air support was not considered to be "good ball." So Sam increased his depth to 300 feet and rigged for silent running. During the noon hour, two destroyers passed overhead or near the *Harder* several times, but she was well hidden under another very welcome negative gradient and was not detected by the sharp-eared pingers. By 1300 the searching destroyers were lost in the distance, whereupon the *Harder* returned to periscope depth and found the sea surface sufficiently ruffled to justify a periscope attack if opportunity came along. At the same time, the *Harder* headed for the northern entrance of Sibutu Passage.

Soon after surfacing at sunset, the radarmen contacted two small patrol craft. They were making 14 knots on a parallel course. The submarine, at 17 knots, soon outdistanced both.

At 2100 that night, with the moon not yet up, the *Harder* boldly entered the bottleneck of Sibutu Passage. The Japanese fleet base of Tawi-Tawi was just six miles away on her port beam. It was a tense period. Radarmen, sonarmen, and lookouts were straining their ears and eyes for signs of enemy patrol boats and night-flying planes. Sam, in trying to visualize the opposition he might encounter off Tawi-Tawi, drew a picture of what he knew of similar patrol measures taken by our own Fleet outside of Pearl Harbor.

There, not a night passed without at least a division of destroyers or destroyer escorts combing the coastal waters of Oahu. Planes, day and night, added close-in as well as distant patrols. Our patrols frequently encountered enemy submarines on observation duty off all our bases—sometimes they turned out to be whales—and gave them severe workings-over with depth charges. Dealey expected similar trouble—and found it. The curious thing about Japanese submarines on reconnaissance duty was that they never fought back at their tormentors. Possibly they feared to jeopardize their mission. Sam had no such compunctions. A destroyer was a prize target to him. He had supreme confidence in his ship and his crew—and belief in his ability to reconnoiter Tawi-Tawi as he had been directed to do.

That was the most amazing and inspiring thing about Sam Dealey—his faith. Not only in God but in man—his faith that every man aboard his vessel would do his best and that his best was good enough.

The *Harder* was heading toward Tawi-Tawi at two-thirds speed, her small wake making but a feeble veil of glowing foam on the ocean's lightly choppy surface. At 2101 a destroyer was sighted ahead. The range was 14,000 yards. One minute later a second destroyer was sighted steaming on in a line of bearing with the first. Such a formation is common in scouting and searching. The ships are nearly abreast of each other but slightly in echelon so as to permit high-speed maneuvering with minimum danger of collision.

"Captain to the bridge!" quietly called the Officer of the Deck into the bridge mike.

"Captain to the bridge," echoed the squawk box.

As always, Sam was cool and cheery and full of his usual Irish wit as he scrambled up through the bridge hatch and took charge. It might have been just a routine dive as he had the word passed for "Battle stations" and sounded the diving alarm.

"Take her to radar depth," he called down to Sam Logan, the Diving Officer in the control room, at the same time motioning with a hitch hiker's thumb to the alert periscope jockey for "Up 'scope."

He crouched before the slowly rising steel tube and as the training handles came above the combing of the periscope well, he seized them, swung to the bearing of the destroyers, and, by a fluttering motion of his fingers, directed the jockey to "Hold it." Since radar depth is shallower than periscope depth, it behooves the approach officer to work in a crouching posture lest too much periscope be exposed to the enemy lookouts.

The range was too great for accurate observations by periscope at this time of night with no moon. However, Sam "guesstimated" that he was looking at the port bow of the target and that her course was about 20 degrees to the right of his line of sight. Calculations of this sort, by long training, become second nature to submariners and they are amazingly accurate.

"Angle on the bow, 20 port," said Sam quietly as he "thumbed" for "Down 'scope."

The *Harder* had not been furnished with one of the new night 'scopes, which not only admitted more light rays to the observer's eye, but was also fitted with a tiny radar outlet that made it possible to obtain exact ranges and bearings.

Dealey, therefore, had to depend on his S J surface radar and he watched its screen intently as the radarman called ranges and bearings to the TDC Officer, Tom Buckner. Paralleling the work of the Torpedo Data Computer, to some extent, was the plotting board at which Lieut. (jg) Phil Sampson was working swiftly with protractors and speed scales. As successive bits of data were plotted, the pencilled courses of the submarine and her selected target, the leading DD, drew closer together. Squeezed in beside Sampson in the crowded after end of the conning tower were Frank Lynch and Capt. Tichenor—Commodore Tichenor, as he was called in order not to confuse his proper title with that of the *Harder's* captain. Like most of the conning tower crew, "Tich" was dressed in scivvy shirt (T-shirt), shorts, and sandals. Some wore no shirts but, universally, they carried a towel tucked into the waistband or draped around the neck to cope with rivulets of sweat from face, hands, and body. In the conning tower of a submarine—a space of less size than a one-car garage—temperatures in tropical waters run high. Submariners do not worry much about reducing diets—especially when the ventilation fans are secured for silent running. Below the attack periscope already gleamed a ring of the skipper's sweat.

The conning tower musicians in this orchestra of death were at their stations. "Enemy base course is zero one zero," sang out Buckner, "with 30 degree zigs on either side. Speed 15 knots, range four thousand."

"Check," agreed Sampson excitedly; "that checks with my plot, right on the nose."

"Take her to periscope depth," ordered Sam, as he motioned for "Up 'scope," "Make ready all tubes."

At this point Sam could not predict which he would fire—bow tubes or stern tubes. All depended on the target's next zig. Things happen quickly in the final moments of an attack.

As the periscope eye broke the surface, the skipper saw that the enemy DD's had zigged to their left and that the leader was heading directly for the *Harder's* 'scope.

"He's zigged, Tom; angle on the bow zero," said Sam, adding in a low voice: "May have to fire down the throat. Looks like that's getting to be a habit with us."

Sam Dealey's attack monologues were an institution aboard the *Harder*. Like many submarine skippers, he talked to himself or perhaps just thought out loud as he worked the periscope. His conning tower companions hung on his every word, for it gave them a picture of what was happening on the surface.

The succeeding periscope peeps made as the range shortened were swift five- or six-second looks concentrated on the business at hand—that leading destroyer. At 3000 yards the targets zigged 30 degrees to their right. "That's just beautiful," breathed the skipper, "just what the doctor ordered. Left rudder," he continued. "What's the firing course, Frank?"

"One four five, sir."

"Bring her to one four five."

"Aye, aye, sir," said Signalman Brostrom, the helmsman, repeating the new course. A veteran of five patrols and a "plank owner" (member of the original commissioning crew), his expert handling of the wheel had won him that coveted job for his battle station.

On came the two enemy destroyers. As the drumbeat of their propellers became louder, those aboard the Japanese vessels little realized that it was the overture to their own March of Death. They were the proud officers and crew of two of the Emperor's newest and best-equipped destroyers. They were the foes of submarines. They were the hunter killer group.

"Forward torpedo room, stand by to fire," Sam said grimly.

In the after torpedo room, the taut crew relaxed. The forward room was going to carry the ball. The torpedomen in the narrow cavernous forward torpedo room worked swiftly on last-minute preparations to make ready six 3000-pound, death-dealing torpedoes. The bare arms and torsos of the men glistened like pale divers with the wet gloss of their skins. Two stood between the vertical tube nests, ready to fire by hand in case of an electrical failure. The senior torpedoman waited, hand on the vent valve manifold, motionless, intent. On the warhead of one of those torpedoes he had written the name of a buddy lost in the *Trout*.

The array of copper-rimmed torpedo tubes before him, viewed from their exposed ends, looked like some odd sort of kettle drums—the main percussion instruments in the *Harder's* Orchestra of Doom.

Back on the conning tower firing panel green ready lights flashed as the preparations for each tube were completed.

"All tubes ready, sir," reported Buckner.

"Up 'scope. Check bearing and fire, Frank."

As the periscope rose, Dealey swiftly aligned it with the foremast of the target, now only 1000 yards away.

"Bearing, mark."

"One five zero," from Frank.

"Set," called the T.D.C. officer.

"Fire."

In rapid succession four torpedoes rasped out of the

tubes on a divergent spread of two degrees. As the fourth fish sped on its way, the skipper signaled Buckner to check fire.

Sam dropped the 'scope and wiped his sweaty hands and dripping face with his towel. As the expert leader of the *Harder's* Orchestra of Doom, he had ended its rendition of the overture to the March of Death. He leaned back and relaxed. The tenseness in his face disappeared. A pause, as though to allow a stunned audience to regain its senses, followed the dull bass thumps of high pressure air catapulting torpedoes from the tubes. Then the thunder of drumbeats from the destroyer's propellers was blotted out in the cymbal clashes of rending metal and the deeper tympanum whoom of torpedo explosions.

As this crescendo began, Dealey gave the signal for "Up 'scope" and carefully checked his results. Meanwhile, Tom Buckner was rapidly feeding new data into the T.D.C. for a shot at the second DD which was almost hidden behind the first at the moment of firing. Sam had fired only four fish from his bow tubes and then checked fire to await developments. As he watched, fascinated, with eyes glued to the eye guards, Number One Torpedo appeared to pass ahead of the first DD, Number Two hit its target near the bow, while Number Three hit the MOT—the very middle of the target—exactly under the luckless destroyer's bridge. Number Four Torpedo was heading to miss astern of the near target.

Dealey swung his submarine right with hard-over rudder to avoid ramming the slowly drifting hulk that had once been a proud destroyer. Tom stood tense, with right hand raised ready to slam the firing buttons as soon as the second target appeared.

About thirty seconds after the submarine started to swing, the other DD came into view astern of and beyond what was left of the *Tanikaze*—we learned its name after the war—which was burning furiously. At this breathless moment, Dealey's famous Irish luck leaped to the fore. The bubble trail of the fourth torpedo was seen to pass under the stern of the blazing wreck and then, as though

Tanikaze

steered by a shamrock-bearing leprechaun, the racing torpedo crashed with a terrific whoom into the second enemy.

Sam turned from the periscope with a quiet smile. "We got 'em both, Tom. We won't need any more fish. Secure from battle stations."

Throughout the *Harder* ran the sort of moderate pandemonium permitted aboard well-disciplined men-of-war at moments of great victory. There were cheers. Men slapped each other on the back. And one by one, those off duty and too excited for sleep drifted toward the messroom where soon fried steaks topped by fried eggs—a big favorite learned in Australia—were being prepared by the ship's cooks. Post-combat meals were a submarine tradition, and they were about the only spoils the victors won. The vanquished would not require human foods.

Suddenly the *Harder* was heeled sharply over to starboard by a heavy rumbling explosion which was probably a boiler on the *Tanikaze* as she sank some 400 yards away. At almost the same instant, a blinding explosion took place on the farther ship and quickly her nose pointed toward the bottom. It appeared likely that her magazines had gone up.

"Have a look, Commodore?" asked Sam. Tichenor and Lynch each took a peek and observed the tail of the second destroyer pointed straight up in the air. The first had already disappeared.

Radio Technician Wilbur Clark, a second patrol veteran on the *Harder*, sat crouched before his sonar stack in the conning tower, gingerly holding an earphone at a little distance from his right ear. The terrific crashes a few minutes before had practically deafened him and he wondered if he had any eardrums left. As silence seemed to fall once more upon the sea above, he cautiously replaced the phones and listened intently, rotating the sound gear to sweep the vicinity.

"No more screws, Captain," he finally reported.

The Orchestra of Doom was stilled. The March of Death was finished. The end of the score had been reached.

Now, like some ghostly, macabre kind of applause, came the ugly and heart-rending sounds of ships breaking up in the depths of the sea. Clearly the microphones registered the crushing of bulkheads, the crashing of loose gear, the inrush of water—all of a goose-pimpling, stomach-gripping caliber. Those are sounds that every combat submariner learns to dread—the death throes of a noble ship. . . . It could be his own.

It was but ten minutes after the first torpedo had been fired—yet it seemed like hours—when Dealey took the *Harder* to the surface.

Sam had the word passed that those who wished to do so might come to the bridge a few at a time for a quick look at the scene where this latest victory had been won. There were plenty of takers for this offer—men who seldom saw the sky or felt the sea winds blowing after leaving port, men to whom the light of day and the twinkle of stars at night had seemed part of the birthright of freedom back in that distant but well-remembered land they called "the States."

It was an eerie stage that looked as if it had been set by Beelzebub himself. To be sure, neither destroyer remained, nor were there signs of boats or survivors. But floating debris dotted the water and a large cloud of steam and heavy vapor hung over the spot where the first destroyer had gone down. Where the second destroyer was swallowed by the ocean before it could burst into flame, the gentle darkness of moonlit sky and sea was broken by the pathetic flame of a lonesome acetylene buoy. Its feeble flicker, designed to guide men lost upon the sea, revealed not a single sign of life or motion other than windblown white caps that seemed to prance in a gayly spirited dance within its narrow circle of illumination. There it floated—a single candle lighted for the dead.

A bright moon sailed in the clear star-studded sky. Sam called his lookouts down from the high periscope shears so that from the lower elevation of the bridge they might more easily spot the loom of approaching ships or planes above the horizon. No craft of any sort were picked up by their powerful night binoculars. A radar search similarly reported: "No ships left!"

Turning to Lynch, as he headed for the wardroom and a cup of coffee, Sam said: "Set a course down to southeastward and let's get away from here before the Japs' night fliers start buzzing."

"Aye, aye, sir," replied Frank. "The last of those two tin cans probably had time to get on the air before she went down."

To which Sam nodded agreement.

With two more destroyers sunk, the Japanese Fleet Commander and his staff at Tawi-Tawi were now thoroughly aroused. The place must have been like a yellow jacket's nest, full of vengeful, vicious—and badly frightened —Japanese sailors. More hard-to-spare ships and difficult-to-train sailors had been sent to watery graves, sunk right in the fleet's own dooryard, as it were. Sunk by accursed American submarines.

"There must be a solid score of them," thought short, bandy-legged, Admiral Ozawa as he gripped his Samurai sword. His cruel, thin-lipped face tensed with anger. How satisfying it would be to chop off the heads of these under- water Yankee assassins who struck down his ships without warning. Perhaps the Admiral had forgotten Pearl Har- bor,* Manila, and the thousands of dead whom Japanese bombers and torpedo planes left in their wake on 7 De- cember 1941. Perhaps he felt that the rules of honorable warfare were written for observance only by his enemies.

Float-type biplane "Pete"

In any case, those Yankee submarines must be de- stroyed or some heads would roll in his own Fleet. They were a menace to his battleships. If he lost more destroy- ers, he would not have enough left for adequate protection

*For a complete account of the Japanese attack read DAY OF INFAMY by Walter Lord. Another volume in the Bantam War Book Series.

of the aircraft carriers, those last hopes of the Imperial Japanese Navy.

Hence, the floodgates of wrath were opened upon the *Harder* and her imaginary hordes of blockading submarine teammates. True, the *Puffer* had sunk two tankers on 5 June some 120 miles to the northeast and the *Redfin* was patrolling to northeastward and was to sink another tanker on 11 June, but, at that moment, the *Harder* alone was in Sibutu Passage. And indeed she felt very much alone as anti-submarine forces massed against her.

Hardly had Sam left the scene of the sinking when radar picked up a plane, probably attracted by the flare of explosions, coming in fast. The sub crash dived but received no bombs and surfaced again—after a forty-minute run.

The battery situation was beginning to worry Sam Logan, the Engineer Officer. The battery charge—so essential for submerged running—had not been completed the preceding dawn before the ship was forced down. As Logan reported to Dealey: "There'll be a batch of anxious hours tomorrow, sir, unless we jam some more juice into the can tonight."

"Go right ahead, jam all you can," replied the Skipper, "but I can't guarantee to keep these night fliers off our neck."

Four minutes after Sam Logan asked permission to start a battery charge, the *Harder's* log records: "2305—(11th Aircraft contact)—Sighted aircraft (float-type biplane) flying at height of 100 feet, coming in off our starboard quarter and almost on top of us. It is believed that he sighted us just as the rudder was shifted hard left. He whizzed by the starboard beam at a range of about 100 yards!"

It was another close shave. Once more those on the bridge of the *Harder* observed no formalities in going below. The only one aboard who seemed visibly annoyed was poor Sam Logan, who begrudged every ampere of juice drawn from his hungry batteries. However, if an air bomb hit the *Harder*, there would be no batteries left to service. Logan found consolation in that thought as the

*Harder* went to 150 feet in almost nothing flat. Only a superbly trained crew, in which every man knew what to do without being told, could have managed such a dive in the time involved.

It was thirteen minutes and fifteen minutes past eleven o'clock when the first two bombs fell. The first was not close. The second, as Sam Dealey observed, was "damn close." He increased the depth to 200 feet.

The eight bells of midnight struck without any more bombs following. At "Rig for depth charge," the conning tower had been abandoned and the watertight hatch between it and the control room dogged down tight. If struck by a bomb or ruptured by a close depth charge, the conning tower crew would surely be doomed, but the compartment below might still be intact. Therefore, it was standard practice and very sensible to bring the personnel down and operate the submarine from the control room.

Usually, when the *Harder* was under counterattack, Sam would be on hand in the control room. There, as the sub ran deep and silent, he would lean his elbows on the table atop the vessel's main gyroscope. Or he would amble over to the scuttlebutt for a drink. Or he would lean against the ladder that leads to the conning tower hatch, an arm hooked over a handy rung, his eyes taking in everything and his tongue ever ready for a low-spoken order or a softly voiced wisecrack. Truly, at such times, the Old Man was a tower of strength for his shipmates, especially those new to the Silent Service, for even the most rugged will admit to a queer feeling in the stomach when their submarines were on the receiving end of depth charges.

More than an hour passed before three distant aerial bombs were heard. It was then about four bells of the mid watch—2 A.M. to the man in the street—when Sound reported contact with an approaching ship. Things being as they were, Sam rigged for silent running and went to 300 feet. He took this action because he knew that all hands aboard were bone weary and needed rest. There is a time to fight, and there is a time to avoid fighting. This was such a time, and so the *Harder* remained deep for the remainder of the night.

Shortly before sunrise on the morning of that 10 June, the *Harder* surfaced to change air in the boat and to cram a few more "amps" into the almost completely depleted batteries. That done, the *Harder* was set for another all-day dive, whereupon the vessel submerged and set course for a point south of Tawi-Tawi close enough to the anchorage so that the concentration of Japanese war ships in the bay could be reconnoitered. Proceeding at one-third speed and bucking the 2-knot current, she made almost no headway all day. Of course, Sam could have used up more juice and thus increased the pace of his progress, but he felt it was greater wisdom to save his electric reserve for submerged running.

Shortly after 0900 the *Harder* sighted two enemy destroyers, hull down. Dealey got set for an approach on them. The mellow call of bong-bong-bong to battle stations resounded throughout the sub. But the attack never developed. The two swiftly moving vessels closed to a range of about 12,000 yards; then they turned away. Their echo-ranging pings faded as the distance grew and Sam secured from battle stations.

The business of sighting destroyers and immediately standing in to attack her most deadly and dangerous enemies was becoming a habit with the *Harder*. That was the *Harder* policy, one in perfect accord with the slogan lettered on her battle flag, "Hit 'Em *Harder*." Perhaps it was not so high-sounding a slogan as Commodore Perry's "Don't Give up the Ship" at the Battle of Lake Erie, but it was one more appropriate to the submarine service wherein there was no thought of giving up the ship. Scuttle her? Yes, as a last desperate measure, but surrender—never! "Hit 'Em *Harder*" will live forever in submarine annals.

The remainder of 10 June was free from alarms until late afternoon. Tired officers and men tried to catch up on much needed sleep, well knowing that such leisure could not be of long duration. The *Harder* clawed her way toward her selected observation spot five miles south of

Tawi-Tawi harbor entrance. She still had about three miles to go when, at 1700, the Sonarman, listening intently before his sound stack on the starboard side of the conning tower, centered his dial on a port quarter bearing. The periscope was down at the moment and Lieut. (jg) Ray Levin was Officer of the Watch.

"Contact, sir!" reported Sound, hushed excitement in his voice; "light and heavy screws. Bearing two two zero, relative."

"Up periscope," instantly ordered Levin and, as soon as the training handles rose above the top of the periscope well, swung the 'scope to the proper bearing.

"Hmm," he murmured to his intent audience, training his 'scope slowly back and forth, "something there all right. Call the tracking party."

"Tracking party to the conning tower," rasped out the squawk boxes.

"Yes," continued the O.O.D., "there are masts—several of them. Better call the Captain. Down 'scope."

In this glassy sea the periscope had to be used most carefully and sparingly.

"Captain to the conning tower; Captain to the conning tower," repeated the Talker.

Already Phil Sampson and Tom Buckner were clattering up the ladder with Tiny Lynch close behind. The amazing skill of this trio in ferretting out the facts about a target's course, speed, and zigs was something that approached clairvoyance and was responsible for the success of many of the *Harder's* attacks. God help an enemy target when these lads, backed by Sam Dealey's sharpshooting eye and the *Harder's* HSN (Hot, Straight, Normal) torpedoes, got on his trail.

As Sam's head came above the level of the conning tower deck, the sound man was reporting: "Pretty wide target, sir. Propeller noises cover about ten degrees on the azimuth dial."

"Several ships, undoubtedly, Captain," reported Levin. "All I could see were masts. Could we have more 'scope, sir?"

"Just a moment and I'll see," said Dealey. "Up 'scope."

Then began one of the periscope monologues for which Sam Dealey was famous. "Um, um," he murmured while taking a cautious peek; "yes, I can see five or six masts—and, oh, man! There's a pagoda!" (Type of mast used by capital ships of the Imperial Japanese Navy.)

"Yes," he went on, "I've gotta have more 'scope. Control: let the ship come up slowly about five or six feet. . . . That's better," as his periscope gained more elevation above the surface. "Man, oh, man! Look at that string of pagodas! Battleships and cruisers! This is the jackpot. Call Commodore Tichenor."

"Commodore Tichenor to the conning tower," spoke the Talker into his mike.

Meanwhile, Sam was feeding data to the tracking trio: "Bearing, mark."

"Two one eight," called Frank to Tom.

"Range, mark."

"One six thousand."

"Angle on the bow—give 'em sixty port," finished Sam. "Left full rudder. What course do I want?"

"Enemy course is one eight zero," replied Buckner. "We better go in on about one nine zero to try to head them off—and pray for some good zigs toward us," he added.

"New course," said Sam to the helmsman, "is one nine zero."

"New course," repeated the man at the wheel, "one nine zero."

Then, glancing around the excited faces of the conning tower crew as Murray Tichenor came scrambling up the ladder, with his voice almost a whisper, Sam said: "Three battlewagons with cruisers and destroyers; man, oh, man, if we can just get a shot. Sound battle stations, submerged. Make ready all tubes."

Tich took a quick confirmatory look and then the *Harder's* periscope was housed (lowered into its well) and her speed was boosted to "Flank" in a desperate try to close the target. Only a change of course toward her could give the submarine a chance to shoot at a decent range.

Sam and Tichenor, with the others watching eagerly, thumbed hurriedly through the ONI (Office of Naval Intelligence) silhouette book for identification of Japanese men-of-war. Both believed that the nearest battleship was of the giant *Musashi* class. With her were two smaller battleships, four or more cruisers, and about eight destroyers.

The sea was glassy-smooth and Sam slowed the ship down after a few minutes so that the periscope, when exposed, would not make too large and revealing a feather on the surface.

Dealey shot his periscope cautiously to the surface for another look just in time to see the nearest battlewagon suddenly enveloped in heavy black smoke. At the same time, Sound reported three distant explosions. At first Sam hoped this might mean that another submarine had gotten three hits on the *Musashi*, but later developments indicated an entirely different train of events. As Sam explained in his patrol log: "Immediately after the smoke and explosions around the battleship, a destroyer, which until then had almost blended in with the big ship, headed directly for us belching heavy black smoke. It is believed likely that one of the float type planes had spotted our periscope while we were trying to identify the units of the Japanese fleet and dropped a smoke float near it; whereupon the battleship's escorting destroyer laid down a quick smoke screen between us and the battleship and then dropped three 'scare charges' as he headed our way. The sound man obtained a 'turn count' for 35 knots on the destroyer. His bow wave and the rapidly closing range verified it!"

"There goes the old ball game," growled Sam. "They'll never come our way now."

"There goes Major Jinkins' limpet bait," added Frank Lynch with a grin which, in spite of his disappointment, brought an answering smile to Dealey's face.

Major Jinkins, when he learned of the reconnaissance part of the *Harder's* mission, had pleaded with the Exec.

to be allowed to paddle his folboat into the Tawi-Tawi anchorage some calm night. His intention was to stick his limpet bombs on the sides of the battleships and blow them to their ancestral Kingdom Come. Lynch had turned the idea down—first, because he did not believe the limpets were powerful enough to do much damage to armored ships and, second, because he considered the danger to daredevil Jinkins too great for the results likely to be achieved.

A few months before this daring proposal by Jinkins, a party of five saboteurs, landed from a submarine, had actually made such an attempt at Singapore. They were led by Major Ivan Bowes-Lyon of the British Army, a first cousin of the then Queen of England. Tragically, after considerable success—four ships sunk or damaged—they were captured and beheaded by the infuriated Japs.

Disappointment aboard the *Harder* at being robbed of this wonderful opportunity to make a record—no allied submarine up to that time had sunk an enemy battleship— had little time to rankle in Sam's thoughts, for the Jap destroyer was racing down upon them. Should the *Harder* evade or accept battle? The decision was not long in the making. To Dealey's inborn aggressiveness was now added resentment for having been robbed of a shot at the jackpot. "Well," drawled Sam slowly, "we're going to have to take a working over anyhow. So let's have a crack at him first."

The submarine was swung toward the destroyer for "down the throat" shots and the skipper, taking occasional quick looks with the periscope, watched the bow of the oncoming destroyer loom higher. The picture had reached the state where the *Harder's* torpedo had to hit—or else. Sonar reported that the enemy destroyer had slowed to 15 knots—probably to permit his own echo-ranging operator to obtain more accurate pinging on the submarine. The pings of the destroyer at this stage could be heard plainly throughout the conning tower. He was certainly centered right on the target. Sam Logan adjusted his TDC setup to allow for the change of speed.

Dealey was as calm as though the whole thing were an exercise—as though his own torpedoes carried dummy warheads and the destroyer were armed only with the hand-grenade sized bombs used in anti-submarine training. His steadfast demeanor in battle was a marvel to all who saw him—and they drew strength from him. During the attack he showed no sign of being under pressure and habitually indulged in his low-toned monologue as he was working the periscope.

Sound reported other fast screws off to starboard, but there was no time to take a look. Things had to happen fast now.

"Stand by forward," said Sam. "Up periscope!"

"All tubes ready forward," reported the quartermaster.

At 1714, with a range of 1400 yards, torpedo run 1100 yards, gyros near zero, torpedoes set to run at six-foot depth, the Skipper ordered: "Fire One!"

Tubes Two and Three were fired with one quarter of a degree spread. Then came the quick order: "Cease firing, all ahead full, right full rudder, take 'er deep."

Theirs was not to stand upon the order of their going but to execute that well-known maneuver to "get-the-Hell-out-of-here." If those torpedoes hit, that destroyer could come right down on top of them. Torpedo tube doors were closed so that the torpedoes would not be subjected to the crushing pressures to be found in the depths of the sea—approximately one-half pound per square inch of surface for every foot of submergence.

"Fifty-five seconds and sixty seconds, respectively," records the *Harder's* patrol log, "after the first shot, two torpedoes struck with a detonation that was far worse than depth charging. By this time we were just passing 80 feet and were soon almost beneath the destroyer. Then all Hell broke loose. It was not from his depth charges, for if they had been dropped at that time this report would not have been completed, but a deafening series of progressive rumblings that seemed to almost blend with each other. Either his boilers or magazines or both had exploded, and it's a lucky thing that ship explosions are vented upward and not down.

"The previously reported sound on the starboard beam was now reported moving in for his share of the fun and started laying his barrages as we passed 200 feet. It is believed that they fell astern. They were loud and close and added their bit to the jolting around, but none compared in intensity to the exploding destroyer we had just passed beneath."

Writing of this phase twelve years later, Ensign Arthur L. Schelling of the U.S. Submarine *Rock*, who was then a Radio Technician, second class, says: "On her fifth patrol, run in Sibutu Passage, we sank five destroyers. The last destroyer exploded on top of us. Apparently our skipper misjudged her speed.

"I had no submerged battle station at the time, so consequently spent most of my time in the radio shack, listening to the battle telephone circuit. I was in the radio shack prior to sinking the destroyer, making myself a peanut butter sandwich. Norman Skiles, RM2c, of Wilmington, North Carolina, who had the Sonar in the conning tower, came in the shack. He was white as a sheet. He said, 'We fired; the Old Man secured the conning tower. I think we missed.' About that time it blew up.

"I dropped or threw the peanut butter jar. Gauges broke, cork and peanut butter flew all over the radio shack. An hour later I went back to my bunk in the after battery, swung up into it, and went—splash! Someone had thrown a whole quart of grapefruit juice into it."

Other explosions, believed to be aerial bombs, landed nearby and all added to make up the most uncomfortable five minutes yet experienced during the *Harder's* five war patrols. Something between twenty and thirty distinct depth charges or bombs were counted, but no one was interested in numerical accuracy at the time. Again the ship was a shambles of cork and loose gear well watered by spurting pet cocks and weeping rivets. Engine room crews were kept busy checking the sea valves which have a bad habit of vibrating open. Inspection of the motor room disclosed that some explosions were so close that water squirted out through the propeller shaft stuffing glands. During the worst period, when the destroyer was believed to have blown up overhead, a barometer in the control room was flung clear across the compartment to smash on the opposite bulkhead. In the forward torpedo room, one of the heavy chain falls used for handling torpedoes leaped from its overhead hook and knocked out one of the torpedo crew, inflicting a severe scalp wound. Even Major Gort Chester, leader of the saboteurs saved on Borneo, who was trying to catch up on his reading, gave up and tactfully inquired if the *Harder* were not almost out of torpedoes. When that happened, obviously she would have to return to Australia.

Two destroyers eventually joined the party, but evasive measures, conducted at 250 to 350 feet, soon left them behind; and at 1905, the tropic night having shut down tight, the submarine surfaced.

Once again, about three miles astern, a lone lighted lifebuoy burned over the spot of the attack. It remained in sight for about fifteen minutes while the submarine cleared the area to the southeastward. The report of JANAC (Joint Army-Navy Assessment Committee) after the war did not credit the *Harder* with a sinking at this time. Nevertheless, Admiral Ozawa reported four destroyers "damaged"—a masterpiece of understatement.

Aboard the *Harder* there was no time for gloating over her victories. Dealey himself never gloated. As we have said, his attack manners were calm. He indulged in no shouting, no fanfare of destruction. After his torpedoes hit, he went about the business of bringing his ship into a position of safety as rapidly as possible. He did not linger to rejoice at the sight of an enemy going down. In his veins ran the milk of human kindness, in his heart was a feeling of humility and humanity that could not find pleasure in the destruction of a beautiful ship and a hundred odd human beings—deadly enemies though they were.

Perhaps he remembered the words of Captain Philip of the old battleship *Texas* at the Battle of Santiago, who called to his cheering crew as their Spanish adversary sank: "Don't cheer, boys; those poor devils are dying." While Dealey never said so, in so many words, one could conclude that he hated the job of killing but knew it had to be done and did his best to carry out his duty.

Actually, there was little time or inclination for celebration aboard the *Harder* that night. After the first spontaneous outburst when the two destroyers took their final dives, the reaction set in. Taut nerves relaxed to leave their owners limp with relief and gratitude for still being alive. All hands desired nothing so much as a bit of peace and quiet—and an indefinite tour of "sack duty." They could not seem to remember when they had last had a hot meal seated at a table. The ship herself needed juice for her batteries, air for her banks of cast steel, high-pressure air bottles; and, above all, she needed solitude in which to send off a dispatch reporting the sortie of the Japanese task force which later, we learned, was the Mobile Fleet under command of Admiral Jisaburo Ozawa, I.J.N.

This last item proved to be more difficult of accomplishment than had been anticipated. While the *Harder* was running submerged at creeping speed and taking her lumps from the enemy destroyers, Dealey, Tichenor, and Levin, the Communication Officer, were not idle. Crowded into the Skipper's stateroom, they were desperately trying to keep their wits and their writing equipment about them long enough to write a contact report of sighting the Japanese task force. With depth charges blasting off above and on all sides, this was a bit difficult. Cork showered down, loose gear fell from desk and shelves, and they themselves had difficulty in staying in their seats during the *Harder's* wild gyrations. Ray's thoughts as to the ancestry of the *Harder's* tormentors could have scorched the dispatch pad on which he wrote as he sat on the bunk and tried to take Dealey's dictation. Finally, it was completed: "Enemy task force sortied from Tawi-Tawi on course south. Three battleships, four cruisers, about eight destroyers. We were forced deep. Sank one Dog Dog. Received minor damage."

After Dealey had initialed it, Levin broke out the coding machine and, with the aid of Radioman Bill Diamond, a brilliant and fast operator, got the dispatch ready for transmission. "Get it off, Diamond," directed Ray, "the instant our antenna breaks water. It is urgent—top priority."

Diamond proceeded to the radio "shack," as the radio room is known aboard ship, and, when the *Harder* finally surfaced, his call for VIXO, the powerful Australian station at Coonawara, went crackling out. The reply came back instantly and the message was clicked out into the blue. No repeats were requested and the proper acknowledgment was received.

Levin, leaning over Diamond's shoulder, felt that something was wrong. The receipt was made too fast and sounded too clear for the distance involved. Diamond, however, insisted that he would recognize VIXO'S "fist" anywhere. Still, Ray was not satisfied and finally confided his suspicions to the Exec. Together they went to the Skipper. Dealey's decision was to check the Baker schedule (a Fleet rebroadcast of important messages from a high-powered station to all action addresses). The *Harder's* message was not rebroadcast.

When Diamond tried to repeat the message, the Japanese station immediately answered up for VIXO and gave the "go ahead." The Australian station then asked the *Harder* to shift to another frequency. This shift was made, but the Jap blocked the channel with intensive jamming. After three attempts, the message was finally gotten through by way of far-off San Francisco, almost half around the globe.

This achievement, sighting and successfully reporting the movement of the Fleet, Dealey considered of importance equal to, if not greater than, that of sinking five destroyers or rescuing six agents from Borneo. Admirals Raymond Spruance and Marc Mitscher were in the Marianas Islands. Their planes were blasting Saipan. Their ears were eagerly awaiting news of reaction by the Imperial Japanese Navy and they undoubtedly agreed with Sam as to the value of his reconnaissance. The *Harder's* report, with one from the nearby *Redfin* on sighting the enemy carrier group, plus later contact reports from submarines *Flying Fish*, *Seahorse*, and *Cavallo*, gave our mighty Fifth Fleet the information it needed.

Admiral Ozawa's departure from Tawi-Tawi, as we now know, was premature. His badly timed move, triggered by deep-dyed heebeejeebies, had launched the treasured Operation "A-Go," by which the Japanese expected to destroy the United States Pacific Fleet "at one blow." His sortie twenty-four hours ahead of the original schedule threw out the timing of other Japanese forces—notably that of the Empire-based air forces. Operation "A-Go" culminated in the Battle of the Philippine Sea, which brought disaster to the Japanese Combined Fleet and the loss of hundreds of their planes in the famed "Marianas Turkey Shoot."

Ozawa jumped the gun on Operation "A-Go" because he believed that a concentration of American submarines existed at Tawi-Tawi. He thought that he had insufficient destroyers to cope with the hordes of destroyer-killing American submarines that seemed to pop up in Sibutu Passage at every turn. Based on this conclusion, he had no choice but to withdraw from Tawi-Tawi while his big ships still had bottoms on which to float.

The entire concentration of Jap-hunting subs was, as we know, supplied by Comdr. Samuel David Dealey and his redoubtable submarine *Harder*. But unhappy little Adm. Ozawa had no way of knowing that.

En route to her base in Australia, the *Harder* received a high priority dispatch. It had been sent by one of Freedom's greatest fighters—an all-time American hero—the Supreme Commander, Allied Forces Southwest Pacific Area. Communication Officer Levin gave a low whistle as the hodgepodge of coded groups slowly yielded the following message:

"To Comdr. Samuel Dealey
 The recent exploits and achievements of your subma-

rine were magnificent. My congratulations and admiration for its commander and crew.

Douglas MacArthur."

Later the General was to decorate Sam Dealey with the Army's coveted Distinguished Service Cross. . . . But that is a bit ahead of our story.

The Communicator carried the dispatch board to Sam Dealey in his cabin where the Old Man was catching forty winks. The Skipper, half awake, read it sleepily.

"Any answer, sir?" asked Levin.

"Yes, Ray," replied Sam, "just say: 'Aw shucks, 'tweren't nothin'.' "

His jaw unhinged, all Levin could do was look at Sam.

"Anything wrong with it?" inquired the Skipper as he wearily lay back upon his bunk.

"Oh, no—no," answered the *Harder's* Communications Officer.

To this day, Ray Levin does not recall if that message was ever sent to General MacArthur. But his bottom-dollar hunch is that it was not.

The Mother sits by the severn side,
  Where Severn joins the Bay,
And the great, gray ships go down the tide
  And carry her sons away.

*     *     *     *     *

Young and eager and unafraid
  As neophytes they kneeled;
And watched their arms, and only prayed
  "Keep stain from every shield."
Naught else they fear as they hunt their foes
  Through fog, and storm, and mine,
Keen for the test of battle blows;
  But God make strong the hearts of those
  Who love, and are left behind.

★★★★★★★★★★★★★★★★★★★★★★★★★★★★★★★★★★★★★★★★★★★★ 4

# No Love for Ships or Seas

Sam Dealey fired his first effective torpedo and sank his first enemy transport in a battle of hair-raising valor shortly after the lunch hour on a peaceful Sunday in the spring of 1918.

The action took place "somewhere in the Atlantic." Coming in at periscope depth, Cap'n Daredevil Dealey nosed his trusty U-Boat into the middle of a heavily armed convoy. After taking careful aim at the largest transport, he saw his torpedo streak across the whitecapped waves and heard a mighty explosion as the missile struck.

The daring submariner took swift evasive action. But not swift enough.

He was captured. Not just taken prisoner but actually grabbed by the scruff of the neck and given a teeth-rattling shaking up by his captor—Lieut. Jerome K. Dealey, U.S.A., just out of training camp and about to head eastward over the Big Pond for some place on the Western Front.

The action took place in the cool shade of the porch that skirted the pleasant little white frame house where Mother Dealey and the still growing members of her brood lived on a quiet residential street in Denver. Young Sam, then twelve years old, was—like other early teen-agers of that time and place—steeped in various aspects of the war which had held most of Europe under its thumb since the fall of 1914 and which Uncle Sam had joined just a brief year earlier.

"You little rascal," shouted Brother Jerome as, half-grinning, half-scowling, he gave his fraternal kinsman, younger by some seven years, a well-practiced shaking down, "what're you trying to do? Kill me? Putting a stick of dynamite under my chair to blow me sky-high."

"Wasn't no stick of dynamite," gritted Sam with that peculiar grin on his face that was reserved for moments of triumph blended with fury, " 'twas only one of those giant fire-crackers they use down at the bandstand in the park on the Fourth of July. I was playing U-Boat skipper and I put the torpedo in a pail under your chair just to see if you'd jump. And," he added with a broad grin, "by cricky, you did! Almost clear to the ceiling!"

Brother Jerome released his grip, gave the youngster a friendly shove with the words: "On your way, kid, and no more rough stuff. Remember our Bond of Responsibility. In another week or two, I'll be on my way to France. And you'll be the head of the house."

At the age of twelve, Sam Dealey was a freckle-faced boy with a ready grin, rather small and light of weight for his years. He had a thick mop of unruly reddish-brown hair that had the gleam—when slicked down with dabs of water—of newly polished mahogany. His eyes, set deep and spaced wide under finely drawn brows, were smoky-brown, flecked with spots of gold that somehow seemed to change into liquid fire on the few occasions when he was really angry. The outstanding trait of Sam Dealey, as boy and man, was his infallible good nature and solidly optimistic view of life.

Born in Dallas in 1906, the son of Samuel David Dealey

and Virgie Downing Dealey, young Sam was a first-generation American on his father's side. On the Downing roster, he was the offspring of pioneers who had come to Texas, by way of Tennessee and Alabama, in the days of the Lone Star Republic from an Ireland which they still loved with fierce pride. In the Civil War, they fought for the Confederacy.

To Samuel David Dealey and his wife were given five children. The eldest of these, George William, was about seventeen years old when his father died in 1912. Next, and some four years younger, came Jerome Kearby. Then two sisters, Ethel and Margaret. And lastly, by far the youngest of them all, Samuel David Dealey, Jr.

Young Sam's father was the youngest of the nine children born to George Dealey and Mary Ann Nellis in mid-Victorian England. Because of business reverses, the family left England for Texas in 1870, settling first in Galveston, later in Dallas. There the Dealey boys grew up to take places of national prominence. One brother, George Bannerman Dealey, as head of the *Dallas News*, in time became the Dean of American newspaper publishers; even as James Quayle Dealey was to become a distinguished historian and Professor of History at Brown University. Had he lived, it is more than probable that Samuel David Dealey, senior, would have risen high in the leadership of Texas business pioneers and Dallas civic leaders. Shortly before his death, he was elected to the Dallas Board of Education by the greatest vote ever cast for that office.

Sam was of the quiet kind. But, once angered, it was well to give him a wide path. He was proud of his heritage which, loosely speaking, might be described as half-Irish, half-Texan, half-Johnny Reb, and all-American. Sam was born in Dallas, on 13 September, 1906. Six years later, his father, a prominent but then land-poor Texas booster, died suddenly, leaving his widow the burden of looking after their five children. Because of ill health, Mrs. Dealey moved to Colorado where she and the three youngest children lived until the early 1920's. George and Jerome, following in their father's footsteps, went into real estate operations in Dallas. When Sam was old enough to enter high school, Mrs. Dealey, Sam, and the girls, moved to Santa Monica. There Sam and Edwina ("Wena") Vawter, high school classmates, formed a friendship which, in time, was to blossom into love and marriage.

After a year or so in Santa Monica, Mrs. Dealey and her brood returned to Dallas and moved into a new house on Dealey Hill in the Oak Ridge section of the town. The earlier Dealey manse had burned down at the time of Mr. Dealey's death. In Dallas, Sam was one of the Mill High School students, with poor showing in "figgers" but good reports in reading. He liked track sports and boxing.

On graduating from high school, Sam's future spread ahead of him—wide and empty. He had no particular aims. Most of all, he wanted to be a rancher. But Sam's brothers, who had been compelled to forego higher education because of stern demands for making a living, decided that Sam, above all, should have an education. The Dealeys, still land-poor and too proud to borrow, decided that the best solution would be to seek the cooperation of Congressman Hatton Sumners to appoint Sam to West Point or Annapolis. Either place was okay in Sam's book. With the help of Colonel Moss, a great Dallas personality as well as the friend and employer of George and Jerome Dealey, the two brothers obtained an appointment to Annapolis for Sam, there being no West Point vacancies. This procedure is not at all uncommon. In fact, some of the nation's best military and naval leaders have risen out of the ranks of boys who went to the "Point" or to the "Academy" without feeling any particular call to either service.

In the spring of 1925, Sam Dealey, for the first time, entered the Yard of the Academy at Annapolis. After passing the entrance examinations, he settled down to the none-too-pleasant life of a Fourth Classman—the lowly life of a plebe. The numerous restrictions imposed upon midshipmen in their first year—and enforced rigidly and raucously by lordly upperclassmen—roweled Sam like a Texas spur. As a Westerner, he had an inborn attitude of independence that rose in undisguised wrath whenever a senior midshipman took him for a ride because of some infraction of a rule so thin that Sam, often, could not even see it. In short, during his first six plebe months, Sam's days were filled with rebellion and his nights were saturated with wrath. As the result of this situation—which was largely of Sam's own making—his standing as a student was seriously jeopardized.

One day, shortly before Thanksgiving, 1925, Sam was marching smartly down a corridor in Bancroft Hall. He was heading for his room—one of the smallest in this the largest dormitory building in the world—when he was stopped by a tall, lean-hipped, and broad-shouldered First Classman. Sam recognized him instantly—Tex Edwards. A fellow Lone Star Stater from San Saba, Heywood Lane Edwards was one of the all-time Greats of the Academy. A member of the 1926 class, he was captain of the wrestling team and a star of the boxing and football teams. As Sam snapped out his name and rank—if lowly plebes have a rank—Tex grinned and said, "Hear you been having plebe troubles?"

"Yes, sir," answered Sam.

A brief pause during which Tex took slow, silent, and careful inventory of the youth before him. He evidently liked what he saw, because he added: "Tonight, after chow, come around to my room. We'll get acquainted and I'll have you meet some other plebes I'm sure you'll like—be seeing you!"

With that, Tex Edwards made his way down the corridor while Sam actually pinched himself to make sure that he was not dreaming.

Holy smoke! He, Samuel David Dealey, Junior, actually had been "spooned on" by no less a person than Tex Edwards himself.

To those who have not attended the Naval Academy and are unversed in its traditions and customs, the significance of a plebe being "spooned on" by an upperclassman is difficult to understand. It granted to the plebe the privilege of visiting the great man's room, of omitting the "sir" in addressing his sponsor, of being helped with studies. It protected the plebe against hazing by upperclassmen of less rank than the "spoon"—especially from those natural enemies of all plebes, the "Youngsters," as midshipmen of the Third Class are known.

To Sam, it meant that a strong protective arm had been placed around his shoulders—that he had a friend among the mighty.

That evening, as soon as supper was over, Sam, still walking with his head in the clouds, hot-footed it to Tex Edwards' room. Midshipman Nix Lidstone was already there. He was a well-set-up youngster of Sam's own age, size, and weight—namely about five feet nine inches tall and weighing about 150 pounds. This meeting led to deep and dyed in the wool friendships on the plebe level, not only with Nix but with two other plebes, Raymond Neal Sharp of Johnson City and William McClure Drane of Clarksville, Tennessee. Because two of them hailed from Texas and two from Tennessee, they dubbed themselves the TNT boys.

But strong as it was in saving Sam from being "braced" by plebe-hunting upperclassmen, Tex Edwards' friendship could not save Sam from the wrath of the God of Two-Point-Five—or Two-Five, as it was abbreviated—that being the passing grade required for all midshipmen at the end of every term. In January, 1926, Sam bilged out not only because of low points in Math and Skinny (chemistry) but also because of the load of demerits piled upon him by upperclassmen who found too many faults with Sam's—to them—too independent behavior. On 10 February, Sam was notified that he had bilged. He asked permission to visit Washington. Obtaining permission, he went to the office of Congressman Sumners in the Capitol. There, after several hours of arguing and pleading, he talked the veteran lawmaker into violating his iron-clad policy against re-appointing midshipmen or cadets who had failed. There was something about Sam that won the older man's heart. When Sam returned to Annapolis and Dallas, he had an appointment to reenter the Academy, with a fresh plebe-start, in the summer of 1926.

Sam was highly elated and for two major reasons: first, he hated to let down his family; second, he hated like the devil to take a licking. And, Sam felt, he had not rolled enough with the punches during his first crack at being a sea-going specimen of the brand that is half-Irish, half-Texan, half-Johnny Reb, and all-American. Sam, at this time, was not driven by any particular love of the sea or urge to be a career officer in the Navy. His main drive was just to make good.

That summer, Sam boned up on his weak mathematical subjects by attending Southern Methodist University at Dallas. And, truly, he put a firm hand to the plow. That he produced a straight and deep furrow was evidenced by the fact that his academic standing, when he returned to the Academy to renew his studies, was greatly improved.

As a member of the class of 1930, Sam stuck to his job faithfully and well. He had no spectacular successes, any more than he had outstanding failures. As the months piled into years, Sam kept within safe precincts so far as the vengeful God of Two-Five was concerned. Throughout his school years, he was in the great middle ground of students who make up the backbone of undergraduates at every institution of learning. During winters, he attended drills and classes. During summers, he went on cruises aboard big old battlewagons. During these latter interludes, Sam revealed that while he was ordinary as a book student, he was extraordinary when it came to aptitude toward the subjects that make for good seamanship aboard a vessel. Not only that, but as a First Class midshipman he showed beyond doubt that he had that elusive and precious thing called leadership or capacity to command. In time, this qualification, plus the sense of visual coordination that made him an expert marksman, were to turn him into a superior submarine commander. But that point of arrival was still far down Sam's highway of life and there were several turns in the road along the way.

Meanwhile, to Sam, graduating from Annapolis was a job that had to be done. He had to keep his nose too close to the academic grindstone to maintain his grades to permit entry into sports activities—except for a bit of class boxing. Sam liked the hops (dances) and other midshipmen parties, but the real highlights of his Academy years were the occasional visits to Annapolis or Washington of Edwina Vawter and her mother. Wena, now a tall, willowy girl with reddish-blonde hair and deep blue eyes, was, even then, the only girl in Sam's life, and he crowded his study hours to the limit when Wena was in the East so as to spend every possible moment with her. The other high spot in Sam's existence was the annual September Leave when he would hurry off to Dallas to spend the better part of a month on Dealey Hill with his mother and visit with his sisters and brothers. The silken cords of deep affection that linked Sam to his family were unbreakable.

There was much purpose but little enthusiasm in Midshipman Dealey's attitude toward his studies. There was not a month during those four years when he did not doubt his ability to make the grade—when he did not fear that, once more, he might be bilged back to Dallas. That his brothers realized those fears was shown in 1929 when they created their own real estate firm with Sam as a full-fledged junior partner. His name was even on the stationery—just to make him feel that he had some place to go if Annapolis became too tough.

His apprehension about making passing marks was so deep that he felt that no engagement announcement should be sent out until it was certain that he would be in the graduating class of 1930. And so he was—neither at the top of his class nor at its bottom, but in the solid and rockribbed middle. Sam had wanted an Annapolis wedding with crossed swords and all the chapel trimmings, but Wena wanted to be married at home in Santa Monica, and Wena won. In June, 1930, Ensign Samuel D. Dealey, USN, and Edwina Vawter became man and wife.

The years of somnolence on questions of defense in case of war began in this country after the Washington Naval Conference of 1921, where limits were set as to the size and number of ships in certain categories. This was followed by the London Naval Conference of 1930 and a

League of Nations General Disarmament Conference at Geneva in 1932.

During the better part of that period the paralyzing touch of obsolescence crept over the entire fleet which was made up of World War I battleships, a handful of cruisers, aging destroyers, and an alphabet soup of submarines, only a few of which were adequate for modern combat conditions. To make the situation worse, the officer corps in the Navy was reduced through resignations without effective steps to fill vacancies through increased admission of midshipmen to Annapolis. It was not a situation that induced young officers to remain in the service; unhappy, dissatisfied, and seeing no future in the Navy, they resigned by the score—and who could blame them?

On joining the fleet, following his honeymoon, Ensign Dealey was assigned to duty aboard the battleship *Nevada*, where he served in various departments until 1934. Like other young officers in his grade, he performed his duties alertly and well; but, like other young officers who were married, he resented bitterly the great slices of time he had to spend at sea away from home. During this phase, if Sam had one outstanding trait, it was the affection he held for his wife and children. By 1934, the Dealeys had a girl, Joan, born in 1931 and David, born in 1933. A few years later, in 1941, Barbara Lee was to enter the world.

As the years went by, Sam became rather weary with battleship duty, but these old battlewagons are traditionally the rings on which Ensigns cut their naval teeth. In 1934, after he had virtually resigned himself to growing old aboard the *Nevada*, his request for transfer to the submarine school at New London for training in the submarine branch was granted.

At the time of his transfer, Sam was not motivated by any particular yearning for submarining. Although he thought that it would be interesting duty, his main reason was that submarine duty would give him more time at home, for the submersibles seldom go on extended cruises from their home bases in peacetime. Also, and not to be overlooked, submariners drew 25 per cent above base pay—an item not to be ignored.

In due time, Sam arrived at New London, entered the submarine school, underwent and passed with high honors a gruelling course of training. On graduating, he was assigned to submarine duty in Hawaii, where he served on several subs, including the S-24. To be sure, Sam was happier in the "pigboats" than he had been in vessels that gave him more extensive duty at sea, but, even so, he toyed seriously with the thought of resigning and returning to Texas to take up civilian life. He even discussed the matter at length with Commander Stanley Moseley, his skipper. The latter, who liked the quiet young Texan and saw in him the potentials of an excellent senior officer, did his best to dissuade Sam.

"He was a quiet officer when he served on the old S-24 and not a colorful one whom you might expect to become famous for his sense of humor," ran the comment to Admiral Lockwood from Captain Stan Moseley, himself a Texan. "I do not believe that he was very interested in continuing in the Navy at that time. In fact, he was seriously thinking of resigning. He discussed this with me and, although I argued against it, I had the feeling that he was unconvinced. What finally made him change his mind, I do not know."

At that time, Sam, a young husband and father of two, was probably suffering from a malady which I have observed in many youngsters in the Navy—especially those who marry early. They find that their service pay has to stretch beyond its elastic limit to cover a multitude of needs; that the family has to be packed up and moved on to a new home and schools about every two years. My own family was moved sixteen times in only seventeen years of married Navy life. Desirable houses, at a reasonable rental, do not grow beside every bush; and, last but not least, they see their contemporaries "on the outside" snugged down in comfortable suburban homes for years at a stretch and drawing salaries that seem fabulous. These combine to make the great outside look mighty attractive

—as the Armed Services today are finding out to their sorrow. It requires a youngster with a lot of the call of the sea in his system to weather this stormy stretch. As one crusty old Navy bachelor put it: "What those kids need in their blood is more call of the sea and less call of the skirt." He was convinced that a married naval officer was hardly worth his salt.

Nevertheless, as we have seen, Sam Dealey did weather that typhoon and, gradually, nostalgia for the rolling plains of Texas was supplanted by the call of the limitless horizons of the Atlantic and the Pacific. The young officer whom Captain Moseley saw next, at a time when the war clouds had burst over Europe, was quite a different man.

"I did not see Sam again," continued Captain Moseley, "until he came to New London in the early 40's to return to submarine duty from destroyer service and, eventually, to put the *Harder* into commission. He was changed in his attitude at this time. He had become enthusiastic and hard-hitting. I guess he was born to fight and bored by the peacetime routine . . ."

Here and there, in the history of humanity, certain groups of fighting men have been labelled as *elite*—specially selected, carefully culled cream of the cream of an army's or navy's crop of fighting men. For instance, Napoleon's Grenadiers were supposed to be one of the finest combat groups ever selected to bear arms under the Little Corporal's tricolor. And yet, compared with the selective progress that enters into the making of America's submariners, Napoleon's Grenadiers were a helter-skelter aggregation of rookies.

This is not alone because submarines are complicated to operate and difficult to maintain at full operating efficiency while under way, but also because, as a bearer of deadly weapons of war, the sub demands alert handling and instant execution of orders. A modern submarine is a single-brained, single-bodied, single-armed and single-handed unit of one single purpose, composed of four score men. The tasks of diving, attack, and surfacing take scores of interlocking motions by dozens of crewmen with split-second timing. But more is demanded than mere mechanical ability. The men of the submarines—from captains to cooks—must have certain well-defined characteristics. They must be alert without being brittle; they must be interested in their shipmates without being nosey; they must appreciate food without being gluttons; they must respect privacy without being seclusive; they must be talkers without being gabby; and they must be friendly without being tail-waggers. They must, in short, be round pegs for very closely machined round holes. The wrong kind of a man aboard a sub, on a long cruise, can become an insufferable thorn in the sides of shipmates. He can, emotionally, cause almost as much damage as an enemy depth bomb. Kipling's famous poem "If," that spells out what it takes to be a *man*, comes very close indeed to describing what is demanded in a submariner. Stability—integrity—compatibility—courage.

Men of the air and men of the deep have much in common. But the submariners, in terms of internal make-up, go their friends of the wild blue yonder at least one better in the matter of exposure to long stretches of monotonous solitude. In The Boats, each man must not only be able to get along within himself but have a God-given capacity for getting along with his shipmates. And, above that, he must be ready, eager, and able to take on a shipmate's job at the drop of a hat. One of the big points of submarine training is that every man, before he can qualify for and receive his coveted twin dolphins insignia, must be able to do almost any other job aboard his ship as well as his own—and with a smile.

In no other branch of military service are men required to remain away from normal human contacts as long as submariners assigned to lengthy patrols that demand long hours—sometimes days—at depths far below the least glimmer of sunlight and far away from the feel and smell of natural air. Moreover, these conditions must be endured with good cheer in overcrowded, sometimes ill-smelling, dew-dripping, steel compartments. Those whose tempers or temperaments cannot stand the strain are soon eliminated.

In Uncle Sam's fleet, the old-time martinet—*The Prussian*, as he was generally known in the American Navy—is now, and happily so, as extinct as *Tyranosaurus Rex*. However, there are still widely different schools of thought as to the maintenance of discipline and morale aboard ship. The "Popularity Jack" who coddles his men is not respected by them any more than the harsh disciplinarian is loved or respected by his juniors. It is a common observation that a taut ship is a happy ship, a ship that will acquit herself well in the final test of battle. The fine balance between laxity and harshness is achieved without difficulty by natural born leaders—lesser men achieve it only by dedication and by devotion to their service and to their shipmates. Sam was one of those natural, inspired leaders to whom the well-being of his subordinates is of equal importance with the performance of his duty. Sam Dealey had been born and reared in a family where the motto was "One for all and all for one." That same loyalty he extended to cover his ship, his shipmates, and his superiors.

When, in May, 1937, Dealey was transferred to the Pensacola Naval Air Station for duty as assistant to the then Executive Officer of that post, he was tickled pink. Two solid years of shore duty—two years of the wonderful luxury of being a regular fireside-based family man. But even an early heaven has its terminal point. In 1939 Sam went back to the battleships, this time the ancient and honorable *Wyoming*—which in two short years was to be a Pearl Harbor target for a treacherous enemy. Again there was sea duty. Again Sam hated the life of everlasting absences from home. Again he thought of how much better the life of a civilian must be. If it had not been because of the increasing pressures of war fronts in Asia and Europe, Sam—at this time—might have left the service. Although he hoped with all his powers to hope that America would not be drawn into conflict, his mental reservations on the subject were so strong that he remained on the job and performed whatever duties the Navy assigned him with willingness and ability. In this respect Sam was not one whit different from hundreds of other Navy officers, young and old in years of service, who saw little ahead in a profession that seemed to be shrinking rather than expanding. Few people realize it, but life in any branch of the peacetime military service—on land, in the air, or on the sea—demands a large measure of abiding love for the work on the part of the man in order to compensate for the handicaps imposed upon his way of life by the demands of his Service.

Then suddenly, for Sam, the humdrum existence of a junior officer aboard a man o' war was changed by the magic of command. Dealey, now a lieutenant, senior grade, which corresponds to the Army rank of captain, received orders to report aboard the destroyer *Reuben James* as Executive Officer, the Second in Command. To a youngster barely ten years out of Annapolis, the job loomed large.

Sure, the *Reuben James* was one of the old World War I four-stackers. But a ship is a ship and the Exec. of any ship is a pretty big frog no matter what size the puddle.

And then came the truly big news: the *Reuben James* was to have a new Captain as well. And who could that be?

Sure—of course. The long arm of destiny reached out and produced Lieutenant Lane Heywood Edwards, USN— Tex Edwards of San Saba and Bancroft Hall.

Now Sam Dealey really felt that there was justice in the Navy and that he was on the winning side.

# Sam Meets Tex aboard the *Rube*

Blustery winds swept over New York's East River and sped dust devils up and down the chopped-up streets of the Brooklyn Navy Yard on the morning Sam Dealey's cab deposited him and his gear at the pier where the *Reuben James* lay moored. If Sam, in his mind's eye, had visualized a spic and span destroyer sleek as a greyhound, he had a most unpleasant second sight coming. The frowsy looking nondescript heap of masts, funnels, and deck gear moored to the stone and concrete dock only faintly resembled a ship.

To be sure, the *Reuben James* was a sick-looking ship that 5 April morning in 1940 when Sam, with a bright right-hand salute to the quarterdeck, stepped on the deck from the gangplank. And why not? About four months earlier, the vessel had almost been lost when her then Skipper and Exec., both of whom had been given general court martials for negligence, had failed to keep her off a reef near the Block Island Channel of Long Island Sound. Since then, the *Reuben James* had been in dry dock in the Brooklyn Navy Yard. Now the major repairs were about finished and, in a few more weeks, the vessel would once again be ready for sea.

After proper introductions to his new shipmates, during which he learned that the new Skipper, whom no one but himself seemed to know, had not yet come aboard, Sam headed for the wardroom, a cup of coffee, and a midday conference with his officers. His first impression, that they were a rather junior but smart and willing outfit, was to be confirmed in the coming weeks and months in port and at sea.

In the absence of Skipper Edwards, who was not expected aboard for another week, Sam took charge of the overhaul job, checked over the ship's organization charts, and took aboard sea stores. At the same time, he took every opportunity to study and understand his responsibilities as Second in Command.

On the morning of 16 April, while Sam was in the chart room of the *Rube*, as she was nicknamed, and working over some ship's papers, the doorway was flung open. In it stood the towering figure of Lieut. Heywood Lane Edwards, the Skipper. Sam sprang to quick attention and salute which Edwards returned swiftly. Then he reached out a bearlike paw that enveloped Sam's good right hand in its powerful grasp. A broad grin spread over Tex Edwards' sunburned face as he shoved his black-visored cap on the back of his head—a familiar gesture of "carry-on" from upperclassman Annapolis days.

"Well, you old gallinipper, you," boomed Edwards' deep rumbling voice. "So we're shipmates at long last, hey? Let me tell you, I've been looking forward to this. You and I, we'll make a great team—have a lot of fun and do a good job."

Even as Tex had been a great influence upon Sam as a midshipman at the Academy, so he was to leave a lasting imprint upon the make-up of Sam as a skipper. This was Tex's first job as Captain of a vessel, but he had built up a fine record on various destroyer assignments up to and including that of Executive Officer. He knew the cans from the keels up. In time, in the course of a dozen months, Sam not only learned how to train men but also learned preliminary lessons in delegating authority—training which was to stand him in good stead in later years.

As planned, the *Reuben James* backed away from her

Brooklyn Navy Yard dock right after Memorial Day. On the day she set course south beneath Brooklyn Bridge—from the heights of which the hatted outlines of onlookers appeared like so many pinheads—the *Reuben James* looked exactly as Sam had expected her to look, but did not, when he first came aboard. Now she was indeed the sleek greyhound of the sea, with not even a gleam of bright work to mar the businesslike gray war color of her hull and upperworks. To the joy of the deck hands, all exterior brass work, in accord with Fleet Regulations, had been removed or painted over. Her guns, trained fore and aft, were neatly canvas-covered, and her gay commission pennant rippled gracefully from the pig stick at the tip of her mainmast, accenting the colors of the United States of America which flew from the gaff halyards below. As befitted a destroyer with an efficient "black gang," as the engineer's division is called, no smudge of smoke issued from her stacks and only a feather of steam streamed from her vent pipes. She looked the proud ship which she was, reflecting the pride of her crew as she headed down stream through East River traffic.

From his post on the bridge, Sam noted that the *Rube* handled well. He listened with happiness to the subdued rumble of her turbines. To be sure, the *Reuben James* was old as destroyers go, but at that moment she did not reveal her wrinkles. Nor did her armament appear as ancient as it actually was. Very little had been changed aboard the *Rube* since the day she was launched in 1920, one of many scores of similar four-stackers. All had lengths of 314 feet, drafts of 12 feet, beams of 30 feet, and displacements of 1215 tons. For their time, they were well powered, well designed destroyers whose sharp, high-reaching bows could slice through ocean waters at a good 33 knots without too much huffing and puffing.

Early in October the *Rube* was transferred from her basic squadron and assigned to Key West for service in connection with the Neutrality Patrol being conducted by the Navy in Gulf of Mexico waters, in coordination with the British in the Caribbean to hunt down German subs

and raiders, as well as to waylay vessels suspected of being
Nazi contraband carriers.

Because of the presence of German submarines off the
Atlantic coast, the Navy High Command decided to assign
destroyers to escort submarines on off-shore trips. Otherwise they might unnecessarily alarm Allied shipping and
actually be fired upon in the mistaken belief that they
were of Hitler's navy. Thus began a problem of recognition signals between submarines and other sea or air craft
which was to plague The Boats in the Atlantic and Pacific
throughout the war and result in loss of valuable lives and
ships.

The Neutrality Patrol was quiet—too quiet. The *Reuben
James* would go back and forth between the Yucatan Peninsula and the western tip of Cuba, altering course now
and then to intercept and identify ships coming through
the straits. It was all rather monotonous, but the weather
was good, and that means a lot to those aboard a highly
volatile can.

While those pre-war days in the Navy were not quite
the kind that try men's souls, they were—none the less—of
the variety that kept men like Tex and Sam on their
professional toes.

At this time, veritable tidal waves of brand-new recruits
engulfed ships of the Navy that were in service. Most of
those very recent landlubbers were rather young. But the
pep, enthusiasm, and alertness generated by the young-
sters was impressive. While Sam and Tex admitted that
recruits were welcome aboard any vessel, they both felt
that something was wrong with a recruiting policy that
brought what they called "kids" into the serious business
of a near-war Navy. Sam discovered that those assigned to
the *Reuben James* were a likeable bunch and decided that
what they lacked in knowledge they made up for in their
utter readiness to learn. That was a universal discovery in
all branches of our military establishments.

Almost since the day when the *Reuben James* began
escorting submarines, Sam had heard the call of the Boats
ringing more and more in his ears. And to his nostrils

came the remembered fragrance of diesel oil and battery gas, smells no submariner ever forgets. Not only did he miss the exciting little ships, but he also knew that, with more being built at every turn of the clock, all sub-trained officers were needed for these intricate weapons of modern warfare.

"I am with you all the way," Tex Edwards replied when Sam asked if Tex would object to his putting in for transfer back to subs. "You're a topflight destroyerman, but you're also fit to skipper a pigboat. Also, I think that for you the quickest way to command—as well as to your all-out usefulness—is the submarine. You put in for transfer and I'll endorse it."

A few weeks later Captain Edwards of the *Reuben James* received the following Navy Department radiogram pertinent to Lieut. Samuel Dealey, his highly-thought-of Executive Officer:

SERVICES LT SAMUEL E DEALEY URGENTLY REQUIRED AS COMDG-OF S DASH TYPE SUBMARINE X BUNAV CONTEMPLATES DETACHING HIM IN APRIL AND ORDERING HIM TO THIS DUTY AT NEW LONDON.

That same day Tex Edwards confirmed the message offering Sam a submarine command.

The battleships are mighty,
They're the backbone of the Fleet:
Cruisers and destroyers, they all look plenty neat.
The Armored Cruiser Squadron is famed on land and sea,
But any doggoned submarine
Is home, sweet home to me.

# Cap'n Dealey's First Command

When Sam, after leaving the *Reuben James*, reported for duty at the New London Submarine Base, he found that whatever refresher course he might need would have to be taken aboard the waddling old S-20 on which he had learned the gentle art of submarining some five years earlier. This vessel, he was told, was to be his ship.

Knowing that the S-20's former skipper had been detached, Sam, on boarding the sub, asked for the Executive Officer, Lieut. Joseph W. Williams, Jr., whom he knew to be temporarily in command. The quartermaster on watch replied that he would find Williams in the wardroom in the after battery. Sliding down ladders with a deftness bred of long habit, Sam headed toward the wardroom where he found Lieut. Williams (now Captain, USN) working on a stack of papers. The two had never met. After passing the time of day, Sam said that he would like Williams to call a meeting of his officers.

"Sorry," replied the Exec., a bit embarrassed, "but there are no other officers on the S-20."

"What?" exploded Sam. "You my only officer?"

"Yes, sir!" replied Williams. "There seems hardly enough to go around these days."

Sam could only agree. He had been through that in the

S-20

*Rube*. He tried to keep this blow from interfering with his new pride of command. Ordinarily he would have had three or four officers in addition to the Exec. But if this was the way the cards were dealt, Sam knew the Navy Game well enough to play it with the cards he had. At New London he would try for more officers.

The S-20 was to operate in and out of New London and to fire the same gunnery and torpedo practices as all other subs. Her primary job, however, was to conduct various experiments—mostly of an engineering nature—for the Bureau of Ships and Engineering. Design and installation of the new subs under construction would be influenced strongly by the valuable information gained from these tests. In this way Sam became unusually familiar with many of the new ideas and devices that went into the construction of the brand-new 1475-ton fleet-type submarines.

Toward Memorial Day, Sam was informed that the S-20 might be selected to carry a novel plan, devised in Washington, into execution. Some bright mind had evolved the idea that it would be a fine thing if some submarine and its crew could be subjected to a well-controlled depth charge attack. Thus the psychological reactions of the men and the minor damage inflicted upon the sub could be examined and explained by the scientific double-domes. Even in those pre-war days, they were infiltrating our naval and military structures.

Sam, with all hands aboard the S-20, volunteered for the job. The destroyer selected to do the depth charging was none other than the *Reuben James*, now stationed in Newport and with Tex Edwards still at the helm as Skipper. On hearing this news, Sam lost whatever qualms he may have had about the trials. If any man in the world could handle a tin can, Tex could.

On the day of the tests, well off shore from New London, Sam made his run with periscope exposed, so that the destroyer could judge his distance from the sub. The *Reuben James* steamed on a parallel course about 200-300 yards from that of the S-20. As she approached the beam of the submarine, the can speeded up to 25 knots, so that the charges would not blow her own stern off, and let go, one after another, a string of five depth charges.

Until the first charge exploded, all hands were pretty edgy. This was new stuff and only a few veterans of World War I had ever heard a depth charge explode, let alone feel that explosion from inside a submarine.

With all W.T. (water-tight) doors and ventilation flappers closed and Joe Williams at his side, Sam kept the periscope trained on the bridge of the *James*. Suddenly, as the destroyer drew abeam, the firing flag was two-blocked (the letter *B*, a solid red flag, hoisted all the way to the starboard signal yardarm), a jet of steam plumed from her whistle, and a splash at the stern told of a 300-pound depth charge being dropped.

"Hold your hats," said Sam. "Here they come."

Unconsciously, men gripped something to hold onto and tensed their leg muscles. The helmsman and plane operators grasped their controls more firmly. The sonar operator removed his ear phones lest he receive a ruptured eardrum. The seconds dragged like hours then—crack!—as of a huge firecracker.

Swish!—as the pressure wave swept through the free-flooding spaces of the superstructure.

Whoom!—and Sam at the periscope saw a huge balloon of water and smoke rise from the sea.

"Look, Williams, look," called Sam, stepping back from the 'scope.

"Sure wouldn't like to be in the middle of that one," solemnly observed the Exec.

"Come the war," predicted Sam, "we'll probably get our teeth rattled a lot worse than this."

Actually, the explosion at that range was barely felt. The S-20 listed slightly away from the pressure wave, then righted herself. The rush and gurgle of water through the superstructure was the most noticeable effect and gave some indication of the terrific power of 300 pounds of TNT. The succeeding charges brought only broad grins.

"I'd like to see what a 600-pounder feels like, Cap'n Dealey, said the grizzled Chief-of-the-Boat. "Those fire-crackers weren't nothin'."

"Well, maybe that will be the next test," Sam replied. "Stand by to surface."

In reporting what effect depth chargings have on submarine crews, Sam very succinctly reported: "They get used to it!"

After the runs were over, the surfaced S-20 headed for the lee side of the *Reuben James*. Captain Tex sent Captain Sam a message: "Pretty lucky! We'll get you next time!"

"Next time," answered Sam, "I'll put a fish under your number one smokestack."

It so happened that the *Reuben James* and the S-20 were destined to be pitted against each other in the solving of many destroyer-submarine problems that summer—a type of intensified training that Edwards, Dealey, and Williams welcomed with open arms.

In mid-October, the S-20 was on special duty in the Portland, Maine, sector when the news came that the *Kearney*, a new American destroyer, had been torpedoed by one of Hitler's U-Boats during an attack on a convoy. War came mighty close to our shores that day. But since deliberate torpedoing of the *Kearney* was not proved, the damage to the ship and the loss of eleven men was not put down as an act of war.

On the afternoon of 31 October, while the S-20 was steaming toward Portland on the surface, her radioman came up to the upper hatch of the conning tower and asked permission to come up on the bridge. The youngster was visibly upset. Wondering what could be the matter, Sam told him to come on up. Sparks climbed through the hatch and told Captain Dealey that he had intercepted messages to the effect that the *Reuben James* had been sunk by German torpedoes as it escorted an England-bound convoy near Iceland during the preceding night.

For a moment, it seemed to Sam as if his universe would reel into splinters. Quickly he got hold of himself. He thanked the radioman for the information; told him to return to his set and to keep him informed if he heard further developments.

The *Reuben James* sunk! Tex Edwards—alive or dead? This could be the *Kearney* all over again—or it could be worse.

Although a news clamp was put on the details of the sinking until all were thoroughly sifted, Sam learned, through the byways of Naval communications, that the *Reuben James* had been hit by a Hun torpedo and had gone down like a stone. One hundred men had lost their lives, including Tex Edwards and all his officers—all friends and former shipmates.

Until that day Sam had tried to keep his attitude toward the war strictly neutral. He had even boasted that he was anti-everything except the U.S.A. That feeling of neutrality was lost with the *Reuben James*.

Then, six weeks later, came Pearl Harbor—and war. From that moment on, Sam had but one purpose in life—to take a submarine into combat.

Everything Sam did aboard the S-20 was designed to increase the combat performance of himself, his ship, and his crew. When he was not conducting tests, there were drills, drills, drills, and drills. His men became so smooth at running combat drills that few other subs could touch the S-20's diving and approach performances.

# 7

# The Cradle of the Subs

Even as the Sea Mother at Annapolis sits by the Severn side, so in tiny Groton opposite New London—with the wide Thames River flowing past its doors—sits the plant whose brains and brawn and machines spawn submarines for the Sea Mother's sons. Here are the sprawling docks, shops, and building ways of the Electric Boat Company, now a Division of the General Dynamics Corporation, which have produced submarines since the company built the USS *Holland* in 1899, the Navy's first submersible. Other plants, both government and private, have built submarines for our United States Navy, but always the majority have been offspring of the parent plant by the Thames' side.

In their cradles, generations of sturdy undersea craft have been launched into their native element and sailed to meet their destinies at sea in peace and in war. Before 1930 the E. B. Company turned out lettered classes of submarines that ran the full range of the alphabet. Then the Navy Department decided to give the names of fighting fish to its undersea men-of-war, but there they soon ran into difficulties. There were simply not enough game fish to take care of the building programs. The Bureau of Fisheries was called into the problem and, although they produced scores of types from the Seven Seas and from foreign vocabularies, the names of game fish had to be generously diluted with those of the less militant denizens of the deep. Even a seal crept in. But in the end result— the sinking of enemy ships—no distinction could be drawn between the fighting fish and those of supposed lesser spirit. All were outfitted with the same muscles and the same teeth, teeth that drew the lifeblood of our enemy.

Here Electric Boat designers and builders, many of whom were Annapolis trained—beginning with that dean of them all, Lawrence Y. Spear, Class of 1890—produced in the 1930's a smaller fleet type which began with the *Cuttlefish* and worked up to the type which, practically unchanged throughout the entire conflict, roved the far reaches of the Atlantic and the Pacific in World War II.

This new boat was a submariner's submarine. Her original characteristics were laid down in 1937–38 by a semi-official group of experienced pigboaters and naval constructors in the Navy Department who called themselves the Submarine Officers' Conference. Their recommendations were presented to the General Board and, after approval by that body, were written by the newly born Bureau of Ships into specifications for the next class of undersea craft which began with the *Tambor*. This new sub, which was produced by the score as soon as the war broke, surpassed in speed, endurance, and offensive power anything then existing in our own or other navies.

As against the S-Boat's 219-feet length, 20-foot beam, two engines, and four forward torpedo tubes, the newcomer had a length of 312 feet, a beam of 27 feet, four powerful Diesels, and six bow and four stern torpedo tubes. And where the S-Boats carried only ten fish, the new pigboats had room for twenty-four fish in its tubes and torpedo rooms. In addition, it had better fire control and sonar equipment, better navigational facilities, and greatly improved living conditions. Its speed of 21 knots on the surface was also highly important. Of its kind, the new vessel was in the high-speed hard-hitting class. It is interesting to note, however, that certain old-timers objected to its so-called hotel accommodations, such as flush toilets, sanitary tanks, cold storage, and air conditioning. One of these new subs was known as Hull Number 257 on the Electric Boat books. It was assigned the name *Harder*. For those who want to know, a harder is a small herring of South African waters. Not a fighting fish, eh? Well, in that connection it may be interesting to know that the deadly torpedo is named after an eel, the *torpedo electricus*. A bit misnamed because the early torpedoes were not propelled by electricity but by compressed air, to which later was added the heat of steam, hence the name—steam torpedoes.

Two nests of torpedo tubes are grouped at the ends of a fleet type submarine such as the *Harder*. Between those nests, six forward and four aft, are the men and machines whose combined goal is to send those fish exactly where they are aimed. But let us go aboard the ship as it lies at its pier ready for operations. The long, flat, narrow steel-clad deck is cleated with strips of teak wood in the interest of swift drying and sure foothold. The steel island, slightly forward of the longitudinal center of the *Harder*, is known as the bridge fairwater. The navigating bridge is inside the forward end, and its light sheet-metal sides protect the heavy, bulletproof, pressure-proof conning tower, the ship's ventilation duct, and the huge, 31-inch main engine air induction—by means of which the Diesel engines draw in the air required for their operation. Rising above the center of the bridge structure are the periscope shears which support and enclose the two periscopes—the eyes of the ship when submerged.

Forward of this island are deck flush installations such as a telephone-equipped marker buoy in case of an accidental sinking, also an escape hatch and trunk with a narrow watertight door reached by an abbreviated companionway from the deck. When first built, the *Harder* had a three-inch gun on its forward deck. Later, it was replaced with a three-inch dual purpose weapon designed to be used against air or surface craft. The Skipper was given an option to decide where he wanted the gun placed, forward or aft of the conning tower. When Sam was asked where he wanted his to go, he answered: "Forward of the bridge, of course! Why aft? Who are we running away from?"

From the bow to the top of the periscope shears ran three sets of antennae wires of stout steel. Well back of the blunt-nosed bow, and folded down into the deck, was the torpedo loading skid for the forward torpedo loading hatch. And, to port of the latter, stood the three-foot metal tube that contained one of the *Harder's* sonar heads. Abaft the six bow torpedo shutters, which cover the outer ends of the tubes and add to the streamlining of the hull, are the bow planes folded up closely—one on each side and operated together. The inclination of these, when unfolded out horizontally from the sides of the ship, determine her up or down direction. Abaft the periscope shears are other hatches, a marker buoy, and, beneath the slatted deck, the mufflers for the main engines. At the stern, some ten feet down, are the twin propellers, the horizontal rudder, and the stern planes. These planes do not fold up as do the bow planes but are permanently rigged and ready for operation. Their tilt up or down governs the inclination of the ship and assists in diving or surfacing.

As for the steel island atop the *Harder*, it had two steel platforms. One of these rail-enclosed spaces is forward of the navigating bridge and mounts a 20- or 40-mm. machine cannon. The other is an after extension of the bridge deck, is similarly armed, and is called the cigarette deck because, located as it is in the lee of the periscope shears, it is the only space on topsides that offers any degree of comfort to submariners in need of a bit of air and a smoke. Back of the forward machine-gun platform rises the chest-high, bulletproof bridge enclosure behind which the bridge watch stands duty when the sub runs on the surface. There was no helmsman on this bridge—only a few essential instruments such as a watertight gyro compass repeater, a microphone, and azumuth circles for taking bearings.

As on other wartime subs, the sheet-metal plates that enclosed the slim steel supports that were the *Harder's* periscope shears had been removed to reduce the vessel's silhouette to enemy spotters. Up and down through these columns ran the ship's two periscopes. The sharp eye of the Number One periscope was no larger than the face of a pocketwatch. Number Two, which gave a larger field, had an eye about two inches in diameter. At the lower end of these optical columns that enabled observers to see from beneath the surface when the periscopes were elevated were the eyepieces in the conning tower.

The slender steel shafts of the periscope antenna (for radio communication) and the radar antenna (for obtaining target ranges) rose just aft of the periscopes. Mounted on the bridge structure, well above its level, were small metal platforms welded to the periscope shears with chest-high steel loops where the lookouts stood their watches. These vitally important members of the organization, when at sea, night or day, constantly swept their respective sectors of sea and sky with powerful binoculars, alert to detect enemy periscopes, torpedoes, airplanes, or surface craft. On their keenness often hung the life of the ship and the lives of their shipmates.

"And," as one lookout aptly phrased it, when being cautioned about the importance of his duties, "there's me, too."

At the base of the steel island, fore and aft, were watertight, pressure-proof ammunition lockers which contained three-inch cartridges for the deck gun.

In recesses in the *Harder's* keel were the underwater soundheads. They picked up the sounds, friendly or hostile, of the sea and its traffic and carried them to the sharply attuned ears of the hydro-phone operators, known as sonarmen. In the *Harder's* broad bottom, as well as in her rather pregnant-looking hull, were tanks which could, by releasing or by applying air pressure, be filled or emptied of tons upon tons of sea water in a matter of seconds. With tanks filled, the *Harder* would become a creature of the dark deep; with tanks empty, she was a surface vessel. Through degrees of flooding, the *Harder* could either ride deep in the water with deck awash or high on the top of the waves, that is, as high as a ship with only 18 per cent of reserve buoyancy can ride.

Leading down from the narrow hatch that gave access from the bridge to the conning tower directly beneath it was a short steel ladder. Just to port of this ladder and facing forward stood the helmsman at his wheel. The steel bulkhead in front of him—he never saw horizon, sea, or other vessels, only a patch of sky if he craned his neck toward the hatch—was mounted with instruments that gave time, speed of ship, depth of submergence, and transmitted orders to the engines or motors. During moments of torpedo action, men of the approach party were at stations along the sides of the crowded compartment. Its center was dominated by the heavy combings of the periscope wells into which the periscopes retreated at the will of the operator. Back of the helmsman stood the Talker above the hatch that led below to the control room which, if the conning tower were the brains of the *Harder*, was the heart of the ship. Directly, by mouth or through microphones, the Talker would pass the word from the Captain to all other parts of the ship. The Chief in the maneuvering room abaft the main engine rooms could also be directed by the helmsman's engine room telegraph.

Just aft of the control room hatch was the station of the peri—scope jockey who, by means of his controls, raised or lowered the periscopes as directed by the Captain or whoever was the observer. When the *Harder* ran submerged, merely cruising along, the bridge watch was stationed in the conning tower where, at stated intervals —perhaps every fifteen minutes, the Officer of the Watch or his assistants would make periscope observations.

Following the conning tower's portside bulkhead toward the stern appeared torpedo firing panels and the torpedo data computer. At the after bulkhead was a small plotting table. The station of the Assistant Approach Officer—always the Exec. who also doubled as Navigator—was opposite the Skipper—while he used the periscope—in order to read instantly the range and bearing of the target shown on equipment before him. The remainder of the tower's starboard side was taken up by the sonar stack, the radar scope, and the Quartermaster of the watch with his ever ready notebook. The conning tower crew were wont to envy the space allotments of sardines in a can.

Below the conning tower was the control room. There the Officer of the Deck also doubled as Diving Officer when the diving alarm sounded. Here was the Christmas Tree which glowed green with signal lights when the *Harder* was properly secured for diving. If one single red light remained on this board, it signified that there was an open hatch or valve where unwanted water could find entrance. This keyspot was under the vigilant eye of the Chief of the Boat.

All stations in the control room are important, but perhaps the most vital one is the flood and vent manifold which is also presided over by the Chief of the Boat. With its coordination, the ballast tanks are filled or emptied. Mistakes at this station have cost numerous lives. Next come the bow and stern plane operators who take the ship up or down, the blow manifold where high pressure air is admitted to the ballast tanks to expel water from them and, last but not least, the trim pump man who shifts ballast water as required to trim the ship most effectively. The radio shack in the after end of the control room, the master gyro compass in the forward end, and the pump room below its deck complete the main stations and equipment of this vital compartment.

A submarine like the *Harder* had no passageways except in the officers' country. Heavy steel watertight doors, built to withstand great pressures, opened from one compartment to the other. One had to duck low and step high to negotiate these narrow openings. Forward of the control room were the officers' and the chief petty officers' staterooms with triple-tiered bunks, the ship's office, the wardroom and its pantry, and the Skipper's cabin—a space about as large as a Pullman section with the upper berth removed. Here, at the foot of a narrow bed, were instruments that gave the Captain instant information on the course and depth at which the *Harder* was running. There was also a telephone that connected with the conning tower.

Forward of this point, behind another heavy steel door, was the forward torpedo room. At its extreme forward end were the shining bronze breech doors of the six forward torpedo tubes. The men who handled the operating of the torpedoes and tubes slept in bunks that were distributed under, along side, and above the torpedo-filled racks that lined the sides of the long, narrow room. Here, too, were the officers' head and shower. With expert handling, it took the *Harder's* torpedomen only about five minutes to reload the tubes after firing the usual spreads of three torpedoes. Another task of the torpedomen was to set the gyros and depth-regulating devices of their long slim 3000-pound charges—750 pounds of which were high explosives packed into streamlined cone-shaped warheads. The men were alert, too, during torpedo attacks, to trigger the fish by hand in the event electric firing connections from the conning tower should malfunction.

Aft of the control room was the *Harder's* compact but highly efficient galley. Here the vessel's specially trained cooks and a baker prepared dishes that had taste, sight, and nose appeal—three essential factors to submariners whose tastes often became jaded toward the end of long and tiring patrols.

"Mother can't make pies the way Butch, the Baker, can make them," was a frequent sob of homecoming submariners.

Below the galley and crew's messroom were cold and deep-freeze storage spaces for all sorts of food, from fruit to fish; meat was a big item. It was taken aboard all boned and ready for range or oven. The ammunition magazine was also below this area. The crew's mess, although it could hold only eight or ten men, was, like the wardroom, one of the *Harder's* great social centers. Next astern came the crew's quarters with folding bunks and nearby head, washroom, and showers. Then followed the two main engine rooms, each with a team of two 1600 horsepower Diesel engines. These either drove the *Harder* through sets of electric generators and motors while on surface or filled the main storage batteries with reserve power for the use of the main motors while submerged. These huge storage batteries were packed into spaces below the officers' quarters and the crew's quarters.

Continuing aft from the engine rooms, one entered the maneuvering room, which could be called the *Harder's* solar plexus. Here highly skilled Electricians' Mates stood watch at the main propulsion controls, taking and executing orders as they came from the conning tower helmsman by way of the musically tinkling bells of the ship's engine telegraph and indicator. Just beyond the steel door at the after end of this vital control spot was the end of the line—the after torpedo room. Here, in addition to the four fish in the tubes, was stowage room for four torpedoes as against ten in the larger forward torpedo compartment. Here, too, were bunks for the men who served these tubes.

Such then was the *Harder* when it was ready for the role it was to play in combat. But even as Rome was not built in a day, so modern subs, despite highly efficient assembly methods, are not put together by the able hands of their builders in a matter of hours.

After a sub's keel is laid on the ground ways of the banks on the Thames, comes the building of the stout double hull. As that rises, so engines and pipes and ducts and wirings and tubes and switches and buttons and connections and levers—miles upon miles, gross upon gross—go into the interior of the sub to provide its system of electric nerves, liquid blood streams, and aircompressing and purifying plants.

Eventually—in seven months under wartime pressures— the submarine is ready to be launched.

★★★★★★★★★★★★★★★★★★★★★★★★★★★★★★★★★★★★★★★★★★★★★★

# 8

# A Submarine is Born

The keel of the *Harder* was laid in the early summer of
1942, and soon afterward Lieut. Frank C. Lynch, class of
'38, was assigned by the Bureau of Ships to represent the
Prospective Commanding Officer during the period of construction. Two senior officers regularly stationed at the
E. B. plant represented the Navy Department. When Lynch
was informed that he would be assigned to the *Harder* at
the time of its commissioning, he began to assemble, man
by man, submariners whom he knew either personally or
by reputation. He garnered many of these men as they
were released from S-Boats that had been turned over to
the British. Thus he collected a group of exceptionally
seasoned hands from many pigboats—all time-tested, all
emotionally and mentally reliable. Outstanding in this group
were such long-time Chiefs as Hiram Delbert Hatfield of
Groton, Connecticut, a radio electrician who probably
could have given Marconi himself a lot of pointers; Carl
Edward Finney of Philadelphia, who had a special gift of
making Diesels hum; and last, but far from least, a past
master in the handling of torpedoes and men, Chief Torpedoman Vernard Leslie Sloggett of San Diego, California. The last named was to become the first Chief of the
Boat of the *Harder*. All three were to win their way to
well-deserved commissions aboard the *Harder*. Lynch him-

self had had wide submarine experience, especially as Engineer Officer. He was then too junior, even in time of war, to serve as Exec., a post which he, if experience alone had been the yardstick, would have been fully able to fill. In time he was to command his own sub and win distinction for skill and daring in the shallow waters along the coasts of China and Korea. In time he was to rise to the rank of Captain, USN.

Attracted by this highly seasoned nucleus of Chief Petty Officers, veteran submarine ratings, released from subs leased to the British, sought assignment to the *Harder*. In fact, there was a waiting list. But Frank Lynch did not want to go too far in anticipating the *Harder's* personnel needs ahead of the assignment of her Captain. Still, bit by bit, he made up a list of motor machinists mates, radiomen, torpedomen, firemen, signalmen, cooks, seamen, pharmacists mates, and electricians mates.

On 19 August, the *Harder* was ready to leave its cradle and enter upon its home element—salt water. It was a festive occasion, as participating dignitaries and spectators gathered in a large group on and around the flag-clad platform built at the *Harder's* up-slanting bow. The launching had been timed so that it would be at the hour between shifts, thus giving the thousands of workmen of the Yards a chance to see another of the creations of their brain and brawn and nimble skills take its first step toward duty in enemy waters.

At the forward end of the lofty wooden cradle, where the *Harder's* bunting-clad bow slanted toward the sky, workmen with acetylene torches stood by to cut the final set of steel plates that held the launching cradle to the ground ways.

A foreman called out the measured perforations in the plates: "One—two—three—four—"

The steel-eating flames of the torches consumed the metal between the perforations. When the grip of steel grew feebler, the cradle began to rock as if the *Harder* were eager to break away.

"Nine—ten—eleven—" The shiver increased in tempo and with it came crackling, screeching noises.

"Now," yelled Frank Bently, who had built subs for Electric Boat since 1925. "Now, Miss Shaforth." At this cry, Miss Helena M. Shaforth, daughter of Rear Admiral John M. Shaforth, wielded the traditional bottle of champagne in its bright silver basket and hurled it with all her might at the *Harder's* bow. The bottle broke and, as its foaming contents streamed down the sub's nose, she was the first to call its name: "I christen thee *Harder.*"

And the band played "Anchors Aweigh" as the cheering crowd applauded.

A proud ship, she glided in her wooden cradle down the well-greased ground ways. Gathering speed, the ship slid gracefully into the water. As the cradle fell away, the *Harder* swayed gently forward in a smooth movement that had all the earmarks of an exquisite curtsy by an elegant lady. She floated high and free. Soon a little company tug bustled importantly up to the submarine to tow her to the fitting-out dock. Then came more weeks of outfitting and operation of the equipment by Electric Boat's test crew, all under the watchful eye of Lieut. Lynch.

When, in the fall of 1942, his orders were issued giving him command of the soon-to-be-completed *Harder*, Sam was as disappointed as he ever permitted himself to be. It would be months and months before the vessel would be ready for sea. On which coast it would have duty, he did not know. No one knew. It was aggravating. Sam had believed that after his training in the old S-20, he would be sent—with a spot of leave which would permit him to see his mother and family in Dallas—directly to Pearl Harbor and be given command of a fighting submarine there. He was mentally prepared to get started on this war right now, instead of waiting months for a new boat to be constructed.

On 20 September, 1942, Lieut. Comdr. Samuel David Dealey first put foot aboard the *Harder*, his first combat command. The affection that was to develop between the two—the Captain who knew no other combat submarine and the vessel that never knew another Master—was slow in coming. In the eyes of Sam, the *Harder* was a barrier that deferred the hour of his entry into war—in the firing of torpedoes that would avenge Tex Edwards and the *Reuben James* as well as his many friends aboard the ships that were destroyed at Pearl Harbor on that tragic 7 December, 1941.

Supervision of the *Harder* shifted from Lieut. Lynch to Lieut. Comdr. Dealey. On that same day other officers reported for duty. The *Harder*, however, would not be turned over to the Navy until 2 December, on which day it was scheduled for commissioning and transfer from the Electric Boat fitting-out docks to the US Submarine Base up the river.

The officers who were to make combat history aboard the *Harder* formed a small but able group. It was headed by Lieut. John H. Maurer, Class of '35. A resident of Washington, D.C., he had just come home from the Mediterranean where he had seen submarine combat duty. Like Frank Lynch, he was to become a top patrol commander and rise to the rank of Captain. He is currently still in The Boats. By virtue of his seniority and all-round experience, Lieut. Maurer was appointed Executive Officer of the *Harder*. He was ideal for the job, as well as that of navigator. Cool, never ruffled, always of an even and tranquil disposition, he was, if that were possible, Sam Dealey's alter ego. If two men were almost look-alikes, it was Sam Dealey and Jack Maurer, except that the latter did not smile as readily as did Sam. But when it came to drive and determination to put a program through come hell and deep water, without stepping on toes or ruffling feelings, they were the pair who could do it and, in doing it, almost read each other's minds.

Next in seniority stood Frank Lynch of the Class of '38. This genial giant, who was born in Kansas and appointed to the Academy from Missouri, had a gift for solving problems that had to do with engineering. At the Academy he had been a hound for electronics and steam engineering. He was full of original and inventive ideas in the field of electricity. For instance, one problem was that of improving night lighting for the conning tower instruments. Lynch solved the problem in a way that received the attention of the Bureau of Ships in Washington. Later, night lighting installations similar to those aboard the *Harder* were made on all U.S. submarines. Frank, too, had a great deal of power and drive. He was the sort of natural leader, in form and figure, that enlisted men are apt to regard as towers of reliability.

Third on the *Harder's* roster of officers stood Lieut. Samuel Moore Logan of Queensboro, Kentucky. Sam, who ran hot, straight, and normal with military punctiliousness, bore the nickname Ramrod. He had been the honorman of his 1942 Class, which was graduated, without fuss or ceremony, some ten days after Pearl Harbor in answer to the cry for Naval officers. Lieut. Logan, who, despite his starchy manners, had a highly workable sense of humor, had also been Number One in his class at Submarine School. Sam was tickled pink to get him. Young Logan had one of those super-mathematical minds that made him a Torpedo and Gunnery Officer just made to send Japs out of this world.

Among reserve officers assigned to the *Harder* were Lieut. Keith Rufus Phillips of West Los Angeles and Ensign Donald Earle Horst of Lebanon, Pennsylvania. Both were untried college men, but Sam found that they, like the rest of his group, had the will to get on with the war. They were all young, eager, and with the light of battle in their eyes.

As the time for the commissioning drew nearer, plans were drawn for the program to mark the transfer and the acceptance of command by Captain Dealey. Home in Dallas, the news that a native son was about to take command of one of the country's latest and most expensive submarines —$7,500,000 was the *Harder's* price tag—was displayed big in the *Dallas News*.

As time went on, from the oldest member of the crew to the newest recruit, all hands developed that blind, childlike confidence in Sam that the Old Man would do the right thing at the right time to get them out of any trouble. Trying to always justify that faith is what puts gray hairs in any Skipper's head. If war merely meant that success was attained by bringing a ship safely through the war, it would be an easy thing, but many risks have to be taken in any battle.

At 0930 on Wednesday morning, 2 December, all *Harder* personnel assembled on Pier No. 8, at the Submarine Base, to which the *Harder* had been moored earlier that morning. Immediately following muster on the pier, the ship's company marched briskly aboard. The crew formed up on the main deck abaft the gun. They faced forward, six abreast and with the tallest men in the rear ranks. Officers and Chief Petty Officers formed two separate lines that faced each other along the length of the forward deck.

At 1000 Captain Cutts, Commander of the Submarine Base, and Captain Forster of the Electric Boat Company— together with Chaplain Collins, USN—came on the pier. They were met at the gangway by Captain Dealey whose status aboard the *Harder* at that moment was that of Prospective Commanding Officer. In line with prescribed procedure, Captain Cutts accepted the vessel from Captain Forster with the words: "I now accept this vessel for the United States Navy from the Electric Boat Company."

Following that moment, Captain Cutts and his party about faced while a Marine bugler, borrowed for the occasion, sounded "To the Colors." On the first note, the colors, jack, and commissioning pennant were hoisted smartly.

A second later, Captain Cutts, turning to Sam, ordered: "Lieutenant Commander Dealey, take command of this vessel!"

With a voice that had a firm note of pride in it, Sam read the orders that gave him command.

Lieut. Maurer ordered: "Parade rest."

After a brief prayer, Captain Dealey ordered his Exec. to "set the watch"—an order that was relayed to Chief of the Boat Sloggett, who saw to it that it was executed on the double.

The *Harder* was in the Navy.

Wena, Joan, and Davy were the first of the visitors aboard, followed by the families of the other officers and enlisted personnel. They were thoroughly impressed with the ship, and Davy had the thrill of shaking hands with "a real live admiral," Admiral Freeland Daubin, who was then in command of the Submarine Force, Atlantic. Rosemary and Martha, eldest daughters of George and Marie Dealey, had come to New London for the occasion. These young ladies enjoyed several personally conducted tours of the ship as each of the bachelor officers sought to please.

In the afternoon, ammunition, stores, and torpedoes were taken aboard the sub. Then Dealey completed his official calls on Comsublant (Adm. Daubin) and the Commander of the Sub Base (Capt. Cutts). A busy and a proud day it was for that eternal boy who lives forever in all real men.

The profound sense of pride and humility that dominated Sam Dealey at the time of the commissioning is reflected in this letter to his family back home:

"Today a submarine was born! The *Harder's* debut into the Fleet took place on the coldest day yet of this year. Nature didn't particularly cooperate. An overcast sky threatened rain, but the temperature hinted more of snow flurries. An icy wind swept across the Thames River and the faithful crowd of friends and families who had come to the ceremony shivered and wished that the shortness of the event could be even more abbreviated. It was soon over, the colors went up, and the commission pennant was raised over the proudest 'skipper' in the whole Navy. The crowd then followed Wena and her party aboard—they had been on the dock—and whether or not they were impressed with the submarine, they were all thankful for its warmth.

"We let them all look through the periscope, climb up on the bridge and into the conning tower, and nearly everything else that is to be done aboard except firing a torpedo.

"To command such a ship as this one is a great honor—and a great trust. I'm satisfied that I have the ship, the crew, and the officers needed for our job, and the rest of it is up to me. When we leave here, we will be expected to get results. We intend to.

"I think I'm going to enjoy this war. Good fortune has certainly given me a generally fine and congenial group of officers to work with. Jack Maurer is going to be a fine Exec. Nothing seems to excite him or ruffle his good nature and he's as thorough as a good submarine officer should be. I'm loading each of the officers with much responsibility and believe their shoulders are broad enough to take it."

Here we see the key to Sam's success as a sub Skipper, the deft Dealey touch of delegating authority, of making each of his subordinates feel himself important to the ship's operations. Some men never acquire this touch; successful leaders find it in early years. Sam Dealey apparently was born with it—the *Harder* was in good hands.

★★★★★★★★★★★★★★★★★★★★★★★★★★★★★★★★★★★★★★★★★★★★★★

# 9

# The Harder Heads for Shooting Country

With a brand new ship under his proud command and enemies waiting to be sunk, Sam Dealey was intent on letting no grass grow under anyone's feet while the *Harder* was gotten ready for war service. For which war zone she was destined nobody seemed to know. Naturally, Sam and his shipmates hoped that Pearl Harbor would be their destination. In the Pacific lay the unexplored hunting grounds. There roamed the big game. In the Atlantic the enemy had little besides U-Boats and occasional raiders.

Returning transferees—sent back as nucleus crews for new submarines—were singing a new song:

> "Sink 'em all, sink 'em all,
> Tojo and Hitler and all.
> Sink all their cruisers
> And carriers too—
> Sink all their tincans
> And their stinking crew—"

Lurid tales were told of Japanese carriers, cruisers, destroyers, tankers, transports learning how to dive to the tune of thunderous torpedo explosions. Scuttlebutt whispered that a lot of old friends and shipmates had been killed or were missing, presumed lost, in the *Sealion* and

*Shark;* that S-36 had been lost on a reef; that S-26 had been rammed and sunk with nearly all of her complement by her own escort vessel; that trigger-happy zoomies had damaged several subs. Good and bad, the stories came back and, good or bad, they brought the same fever to "get out there and sink Japs." Patriotism, revenge, and sometimes just sheer desire to prove oneself in the acid test of battle, competed for the thoughts of men. . . . And time was mighty precious.

There was little of that all-important time for speculation aboard the *Harder* during the part of December following her commissioning. The days were filled with working parties loading ammunition, sea stores, torpedoes, fuel, fresh water. The nights were filled with last-minute work by E.B. technicians making final tests and minor installations. Sam itched to chase the whole kit and caboodle over the gang plank and take his ship and crew to sea.

Finally she was pronounced ready and, on the morning of 6 December, a clear and cold Sunday, Dealey backed away from the E.B. dock and headed out for the deep hole south of Fisher's Island. He wanted plenty of water under his keel for these first dives. The ship, he knew, could stand any pressure to which the comparatively shallow waters of Long Island Sound could subject her. But he did not want any inexperienced diving officer or planeman ramming her nose or her delicate sound heads into the bottom.

Under the keen eyes of the Exec., Jack Maurer, the only combat-tested officer among them, preparations for the day's work were swiftly made. Hardly had Dealey gotten his submarine turned and pointed down the river before Jack reported the ship "secured for sea," and before they had cleared Southwest Ledge Light at the entrance, the word came up the conning tower hatch: "Cap'n, Mr. Maurer reports rigged for diving."

"Aye, aye," acknowledged Sam, adding with a pleased smile, "the boys are on their toes this morning—rarin' to go!"

"Yes, sir," volunteered Frank "Tiny" Lynch. "Everybody wants to get on with this war."

And that was the motif of the day: everybody, including the ship, was rarin' to go.

No submarine's first dive is ever perfect and no skipper ever gives those first commands: "Lookouts below! Clear the bridge! Dive, dive!" without a bit of gooseflesh on his arms and a few chills up and down his spine. Is she properly compensated? Will she head for bottom like a stone? Will the main engine induction valve close? . . . It did not in the *Squalus* and twenty-six men died. . . .

It was, therefore, with a sense of great relief that Sam and all hands felt the ship start to level off after her first headlong plunge. There was no dreaded, spine-chilling crash of water flooding into a compartment as Frank Lynch expertly got the ship under control and reported: "Periscope depth, sir."

That night, in his just-begun diary, Sam wrote: "The ship handled well submerged and the crew behaved like a bunch of old-timers. They'll be all right in the war zone. I guess it's always a relief to complete the first dive on a new sub successfully. This was no exception. Things went almost too smoothly. Exercised battle stations submerged at periscope depth and at 100 feet. Am taking things slowly and aiming for precision first. Speed can come later."

As the days went on, the dives and drills became progressively smoother. Small mistakes were made, but all aboard were doing their best, including, of course, the skipper. But even Sam, despite his exacting standards of perfection, was not impervious to the tricks of Fate.

The *Harder*'s routine, when she docked upriver at the Submarine Base, was to head down for Long Island Sound every morning, usually before daylight, for training runs. Since railroad and highway bridges cross the Thames at this point, it was the habit of submariners heading out of New London to slow down a bit above the bridges in order to fill their tanks with water enough to flood down until the decks were awash. This lowered the periscope shears sufficiently for them to clear the underside of the structures and thus save the trouble and traffic delays caused by the opening of the draws.

On one particular morning, the tide was ebbing—and it had been on the ebb for some time. This caused fresh water, which is heavier than sea water, to flood the lower portion of the river. Somehow no one aboard the *Harder* took this into consideration. So when Sam, on approaching the bridges, ordered the ballast tanks to be partially filled as he had on previous occasions to trim the vessel down to deck-level, the sub sank deeper in the water than it had in past instances.

"We are taking water in the engine room! It's coming in through the main engine air-induction line!" This cry of alarm from the engine and maneuvering rooms was shouted by John P. Lonas, another veteran Chief Motor Machinists Mate.

"Blow all main ballasts," shouted Sam from the bridge.

One of the new Junior Officers, scared by the mishap, sounded the hoarse call of the surfacing klaxon by pressing its bridge lever three times. This added to the already large amount of excitement among the new hands. However, order was restored in jig-time as the *Harder,* tanks empty, floated high upon the river and well below the nearest bridge.

"We have lost all power on the main motors, sir," reported Frank Lynch. Water spraying into the maneuvering room had short-circuited the main controls. So the proud *Harder* had to drop the hook and send out a call for a tug to haul her back to the Submarine Base.

While Sam took quite a riding on that one from his fellow Skippers, he took it with a grin and in his stride. After quick repairs, the sub went to sea again. More drills, more dives. Now the *Harder* began going deep and staying at sea around the clock. One noon, Sam sat the *Harder* on the bottom while all hands had lunch. He did it to teach the new men how it felt to live under water and it worked like a charm. Of course, not all dives went smoothly because of the inevitable percentage of green men fresh

20 mm. Cannon

out of school aboard the *Harder*. Every sub has to take its share of brand-new grads, regardless.

On one occasion her stern planes became jammed as the ship dived. There was a ten-degree down angle on the boat at the time it happened. But by quick blowing of the bow buoyancy tank, the sub was leveled off at 100 feet. Nothing happened other than smashing a lot of dishes in the wardroom pantry and in the galley. The wardroom mess boy, Robert Moore, and the ship's Chief Commissary Steward, Audley Carver, swore like throat-cutting pirates—but after all, there is no use crying over spilled dishes.

All sorts of trials were given the *Harder's* equipment, installations, and operations to insure that, at some crucial moment, there would be no failure. Anchor tests, high-speed engine and motor runs, crash dives to see how much they could beat the contract time, deck gun and 20 mm. cannon firing, and dozens of others followed in seemingly endless succession. Sam, like the perfectionist that he was—ably seconded by his Exec., Jack Maurer—let no imperfections slide by. These were not just exhibitions or dress rehearsals; tomorrow they might be the real thing out in the war zones where you play for keeps.

One drill that Sam carried out surprisingly well was the "balancing" test. In that operation the submarine's submerged trim is adjusted to perfection. Then the ship is stopped and lies doggo, as though trying to outfox those blood hounds of the sea with microphone ears—enemy DD's. With a perfect trim, a submarine will balance where she is halted for minutes—sometimes hours—especially, if she is sitting on a sharp thermocline.

Long Island Sound is notoriously bad for balancing because many rivers and streams pour fresh water into it, causing unpredictable water pockets—air pockets, to the birdmen.

However, Sam scratched his balancing tests off his list on the very first attempt and then proceeded out into the Atlantic for his deep submergence trial. This was important because the *Harder* and her sister-ships had been designed to operate at great depth. Just what that depth was is secret.

On the subject of his wardroom officers, Sam's diary said: "I am mighty pleased with Jack Maurer's work. He's a detailist and that is exactly what is needed in training a new crew. Enough attention to the little things and the *big* things will take care of themselves. Can't complain of Frank's work with that Engineering Dept., either. He's a hard worker and a swell shipmate. His young assistant, Ensign Don Horst, continues to surprise me.—Don falls right into this Navy life as if he had been "Navy" for years, instead of months."

By this time, Ensign Thomas Buckner of Nashville, Tennessee, a Naval reservist, had joined the party to take over various Junior Officer duties. Tom—with his slow smile, slow speech, soft accent, and eager attitude toward anyone and all things—soon endeared himself to all aboard the sub. The fastest things about him were his quick powers of observation, his sense of humor, and his facile pen as a cartoonist with a bite.

By mid-January, 1943, the *Harder* had made more than a hundred dives and in excess of sixty practice approaches. Now came a period of galling and grueling uncertainty with respect to the day-to-day moves of the *Harder*. The work went on, but the old routine of getting home nights, or even weekends, went down the drain.

While in non-home ports, Sam spent most of his spare time studying, with professional thoroughness, the mimeographed copies of submarine combat reports sent in by commanders of subs in active theaters. Sam, on reading about sinking techniques and stowing them away in his mind for future use, thought it ironical that the U-boat problems that gave the Allies the biggest headache in the Atlantic were the same problems that created the most sleepless nights for the Japs, namely, relentless submarine warfare!

The time for the *Harder's* departure for a combat zone was drawing near. Sam was not quite sure if he would draw European waters or the Pacific. He hoped that it would be the latter. Frankly, a vast pressure head of impatience had been building up within Sam. He had had his fill of drills and runs and trials. The *Harder* and its men had made good in the realistic check-out torpedo approaches and firing runs conducted under the sharp eyes of specially appointed training officers. These seasoned and hard-to-impress submariners, Commander Erck and Commander Peacher, failed to hide the fact that they were truly startled by Sam's almost phenomenal ability to estimate angles on the bow, ranges, and zig-zag patterns. Nearly every attack resulted in slipping a dummy torpedo right under the old *Sapphire's* stack—the very middle of the target. His precision of judgment was uncanny. They had seldom seen a sharp-shooting equal of the Torpedo Totin' Texan. In the check-out tests, the *Harder* got the highest possible passing marks. That, to Sam, was the last hurdle. Now the *Harder* was ready for real action.

However, making new installations designed to increase the *Harder's* performance and combat efficiency kept the ship in New London during the early months of 1943.

Then, at long last, dawned Sunday, 26 April, 1943, the golden day of departure. The rising sun was still barely above the horizon when the *Harder*, for the last time, all her amateurish days of learning over and now a real professional in the game of death and destruction, slipped beneath New London's bridges and pointed her bow toward the open sea—destination Pearl Harbor; first stop, the Panama Canal. As she stood out through the supposedly mine-free, swept channel past Montauk Point, a lot of thoughts still looked backward toward old New London, where families and friends and associations of months —perhaps years—still remained. New London is not a town one forgets easily.

That first night out, the weather was ideal. Through the open hatch above him, Signalman Wayne Bostrom, standing his watch at the wheel in the conning tower, caught, as from the bottom of a well, occasional glimpses of the slowly swinging star fields and the faint bluish light of the new moon. Bachelorlike, his thoughts probably looked backward—and forward. Panama can produce some mighty good-looking senoritas.

Driven by his sense of responsibility for his new ship and relatively inexperienced crew, Sam Dealey had Alabama Moore rig a cot for him in the far end of the conning tower. It was not far enough from the heart and brain center of the ship to completely isolate him from the inescapable ship control noises, and he slept only in catnaps and heard practically every order that was passed— softly voiced though they were.

Above the bridge, silhouetted against the starry sky on their lookout platforms, Red and two other lookouts stood two-hour watches. A longer stint of constantly peering through binoculars was bad for the eyes . . . and the eyes of lookouts are important. These were dangerous waters, the hunting grounds of enemy subs and the cross-Atlantic lanes of in- or outbound convoys that plowed along at painfully slow speed, as completely blacked out as human provision against carelessness could provide.

On the *Harder's* bridge structure and cigarette deck there were no lights. Smoking on topside at night was strictly forbidden. Even the faint glow of a cigarette might be caught by watchers on night-prowling Nazi U-Boats.

The blacked out convoys just mentioned had to be avoided for several reasons. Foremost among these was the fact that they were guarded by destroyers with guns manned and loaded and depth charges ready in the racks. When it came to intruders, especially submarines, the tincans did not ask questions first. They asked no questions. Period.

The *Harder* lookouts had been selected by Lieut. Maurer, her Exec., through careful tests and eliminations. To be a first-rate lookout in Jack Maurer's book, a man must not only be sharp-eyed and alert, but also possess good powers of evaluation. This, so that unexpected sightings would not send him into a dither. Moreover, he must be able to make articulate reports of what he saw—swift, clear, and to the point, so that there would be no delay in the issuance of orders based upon the lookout's report. On a sub the lookout is a key man.

At 0445 on the morning of 27 April, Jack Maurer was on the bridge taking his morning star sights when Sam joined him. They agreed that in a few more hours they would be south of the convoy area as defined by Operations at the New London Submarine Base. Just as the sun rose, the *Harder*—her batteries jammed with juice—dove to a comfortable cruising depth of 100 feet for the daytime submerged run.

At 0900, she glided up to periscope depth. Sam, on looking through his Number Two observation scope, was aware, with a tingle of skin-crawling gooseflesh, that his field of vision was filled with ships in convoy and destroyers in escort.

As he took a quick last look, he beheld a fast tincan peeling off from its convoy position. She headed straight as a taut string toward the *Harder*—brimful of business, smoke rolling from her stacks like a black knightly plume and mean as the devil, with a threatening foam-crested bow wave that rode high at its knife-sharp bow.

"Down periscope, left full rudder," spoke Sam in his usual low-level voice. "Take her deep. Slow to creeping speed and run silent."

It was only then that Jack Maurer, who was standing near the scope at the time, realized that something unusual and dangerous was afoot. Sam told him what the scope revealed.

Now sonar and hydrophones reported sounds. The destroyer's pinging came close, but there were, as yet, no signs of depth charges.

"Clear the conning tower; all hands lay below to the control room," ordered Sam—a precautionary measure in case the *Harder's* steel horizontal cylinder of a conning tower should receive fatal damage from a close ashcan, as a depth charge was called. When the conning tower was empty, Sam slid down the ladder to the control room and Chief of the Boat Sloggett dogged the communicating hatch tight above him. Now, if the area of the periscope sheers was hit, the lives of those in the sealed-off compartments below were not necessarily endangered by an unstemmable influx of seawater.

For two hours, while the *Harder* ran silently and deep, the watchdogs above kept sniffing for her trail with their electronic noses. But they never caught the evader's scent. Eventually they ceased. Chief Hatfield, listening at the boat's sonar ears, reported no more screws.

Wrote Sam in his diary: "We expected depth charge attack during first stages of our hide-and-seek game, but found evasive measures effective as we left the convoy and escort far behind. It was a rough way to break in the crew, but everyone took it well enough. Frank's handling of the boat at deep submergence was excellent. Here's hoping the next convoy we encounter will be one of the Japs."

Sunday, 2 May, brought clear skies and flat seas. Just to keep his navigational hand in practice, as well as to allow

Jack Maurer a chance to catch up on sleep, Sam shot the noon day sun. The bridge watch, at the time, consisted of Lieut. Keith Phillips, OOD, Ensign Don Horst, Assistant OOD, and Signalman Wayne Bostrom as Quartermaster. Because he felt certain that the *Harder* was in safe waters, Sam had permitted her to run on the surface in the daytime. This to make up for time lost while running submerged.

Captain Dealey was heading from the cigarette deck toward the bridge proper when, at 1209, the port forward lookout sang out: "Aircraft bearing two seven zero. Distance 5000 yards; altitude about 3000 feet!" As he reached the conning tower hatch, Sam passed his sextant below, took out his pipe, and clamped it between his teeth. At that time, he usually smoked it dry in the forenoon. Then he leaned against a corner of the bridge to watch the proceedings.

"The plane is a PBY," came a voice from the periscope shears. Sam concluded that it was a patrol bomber of the Caribbean Sea Frontier out of St. Thomas. The *Harder* was flying her colors in full view of the oncoming plane.

The submarine was also well within the safety lane assigned her by the Chief of Naval Operations for the trip to Panama. Nevertheless, the plane looked like it meant business as it headed directly for the *Harder*.

"Bostrom," called the OOD, "give him the recognition signal."

Out flashed the challenge of the day from the Aldis lamp, but the zoomie gave no sign of having seen it. (Light flashes from Aldis lamps were frequently mistaken by aviators for machine-gun fire.)

"Fire the emergency flare," called Keith Phillips.

Still, as Sam expressed it, "all signals were ignored by the dauntless airmen." Ominous, dull, flat cracks could be heard above the rhythmic roar of the plane's engines. There could be no mistake—those were machine guns.

OOD Phillips kept his head well and no old-timer's voice could have been steadier as he sang out: "Lookouts below; clear the bridge; sound the diving alarm; left full rudder."

The men who had stood in their loops high on the *Harder's* steel shears had vanished through the hatch and Bostrom was halfway down it when the PBY thundered in—guns cracking. For one brief second—as the craft cast its heavy shadow over the sub—Dealey, Phillips, and Horst, who were still on deck, wished that they were manning the boat's 20-mm. cannon.

"Man," said Horst later, "but wouldn't we have liked to hose that pilot down with a stream of lead!"

Fortunately, Phillips' quick decision in turning the ship toward the approaching plane saved the day. The gunners' aim was spoiled and they failed even to hit the hull of their slim target on their bow to stern run. Instead, the bullets ripped into the water along the starboard side close aboard.

Throughout the entire incident, Sam had remained quietly out of the way in a small corner of the bridge. He had taken no hand whatever in the proceedings. This attitude on his part gave ample proof of his faith in his officers that they could be relied upon to do their jobs well. However, as befits the captain of a ship, he was the last man down the hatch and heard the unpleasant patter of bullets alongside as he slammed the cover.

As the *Harder* slid through the mirror of smooth blue sea and was swallowed up by the kind of magic that made Alice vanish through the looking glass, the PBY executed a snappy climbing turn and, streaking out of it, roared back toward the *Harder*, the swirl of whose propellers must still have been visible to the attacker.

First came a rain of machine-gun bullets. Next, the crack-whoom of a depth bomb.

Poorly placed, the bomb was nevertheless near enough to give the *Harder* a good shaking-up. Close on the heels of the first whoom came another of the same. It was even more distant and won only sneers from the bridge watch who knew that the PBY carried only two bombs.

There had been no time and, as it developed, no need

PBY

to abandon the conning tower. Actually it was so tightly packed with extra hands that there was very little jostling around.

After a bit, when damage control parties had reported all serene, Sam took the Talker's microphone and, speaking throughout the ship, said that now the *Harder* and her men had undergone their baptism of fire. The fact that the bullets were fired and the bombs were dropped by men who were on their own team was a double warning to be forever alert and to take nothing in the sky or on the sea for granted. The reaction of the crew was excellent. They had dodged their first depth charges. They felt themselves already old hands.

Sam's diary that night carried the entry: "The aviator's poor approach was exceeded only by his poor marksmanship. . . . But whose side are these crazy aviators on?"

As he thought about the incident and recalled that the

acts of hostility were staged in spite of the colors and two sets of recognition signals, Sam's anger, always slow to boil, began to seethe within him. He was not angry at the young men aboard the PBY whose lust to kill had been so easily triggered. Instead, he directed his wrath at the Nazi, Fascist, and Jap expansionists whose thirst for blood and battle had forced the young men of America to learn how to become air-borne Deputies of Death.

Being now in tropical waters, many of the new submariners aboard the *Harder* were properly impressed—in fact, quite thrilled by their first sight of schools of flying fish. As Sam described them, "they streaked over the surface of the sea like silver darts." The sub also came upon two love-making or playful whales that passed rather close aboard. The deep-swimming whales were at first—when scanned by sonar—believed to be submarines. Aboard the *Harder,* a Junior Officer of the Deck was inclined to send for the Captain. He was convinced that the situation required a call to battle stations. However, he was persuaded that the situation was well in hand. Those two cruising lovers never knew of the threat to their romance. Poor devils, whales had a rough time in World War II.

Throughout the long journey to Panama the weather and the seas were friendly—a welcome kindness on nature's part toward the new men aboard the sub. Days and nights were filled with drills in addition to regular submarine watches. "School of the Boat," instruction in all equipment of the ship and notebook work for all unqualified men, kept the officers and men fully occupied. Sack time was always at a premium.

One exception was the night before the ship entered port at Panama. The *Harder* ran through a school of flying fish so big that winged fish by the dozen zoomed out of the sea, knocked themselves out against the conning tower's exterior plating, and fell on deck. All hands had fried flying fish for breakfast that next morning—Andy Sammut could do acts of magic with a skillet. It was Tom Buckner, doubling in brass as Commissary Officer, who had the idea that the winged visitors would make a welcome change in the diet. Calling a few willing hands, he collected the wildly flapping fish and turned them over to the cooks for further handling.

Alas, from then until the approaches to Pearl Harbor were sighted, there were no more exciting incidents. At Panama, Jack Maurer and Don Horst received pleasant surprises. The former had notice of his promotion to Lieutenant Commander, the latter to Lieutenant, Junior Grade.

Once out the westward exit of the Canal, the *Harder* made a great circle course for Hawaii. In mid-May, day on day, the Pacific lived up to its name, but after a week or so the going was not too pleasant. In high winds and seas the sub would roll and pitch like a bronco. It was hard enough at times for weary, would-be sleepers just to stay in their bunks without attempting to sleep.

One sunset the *Harder* surfaced suddenly and with a steep up-angle, just as Ship's Cook Sammut was about to dish out the evening meal. A stream of sulphurous language echoed through the ship. Tom Buckner rushed into the galley to see what all the howling, up-state New Yorker's commotion was about. He found the cook seated on the deck with spaghetti running out of both ears and a lap full of baked beans.

Along with much cussing, Sammut made the sage remark: "I hope the country realizes the sacrifices I have to make in order that democracy may live!"

All hands enjoyed the incident so thoroughly that no one minded the makeshift dinner served that night. Sam regarded little events like that as perfect safety valves to relieve tension in the crew.

Under the broiling sun, Keith Phillips became as brown as a Mexican. On the bridge one day he noticed Sam rubbing vinegar on his face to take the sting out of sunburning. Grinning broadly, he said he would write his good friend Rosemary Dealey that the old man has been pickled ever since the cruise began.

Said Sam to himself: "I suppose I do have the fragrance of a dill!"

While en route, the wardroom established an efficient

system for keeping its tablecloth clean. For a while, in New London, the mess bills were getting alarmingly high because of the many dirty tablecloths to be laundered. But soon after the Hawaii-bound cruise started, it became a wardroom rule that whenever someone spilled anything on the cloth, he had to buy candy bars from the ship's store for every wardroom occupant. It was amazing how careful everyone became not to splash food around. A cloth used to stay clean two days; under the new system it lasted a week to ten days! Since Sam had put himself on a strict diet, he had twelve candy bars owed to him on arrival in Honolulu.

When at last they entered Pearl Harbor, the great Naval station of the Pacific, the *Harder's* people were forcibly impressed with the extensive damage done by the Japs. They saw, with anger running hot in their veins, the valiant ships that had been left as rusting tombs for the men who were trapped within their hulls when they went down. Sam felt thoroughly choked up as he recalled the men he had known who now rested in slimy graves within the walls of dead ships. That gave him a little more unfinished business to take up with the Japs.

Steaming on, the *Harder* reached Pearl Harbor's Submarine Base. Sam was surprised and elated when he heard a band and found many friends at the dock to welcome him into the fold. Ice cream, cold milk, and fruit juices were brought aboard for the crew while the band, led by famous Eddie Peabody, played such lively tunes as "Anchors Aweigh" and "There'll Be a Hot Time in the Old Town Tonight."

In my new role as Commander Submarines Pacific, it was my job and pleasure with the operational members of my staff to go aboard newly arrived submarines as soon as the gangway was rigged. So it was with the *Harder*.

Best of all was the moment Sam caught sight of his brother, (Bud) Jerome, whose uniform fit his short, straight, and manly figure to a T. He had a five-day leave from his Military Police Company on the Island of Kauai. Then, and during future overhauls between patrols, the two were to spend many hours talking over old times and making plans for the years to come.

Bud spent his leave living aboard the *Harder* with Sam, the officers, and crew. They all joined in wishing Bud were a regular member of the outfit.

After receiving services for a few voyage repairs alongside a tender, the *Harder* was popped into the ARD-1—a 2500-ton floating drydock assigned to Sub Base Pearl. There a round-the-clock job of bottom scraping, propeller polishing, and antifouling painting was done. The sides of the old ARD-1 fairly smoked in those days just from the friction of going up and down so often. Time was really pressing in the Pacific and subs had to be sent to sea with clean bottoms so their speed would not be impaired.

Targets were increasingly plentiful and the performance of our torpedoes was increasingly disappointing. Drastic changes going all the way back to the Bureau of Ordnance were indicated. Submarine captains returning after war patrols in Asiatic waters wore long faces and told sad stories of the big ones that got away "because my damned torpedoes prematured [exploded before reaching the target]." Most of them were about ready, as they expressed it, "to go over the hill."

# Preview of Pacific Theatre

When I stepped aboard the *Harder* on her arrival that 23rd day of May, 1943, to be greeted by Sam Dealey's best smile and a bright right-hand salute from all on deck, I was not a happy man. I remember that period of the war only too well. I had arrived at Pearl in February, 1943, from "down under," where I had served in General Mac-Arthur's Southwest Pacific Area, to try to fill the shoes of Admiral English, my predecessor as comsubpac, who was killed in a plane crash. I inherited a fine bunch of young-sters who wanted to win the war single-handed, and it was one of my most important jobs to give them torpedoes that would explode when they hit—not before.

Our Big Boss, Admiral Nimitz, Commander-in-Chief, Pacific Fleet, himself a submariner for many years—and with the tangy smell of Diesel oil still in his nostrils—was our biggest booster, but he felt, as I did, that something was rotten in our setup.

"Lockwood," he said, "either our torpedoes are defective or the Japs have some secret defense which triggers them prematurely."

Too many enemy ships were steaming away after our torpedo attacks instead of heading for Davy Jones' Locker. Well, the trouble was in our magnetic exploder—but that is another story. We eventually whipped the problem, but this happy situation had not been reached when the *Harder* made her initial appearance at Pearl.

Hence, after a quick look at Sam Dealey's ship—brand, shiny new out of New London—to get an idea of her morale and material needs, we adjourned for lunch at my quarters on Makalapa Hill. There we talked torpedoes and East Coast training methods. Sam impressed me, as he did my staff, with his earnest manner, his cheery Will-Rogers sort of grin, and the cut of his jaw. In spite of his cherubic, youthful appearance, he seemed to have tucked a lot away under his hat and was impatient to get into the fight.

"I've got some unfinished business to take up with the Japs—and with the Huns, also," remarked Dealey. "Guess I'll have to take that out on the Japs, too."

Of course, he did not know how his exploders would act in a war shot. But he had confidence in his torpedo crew and said they had made a lot of hits for him in training. He guaranteed that his fish would run hot, straight, and normal right into Hirohito's front yard.

As a matter of fact, his torpedo attacks against fast targets outside Pearl Harbor under the careful eyes of Captain John Brown, Commander "Fearless Freddy" Warder, and others of the Training Command, showed that he was, in truth, a Torpedo Totin' Texan. His officers and crew also reflected plenty of ship spirit—a most important factor in any man-of-war, especially a submarine.

There was nothing about Sam Dealey at the time—in his bearing or manner of speech—to indicate that he would be in any way different from others of his kind. Which, for that matter, he was not. To me, one of his most interesting aspects has always been that he was thoroughly representative of the men who command our submarines.

Since our first boats were acquired at the start of the twentieth century, they have been employed in two World Wars and a Police Action. During this half-century some submariners had opportunities to show the stuff that was in them, to act with mental brilliance, spiritual strength, and physical courage under challenging conditions. Others, lacking such opportunities, never had a chance to display their potentials.

Sam was lucky enough to be in the first category. With his splendid array of command talents, it is surprising to find that Dealey was not extraordinary or uncommon as a son, brother, husband, and father. He was just an ordinary God-fearing, home-loving human being—even as you and I. He loved his home and family. It meant much for him to give it second place in order that he might serve his country in the Navy. He hated war, but still he was ready to make the full sacrifices he had to offer in order to help bring victory to the cause he knew was right.

To me, the thing that made Sam such an outstanding success as a combat skipper was not primarily his absolute fearlessness, but his amazing ability to make instant and correct decisions. Where others might have hesitated—held off for better evaluation or a bit more data—Dealey instantly bored in to the attack with seemingly instinctive knowledge of how it should be done.

The *Harder's* arrival and brief refresher course of training at Pearl Harbor in May–June, 1943, came at a period when plenty of hot irons were in the fires of war and our Pacific fighting forces were scrabbling around for asbestos gloves wherewith to retrieve them. The war was then a year and a half old and what had been, initially, a private war of the submarines had now become a general melee. Action by air, land, and sea raged far and wide in the Pacific. Although Guadalcanal had been secured in January, 1943, after the evacuation of its remaining troops by vessels of the Tokyo Express, the Solomons Islands were still far from cleared of the enemy.

Fleet Admiral Yamamoto, reputed to be the brains of the Japanese Navy, had been ambushed and shot down in April by Army fighter planes just as he was about to land at Buin, a Jap base in the Solomons. However, the Imperial Japanese Navy tightened its belt and gave no sign that their top admiral had been indispensable. Enemy light craft carried on with their usual boldness and determination and kept alive the tradition of the Tokyo Express by

**U.S.S. Narwal**

nocturnal attempts to land reinforcements and supplies for their remaining Solomons' garrisons. Frequent clashes with our cruiser-destroyer forces occurred and, in these night battles, our radar-controlled gun and torpedo fire proved of great value. Even so, our losses in cruisers and destroyers mounted.

In the air, Australian- and Solomons-based American planes shot it out in continual battles with Jap Bettys, Zekes, and Zeroes. Together with New Guinea-based PT boats, our planes in March had inflicted a crushing defeat in the Bismarck Sea to an enemy convoy with six thousand troops bound for Lae in Papua, as the southeast end of the New Guinea group is called. Not one of the eight crowded transports and only four destroyers survived the slaughter. Nevertheless, the enemy continued a precarious supply line to his short-rationed troops in New Guinea by means

of submarines or by bringing in barges at night from Cape
Gloucester.

In Australia and New Guinea the Supreme Commander
Allied Forces, Southwest Pacific Area, General of the
Army Douglas MacArthur, with headquarters at Brisbane,
also was beset by urgent problems. His army of Australian
and American troops, after beating back the Japanese from
a thrust at Port Moresby, was struggling up the Papuan
coast through mud and swamp and jungle toward Salamaua.
He lacked sufficient troops and adequate landing craft for
his amphibious force, but the VII Phib Force and the
Seventh Fleet were rapidly developing. 30 June had been
set for a new advance up the tail of the New Guinea Bird
to Nassau Bay.

In the far north—Admiral Kinkaid's Aleutian sector—
Attu, after a stubborn defense, had fallen to the amphibious forces of Admiral Rockwell. It was assaulted on 11
May and reported secured on the 30th of that same month.
Submarines *Nautilus* and *Narwhal* contributed to this success by landing each about 100 Army scouts on the enemy's flank. Kiska was marked for the next invasion in this
area.

In the submarine forces, all was not well. Not only were
their Mark XIV torpedoes equipped with Mark 6 magnetic
exploders performing badly, but an inexcusable news re-
lease had needlessly endangered the lives of every submariner and submarine in the Pacific. A public official who
had visited front-line bases, on his return to the States,
boasted in the press that American submarines did not
fear Japanese destroyers because their depth charges were
not powerful enough to damage our boats and not set deep
enough to reach them. The gratitude of the enemy for this
information can be readily imagined.

Notwithstanding these handicaps, American, British, and
Dutch submarines in the Pacific theatre were sinking enemy ships. At the end of April, 1943, the Allied score
stood at 258 enemy merchant ships sunk for a total of
1,105,113 tons. Added to this were 39 men of war, including a carrier, a heavy cruiser, a light cruiser, 16 destroyers

or other anti-submarine craft, and 9 submarines. The enemy was beginning to learn, even as the Allies had learned in the Atlantic, the crushing burden of maintaining long supply lines exposed to enemy submarine attack. These successes had cost the American submarine forces 10 boats sunk presumably by enemy action and 4 lost in operational disasters. Lost, with these ill-fated submarines, were about 550 officers and men—not including those taken prisoner, some of whom were returned at the end of the war.

These stark statistics were grim evidence of the bitterness of the war being waged at sea.

Not that there was any doubt in the minds of submariners in the Pacific, South Pacific, and Southwest Pacific that a war was on. In a small organization—such as was our submarine force before World War II—an outfit in which nearly everyone had friends in all the boats, the death or imprisonment of 500 to 700 men struck blows at the heart of the entire undersea service.

Nor was there any doubt in the mind of Comdr. Submarines Southwest Pacific at Perth, Australia, or in my mind as Comdr. Submarines Pacific at Pearl that we were fighting a determined and deadly enemy as we sweated out those agonizing ten days after a submarine failed to return to base before reporting her "missing presumed lost."

Submarine construction was speeding up at home; a report from New London stated that building time had been cut to 336 days and would shrink even more. Splendid new submarines were arriving at Pearl at the rate of four or five per month, and at the time of the *Harder's* arrival seventy-five were operating out of Pearl Harbor.

Occasionally a new submarine would arrive whose personnel had not worked up to a fighting pitch and the full grasp of the deadly seriousness of war. Even though the *Harder* had few combat-tested officers or men on board, her fighting spirit, as exemplified by her Skipper, Comdr. Sam Dealey, was excellent.

Even when new ships arrived with a low head of Jap-hating steam, it did not take long for association with veterans of combat patrols to stoke the fires. Those men

Papua

had learned the ghastly truth that in enemy-controlled waters, it is sink or be sunk; kill or be killed. A good Jap was one whose bloated body you saw floating face down in the water. Capt. Babe Brown, the Subpac Director of Training, and his team of battle-tested Division Commanders dealt out a brand of elder brother, starkly realistic training at sea and on a War College type game board ashore into which they had worked all feasible types of enemy counter-measures and the best methods of successful submarine commanders.

Among these last named at that period were such stalwarts as Bull Wright, Freddy Warder, Bob Rice, Donk Donaho, Peedee Quirk, Chester Bruton, Bert Klakring, Bill Post, Art Taylor, Bob Gross, Rebel Lowrance, Bill Brockman, Creed Burlingame, Barney Sieglaff, Mike Fenno, and Mush Morton* to mention only a few. Three of these

*For the full story of this great captain read WAHOO by Rear Admiral Richard H. O'Kane, Ret. Another volume in the Bantam War Book Series.

high-scoring skippers—Brockman, Fenno, and Donaho—
were, even then, on speaking tours in the States in an
endeavor to attract more recruits to the lowly, unglamourized
pig boats. The training included, whenever possible, a
night and day attack—without firing torpedoes—against
one of our own convoys coming in from the West Coast.

When a submarine left Pearl Harbor headed west, she
was trained and conditioned to a fine edge of perfection—
and even so was the good ship *Harder*.

One of the most popular men aboard the *Harder* was
Audley Carver, a great cook as well as Chief Commissary
Steward. He was taken ill and his case diagnosed as ap-
pendicitis. To fill the vacancy, J. W. Thomason, Ship's
Cook First Class, was taken aboard and given the duties of
Commissary Steward as well. Thomason hailed from Fort
Worth, Texas. A high-income and high-powered sales pro-
moter before he enlisted in the Navy, he soon proved
himself an equally high-class wangler in filling the store-
rooms of the *Harder* with taste-tickling items. Incidentally, he had also learned how to be a first chop cook who
knew his way around on a galley range.

Between them, Commissary Officer Buckner and Commissary Steward Thomason found food stuffs for the *Harder*
that were not standard for subs. Thomason, however,
ruled his galley with a rod of iron. One day he had turned
out a batch of cherry pies. He set them out on a mess
table to cool. MoMM Joseph Sauvageau of Poquonnock
Bridge, Connecticut, came along, saw, and was conquered.
With his knife he cut out a slice of pie. In cold anger,
Thomason threw the whole batch of pies into the garbage
can. He narrowly escaped being put on the report for
wasting food, but from that time on, no one took anything
in the galley without Jack's consent.

At this same time, Tom Buckner was busy along other
lines. Before the *Harder* left New London, he had written
a letter to Dinah Shore, the singer and movie actress with
whom he had attended school in their native Nashville.
He asked her, with the permission of the Skipper, if she
would be the *Harder's* Guardian Angel and send him a

few photographs to be placed strategically about the vessel—in wardroom, messroom, and other places.

It so happened that, aboard the *Harder*, so called cheese-cake pictures and cheesecake conversational subjects were frowned upon as being out of bounds. Hence Sam was happy to have the sweetly ladylike personality of Miss Shore represent the glamour sector of the fair sex aboard his ship. The only other art in the *Harder's* wardroom were the photos of wives and children of the wardroom gang. Therefore, when Tom Buckner, on arrival at Pearl Harbor, found a group of autographed pictures of Dinah Shore in his mail, he immediately set about having them framed and placed in bulkhead positions previously decided upon.

It was a bad stroke of lightning when Chief Carver was laid low. But it was even worse when a bolt hit again, just a few nights before the sub was to leave on her maiden patrol.

On that evening, Buckner and Don Horst had been at a movie on the Submarine Base when, in coming back aboard the blacked-out *Harder*, Ensign Buckner vanished right before Don's eyes. He had fallen through a grating in the deck that had been left open by accident. While an ambulance was called, Lieut. Horst and crew men who were aboard hoisted Buckner out on deck. It was obvious that he had a broken leg.

When Buckner realized his plight—that he had to go to a hospital and that it could be a long time before he rejoined his ship, he came close to tears. "Look here, you Donald Earle Horst—if you don't get me back aboard the *Harder* when I get out, I'll clean your shovel—so help me, I'll mow you down."

That phrase, "I'll clean your shovel," was the most dire threat Tom Buckner could make to any man for any reason. Don promised that he would move Heaven and earth with the Old Man. Tom had nothing to worry about on that score. The next day, Captain Dealey called on the young Tennessean at the hospital and told him that his berth would be held open. Not only that, he took it upon himself to look up the Commanding Officer of the Naval Hospital and to make a personal plea for expediting the recovery of his most junior Junior Officer.

"Well," grinned the Captain in command at Aiea Hospital, "if you put it that way, Mr. Dealey, I'll knit the young man's leg personally." That big, quick warm Irish grin of Dealey's lit the path for him wherever he went.

When the last war call has sounded,
And the fleet will sail no more,
When a lasting peace is founded,
And no enemy threatens our shore,
When at last they write the story,
And the reason for vict'ry is seen,
You will rise in honored glory,
You mighty submarine.

★★★★★★★★★★★★★★★★★★★★★★★★★★★★★★★★★★★★★★★★ **11**

# The *Harder* Comes of Age

After what Sam considered an interminable delay to his progress toward the war—actually only two weeks—the *Harder's* training period came to an end. Her last torpedo training shots scored three runs under the bull's-eye of a speeding destroyer.

"I wish they had been hits on a Jap ship," wrote Dealey. "Well, it won't be long now."

And so, on the afternoon of 7 June, the *Harder* backed away from Pier 4 at the Submarine Base.

On the stroke of the bell at 1330, Jack Maurer, the Exec., passed the word: "Take in the gangway. Take in all lines. Starboard, back two-thirds," and, with Sam Dealey watching casually, Jack backed the *Harder* around in a graceful arc until her prow pointed out the channel. Then a boil of water at her stern signaled the bite of her screws as the engines were put ahead and, with the *Searaven* and an escort vessel following, the *Harder* stood out to seaward. As Sam and his silent crew passed the crumpled wreckage off Ford Island, which had once been the proud ship *Arizona*, and the whale-like bottom of the capsized *Oklahoma*, they registered a silent vow that many a yellow-belly would pay for those murders.

That night Sam's diary recorded: "One and a half years

**U.S.S. ARIZONA**

ago the war began. Pearl Harbor was bombed. Today we start for the war zone.

"Many folks came down to see us off in company with the submarine *Searaven* and escorted by a patrol vessel.

"After clearing the harbor, I announced over the loud speaker to the crew that our destination was the Empire War Patrol area. The news was greeted with cheers throughout the ship, as I knew it would be.

"We are headed right for the enemy's back yard. Remember the song—or was it never written? 'Goodbye, Mama, We're off to Yokohama!' "

After dark the parting escort vessel flashed the traditional message of farewell, "Good luck and good hunting," reversed course, and the *Harder* was on her own.

En route to Midway Island, a four-day journey, Sam held daily dives, fire control and battle surface drills, plus other exercises for perfection in essential training.

As day broke on the morning of 11 June, the sun rose clear from behind the cumulus clouds that usually rim the horizon in the central Pacific at dawn and dusk. Other scattered wool packs dotted the sky. Skipper Sam Dealey, Navigator Jack Maurer, and the lookouts on the periscope shears of the *Harder* strained their eyes for Midway where the *Harder* was to top off her fuel tanks. This she undertook promptly upon arrival at 0800 at the tender dock in the lagoon after a hazardous trip up the narrow dredged channel through the coral reef. With the long ground swells astern of her and boosting the sub along, Sam felt as though he were riding a cross between a roller coaster and an Hawaiian surf board. It took fast work with the helm and plenty of speed to keep the ship from swinging crosswise of the channel and smashing into the side.

On Midway the atmosphere was even more highly charged and warlike than at Pearl. Only a year before, the decisive carrier battle of Midway had been fought and won by U.S. forces almost within sight of its shores. The island itself, serving as a base for all available Army aircraft which could be gotten out from Pearl, had been badly worked over by Japanese bombers. One burned-out seaplane hangar, a gaunt frame of bent and twisted steelwork, stood as a grim reminder of those flame-blasted days.

If any superheat were needed for the *Harder's* war spirit or training, Midway certainly provided it.

Lieut. Max Kerns, a last minute replacement for Tom Buckner, whose home was in Melrose, Massachusetts, and Lieut. (jg) Don Horst had business ashore and obtained permission to visit the Ships Service Store and the Post Office. They purchased a few personal items and then posted a large packet of letters. Among the letters they posted were some three dozen to some of the most luminous glamour girls in Hollywood. Each of those letters, all written by the officers of the sub, excepting Sam and Jack Maurer, asked each star if she would be the Guardian Angel of the *Harder*. It was all part of a gargantuan gag staged for the benefit of Tom. His wardroom pals thought it would be fun, when Tom returned, to find the space literally littered with personalized photos of regal movie queens to offset his own personal Guardian Angel.

The _Harder_ departed Midway at 1600, under air escort, and set a course for the tiny island of Hachijo Jima, more than 2300 miles to the westward. During the first few days, when the weather held fair, drills of all sort were continued. There were, of course, breaks for rest and recreation. These, Sam knew, were essential for efficient human performance. When not on the bridge or in the wardroom or prowling the ship, as any skipper must be to maintain efficiency and morale, Sam would study a digest of patrol reports which had been made on his assigned area or catch cat-naps in his stateroom. He was soon to know, by first hand experience, that in combat waters, submariners generally get next to no sleep and that the Old Man catches the least shut-eye of all.

The provisioning of a submarine is an art and an operation of comparable importance to the combat loading of attack transports. Everything must be stowed so that it may be taken out of storage in the proper order. All fleet submarines were capable of being provisioned for seventy-five days, although the standard war patrol was only sixty days. Storeroom and refrigerator space was at a premium, so that once stowed, the supplies could not be shuffled about—at least during the first part of a patrol. Unless care was exercised, a crew might find itself condemned to eat its way through a wall of string beans or chicken soup or spam before some variety could be introduced into its diet. Ship Cook—Acting Commissary Steward—Thomason never got himself caught in that kind of a bind. He and Ship's Cook Sammut, with their mess cooks, personally supervised the stowing of every can, every pound of fresh meat, and the large quantities of fruit and vegetable juices so vital to men who enjoyed little sunlight.

The officers' mess of the _Harder_—like that of all other submarines in wartime—served the same food as was provided for all hands. A few extras—somebody's favorite breakfast food or some other lad's special jam—might be included in the wardroom's monthly mess bill, but these items were not numerous. The mess arrangements were presided over by Cabin Steward Rufino Guiang of Zambales Province, northwest of Manila, and Cabin Cook Robert "Alabama" Moore, who, despite his nickname, actually came from Mississippi. Both were excellent cooks in all departments. Guiang specialized in rice and curry dishes; while Alabama's salads, even with the limited ingredients available at sea, might have made Oscar of the Waldorf look to his laurels.

Coffee, of course, bubbled in the galley and wardroom urns all around the clock, and during the night, snacks in the form of meat-filled sandwiches were always available. For some obscure reason, introduced by Thomason, custom aboard the *Harder* was soon to dictate that, after combat, when possible, steaks under blankets of fried eggs were served to celebrate victory. This habit had been brought north from Australia where steak'n-egg was a national dish.

Every evening, Chief Radioman Hiram Hatfield would distribute typed-up copies of news summaries broadcast by HAIKU, Cincpac's station, to the fleet. When conditions permitted, men off watch would listen to newscasts and other programs, mainly music, out of San Francisco. Nearly all looked forward to the hour when they would hear Radio Tokyo and catch the voice of Tokyo Rose, whose honeyed verbal poison was the main hate and the main joke among Americans. When, after several days of westward cruising, the *Harder* finally picked her up, Rose proved to be rather disappointing. Her novelty scent soon wore off and became odoriferous.

Some subs held divine services at stated hours on Sundays. Not so aboard the *Harder*. To be sure, now and then Bob Moore would hold informal and well-attended prayer meetings. At these he would play sweet stuff, as the jam-cats put it, on his trumpet. In the crew's messroom, the main recreations were chess, checkers, and salvo.

Bunking conditions aboard a fleet-type submarine were probably the most crowded part of the men's crowded lives. In the after battery compartment where some forty-odd men slept, the fold-up pipe berths were three high. That situation did not change throughout the patrol. In the forward and after torpedo rooms, however, conditions were subject to change. When a sub headed out for the shooting country, all tubes and all reserve torpedo racks were full. The torpedo crews and others who slept there were wedged in above, below, and alongside of cold-skinned, unyielding bedfellows who packed a 750 pound TNT or torpex wallop in their warheads. They had the comforting assurance, however, that no matter how unreliable those warheads might be in performance against the enemy, they could not possibly explode until they had run an arming distance of about 400 yards from the submarine.

As the fish were expended, elbow room in the torpedo rooms increased—and they then became available for 16-mm movies. However, at times accommodations had to be furnished to extra passengers, refugees or dunked aviators. Then, since there are no spare bunks in a submarine, a system of "hot bunking" was resorted to. This meant that a man coming off watch climbed into the bunk of a man who had just gone on watch. And always when conditions of any sort reached the semi-unbearable stage, some comforting soul would give voice to the time honored crack: "Cheer up, sailor; it's the same in the Army."

In the wardroom, at the end of day, the *Harder's* officers would get together around the small rectangular table to hash over the day's happenings, tell stories, or sing popular songs. Sam knew more lyrics and music than a tin pan alley tune-booster, from such old time favorites as "In the Gloaming" to more timely but transient tunes such as "Don't Fence Me in." Irish songs and plaintive old plantation melodies Sam knew by the dozen; cowboy and hillbilly tunes by the score. So did Frank Lynch and Tom Buckner; but Tom, alas, was not on the first patrol because of his broken leg. The others in the wardroom—Maurer, Kerns, Logan, and Phillips—strummed happily along. Now and then Alabama, in his pantry, would play a sweet'n low accompaniment on his trumpet.

Bob Moore was a product of Hattiesburg, Mississippi.

But, through hard-won education in studies for the pulpit, he was by no means a typical plantation Negro of the deep, deep South. On the contrary, his English, when he wanted it to be that way, was well above the national average. But Robert Moore knew that, aboard a submarine, the comedy youall plantation vernacular that made minstrels so popular would be laugh-productive. Hence, in order to spread laughter and amused grins where he could, the nearly-Reverend Robert Moore frequently donned the verbal garb of Alabama the Minstrel Man— and produced what he grinningly called Uncle Tom stuff. It was a line of talk, words, and jokes that made him widely quoted and much admired throughout the ship.

For the first three days out of Midway, Jack Maurer was able to get his sights and do his navigating under ideal conditions as the *Harder* pressed westward under blue skies in moderate seas and low winds. But on 15 June, the wind shifted from southeast to northwest during the night. The barometer plummeted and the seas picked up. With the coming of daylight, a very heavy sea was running. The *Harder* slowed to one-engine speed, which in the raging storm meant about 8 knots. The lookouts were reduced from four to two in order to lessen the chances of having a man overboard.

The gods of wind and rain and waves took a breathing spell on 17 and 18 June. At 0800 on the morning of the 18th, Sam was on the bridge as Jack Maurer came up from working out his early morning star sights. "According to my plot," said Sam's alter ego and second in command, "we are just entering the 600-mile circle from Tokyo."

Sam viewed the clearing skies and the abating seas. "Too bad," he said, "that dirty weather could not stay with us long enough to let us get by the Jap air and sea patrols at Hachijo Jima."

The latter island is in the group of earth dabs that spill southward out of Sagami Nada, the outer bay of the shallow, tightly enclosed expanse of water that gives Yokohama and Tokyo a harbor that is virtually attack-proof from the sea. With Mikura Jima, its northern neighbor, Hachijo

Jima forms a major gateway for west-east shipping to and from Japan. It was an important Japanese patrol point for sea-borne as well as winged patrol craft during the war.

But Sam was to have his weather wish. As his log stated for 19 June: "During night barometer dropped. Sea and wind picked up. Very heavy seas by morning. Taking occasional waves over the bridge. Sky hazy and overcast.

"Intermittent light and heavy rain squalls throughout day. Perfect weather for slipping into area unobserved. Heavy weather has apparently grounded Jap planes covering this area and has chased patrol craft and sampans into harbor."

At 1800, the watchful _Harder_ was pushing forward; to Tokyo the distance was only one hour by air. Observed Sam in his log: "About one hour's flying from Tokyo air bases and still no planes. Too bad that this ship does not represent another and bigger Shangri-La for a Doolittle Return Engagement Over Tokyo."

Slightly more than an hour later, a lookout sang out: "Land on the port bow, sir. Bearing about 350."

The distance plotted eighteen miles. It was undoubtedly Hachijo Jima.

At the same time contact was picked up by the SD (aircraft warning) radar, but the SJ radar, designed for use against surface targets, although coached on the bearing of the island, did not show a pip on its screen until the range had shortened to 23,000 yards. This 10-CM radar was new to the submarine service and its full capability had not then been developed. Later, it was to prove an almost indispensable aid to night battle.

Sam, undaunted by the near proximity of an enemy base, passed it at 2200 only five miles to port. In the blackness of the night, no shipping activity in the open roadstead nor outlying patrol craft were noted. No lights were to be seen in the port and all navigational lights had evidently been turned off for the duration.

There were tense moments during this first entry into enemy home waters and the binocular-equipped bridge watchers strained their eyes for the first sight of an enemy—

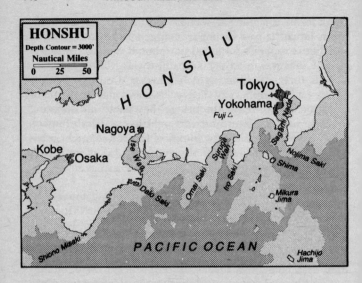

Honshu

many submarines gave prizes of cigarettes, etc., to sharp-eyed lookouts. Dealey, however, found time to congratulate navigator Maurer on making an excellent landfall under minimum conditions for favorable navigation.

It was near the pearl-gray hour of the false dawn on 20 June when the *Harder* entered upon Area 5, which was to be her first scene of battle.

Tracing it on a chart, one would find that the eastern end of this area is Omai Zaki, a lighthouse west of Suruga Wan. The western end of Area 5 is Shiono Misaki light, whose long white beams cover the dark waters for ships that head for the busy ports of Kobe and Osaka. The stretch of coastline from Omai Zaki to Shiono Misaki runs some 135 miles. At its exact center stands Daio Saki, marking the entrance to Ise Bay and the harbor of Nagoya.

All ports in this central section of the Honshu coast are highly industrialized, which promised well for the *Harder's* probable supply of targets. All along this coast runs the Japan Current, which the Japs call the Kuroshio, heading northeasterly at a speed of 1 or 2 knots.

During the hours Captain Dealey had a chance to spend in the privacy of his stateroom on the way to the shooting country, he had given much thought to the plan of attack that would direct the movements of the *Harder*. On occasion, he had thrashed the subject out in talks with Jack Maurer.

The *Harder's* job was to find and sink the enemy's ships: cargo vessels, transports, battleships, carriers. In those days, the rule against expending scarce torpedoes upon destroyers and the less important men-of-war was still effective.

Having studied previous patrol reports covering the area, both men knew that commerce in the region fell into two well-defined routes: One was the deep-water route from Omai Saki to Kashino Saki; the other closely hugged the shore (inside the 100-fathom curve), conforming to the contour of the southern Honshu coast line.

During the night, the *Harder* ran at a smooth 15-knot pace toward Omai Saki to the tune of its own muffled engine exhausts and under a wide and starry sky that gave full illustration of Stevenson's poetic description. Max Kerns, as O.O.D., sniffed—expanded his nostrils—and sniffed again. He threw a quick glance toward Don Horst, his Assistant O.O.D. In the darkness he could barely see him. But he heard him. Kerns was sniffing too.

"What do you make it?" asked Kerns.

"I dunno, but it might smell like Christmas in a harem," Don replied.

"Lookouts!" called Max, "do you lads notice anything peculiar, like a funny kind of smell?"

"Yes, sir!" came a swift reply. "Smells like some kind of a flower garden."

"See any land? You fellows been asleep? Quick, take an all around looksee!"

In seconds, all reported: "No land in sight."

"That's the way I figure it, too," observed Kerns. "We should be at least twenty-five to thirty miles from the nearest land."

"Well, sir, if we were up the Yangtze River," kidded Roland Provencher, standing watch as Quartermaster, "we might be passing a 'honey barge.'"

"I don't know what it is—but it might mean something." Then a little louder: "Conning Tower."

"Conning Tower, sir," came the reply from the man at the helm immediately below the conning tower hatch.

"Ask the Captain to come to the bridge."

A bare thirty seconds later, the Old Man, attired in a pair of striped pajamas and with his red-lensed night vision goggles pushed high on his forehead, rose quickly through the hatch onto the bridge proper.

Before anyone could say a word, Sam was aware of the fragrance. Kerns noted his awareness and said: "That is why I called you, sir. It may mean nothing—but, on the other hand . . ."

"You did quite right, Max. When in doubt, always call the Skipper. That's what he gets paid for. And I think I know the answer—it's the land smell. The combined smell of the forests, the fields, and the gardens carried out to sea by a gentle wind. I'm glad you called me. It's an experience I would have hated to miss."

Returning to his cabin, Sam wrote in his log: "During night thirty miles off Honshu all members of the bridge force smelled the beach. A distinctive, almost perfume-like fragrance, suggestive of camphor wood and eucalyptus trees. The wind was from the beach and the scent became stronger as we moved in. It is suggested that all navigators keep this aid-to-navigation in mind when approaching Honshu in reduced visibility."

That day and the night that linked 20 June with 21 June, Sam and Maurer hardly left the conning tower when the *Harder* ran submerged or the bridge when she slipped quietly along on the surface. Only one contact was made throughout the day—a mere patrol boat. But during the afternoon, depth charges were heard in the distance. To Maurer, and the very few other combat veterans aboard, this was old stuff. But even so, one never gets quite used to being cooped up in a self-propelled sardine can with foes lurking here and there ready with several kinds of can openers, all of them fatally unpleasant. Thus the new hands aboard the *Harder* heard their first real depth charges. They were far away and not intended for them. But even so, they were meant for somebody and, almost any hour, others might be headed for the *Harder*. The real question in their minds was: on which depth charge, if any, was the *Harder's* name written?

"Those depth charges," Sam said conversationally to the men present in the control room during a submerged daylight run, "I believe were all set too shallow. The main thing is to get down deep and fast."

"How far down would you say, sir?" asked Sloggett, who as Chief of the Boat stood at his post just forward of the diving plane station on the port side.

"Oh, a few hundred feet should be enough," replied the Skipper. "I think the Nips don't set them deeper than, say, 250 feet, because that's about as deep as their own pigboats can go."

As Dealey and Jack Maurer studied the chart in the control room, plotting their strategy for the night surface run, Jim MacMasters, the ship's yeoman who kept notes for Sam's daily write-up of the patrol log, stood by, notebook in hand.

"This Kuroshio Current is something we've got to lick and also to use," observed Sam. "The chart says its strength is from 1 to 2 knots, but all this morning we have been heading into it at 3 knots and still we are losing ground. Tomorrow, for our submerged daylight patrol, we had better go well down to the southwest and drift along with it. That way we'll save juice for making attacks."

During the afternoon of 21 June the *Harder* observed what was evidently a picket line five or six miles off the beach and across the entrance to Ise Wan. Sam decided to go through or under them that night to see what went on inside the line.

At last the long summer day was over. The *Harder* surfaced and headed for Daio Saki. They sighted it at 2230 and found, to their surprise, that the light was lighted and showing apparently at full intensity. This indicated that too much shipping passed that way to permit blacking it out. Half an hour later the sub's radar picked up a patrol vessel dead ahead at 4500 yards. Bridge lookout sighted it at the same moment.

"Hard left," was Sam's quick order to the helmsman, hoping he would not be forced to dive and thus lose the advantage of his higher surface speed and maneuverability. The *Harder* was not sighted. However, the change in course put the sub within three miles of Daio Saki—well inside the 100-fathom curve.

"Turn on the fathometer," was the next order. This automatic leadsman was both instantaneous and accurate in reporting the decreasing distance between the *Harder's* keel and bottom.

"Patrol vessel on port beam—4000 yards," reported the port forward lookout.

What to do? If he had been sighted, diving would bring on immediate attack. Sam decided to bluff it out. Only Jap vessels were supposed to be in these waters. So he would play Jap. As the *Harder* sped on its way at a 15-knot clip, Sam and all the bridge watch felt sure that their ship had been seen. But the patrol made no effort to challenge or fire. The bluff had worked.

That's one thing Sam had learned from Tex Edwards' brand of poker. In a poor deal, play as if you held the winning hand.

"We were now," Sam states in his log with great modesty, "definitely inside the picket line, with visibility conditions favorable to us."

"Captain to the bridge."

He had barely risen from his chair when the musical bong, bonging of Battle Stations sounded through the ship. "Battle Stations, Torpedo," squawked the loud speakers. He reached the bridge to receive an excited report from the OOD, Sam Logan. "There is a two-ship convoy with one escort on port bow. They are heading about southwest. Distance 11,000 yards. We are tracking him by radar."

Nodding concurrence, Sam ducked down the hatch to the radar screen in the conning tower. From the pips on the screen, it was obvious that the leading ship was the larger.

"We will make our first set-up on the leading ship," outlined Sam to Maurer. "This course will lead us into pretty shallow water, but we'll just have to risk it."

The range closed rapidly and at 6000 yards Sam could see the target through the Number One periscope. "Clear the bridge. Take her down," came his order. "Hold her at 40 feet."

Down tumbled the lookouts and the bridge watch. The klaxon sounded its hoarse double call. Dogged was the topside hatch; in position were all hands throughout the sub as Sam continued his radar approach. When only 2000 yards lay between the *Harder* and its victim, Sam went to periscope depth and stood by to fire his first real torpedo at a real enemy.

"Stand by to fire four fish," he said quietly.

"Forward Torpedo room, stand by to fire four fish," repeated the Talker.

Suddenly Sam remembered he had not told Chief Torpedoman Mays in the forward room to write Tex Edward's name on that Number One torp. "Too late now," he mused half-aloud.

"Sir?" queried Maurer.

"Oh, nothing, Jack," replied Sam. "There'll be another time."

"Yes, sir," said the mystified Jack, "we are coming on the firing bearing, sir."

"Fire one," ordered Sam quietly, and a slight tremor of the ship followed as the torpedo rasped from the tube in acknowledgment of his order. The other three followed at short intervals, but a heavy explosion at fourteen seconds after the order to fire advised the submarine that her first war shot torpedo—the one that should have borne Tex Edwards' name—had exploded prematurely.

Had Sam been a cussin' man, he would have let loose a string of invectives—rules of the ship or not—and been thoroughly justified. Here was his very first torpedo—one fired as his thoughts went back to Tex Edwards and the *Reuben James*. And it had blown high and wide, but far from handsome. In his log he resignedly noted: "A bit disconcerting for my first shot of the patrol."

But any fears he may have had that his target had time to use the explosion to take evasive action were banished when he heard the other three warheads hit the ship with explosions so heavy that their reverberations in the water rocked the *Harder* on her keel. Noted Sam: "Torpedoes #2, #3, and #4 hit the target with shattering explosions that rocked the submarine. Flames from three parts of target enveloped entire ship. It was ablaze from bow to stern in a matter of seconds, with the flames shooting 100 feet into the air. I don't believe anyone aboard could have survived the explosions or the fire for thirty seconds.

"Shifted attack, swinging ship and periscope, to escort vessel on starboard hand, but watching flames of the burning target had completely destroyed my night vision."

As he stepped back from the 'scope and before he could even straighten up from his bent position, he said—and rapidly: "Take her deep. Right full rudder." Without waiting for the helmsman to repeat, Sam continued: "All ahead full. Rig for depth charge. Shift steering below. Clear the conning tower and let's get into deep water as quick as we can!"

This was it. This was the time when all the drills and trials and exercises Sam and his crew and his ship had conducted had to pay off. In a few more seconds ashcans from the escort vessel would be on their way down. In a few more seconds the *Harder* would have to be at a safe depth—or else.

To survive, the *Harder* had to be below the terrific pressure areas created by those 300- to 600-pound charges.

To be caught above them meant being blown to the surface where the escort's guns could make short work of her before she could get under again.

All hands leaned aft to keep their balance as the *Harder's* bow pointed down, down, down. The conning tower crew quickly slid down the ladder to the control room, secured the lower hatch, and took up their new stations.

The first depth charge arrived just as the *Harder's* depth gauge needle passed the 100-foot mark. Click! Crack! Whoom! Then came a veritable tidal wave surge of water through the freeing ports and superstructure which swayed the submarine, first away from the direction of the blast and then toward it as the displaced water rushed back to fill the void created by the explosion. This is a terrifying sound even under training conditions, but it can be practically heart-stopping when born of the deadly hatred of an enemy whose aim is to crush out your life and that of your tiny ship under measureless tons of sea water.

Fortunately the first depth charge was not too close, so that the *Harder's* people had a chance to brace their feet and their nerves before the next test of their fortitude—a test of slightly different character.

As the submarine plunged bottomward in a desperate attempt to find safety below the ashcan pattern, she did not respond properly to measures intended to level her off and overshot the ordered depth of 300 feet. She found— the bottom. Found it with a shock that threw men, dishes, and unsecured equipment into heaps and completely wrecked the QC-JK sonar head. Even this near disaster was not without the lightening touch of Sam's Irish humor. He recorded that they had made their first landing on the shores of Japan. The *Harder's* sonar gear, he added later, had not been performing well anyhow.

With his ship stopped and on bottom, the skipper took advantage of the situation by shutting down all sound-producing machinery and lay doggo, awaiting the next counter attack. He had not long to wait, for immediately a string of depth charges, well-placed and at regular intervals, crashed above the sub to the accompaniment of throat-gripping water noises.

As the submarine crashed the bottom, Don Horst, the Damage Control Officer, was off like a broken-field runner to look for damage forward. In the torpedo room he found a most unhappy Chief Torpedoman Elmo Mays in charge. One sonar head was jammed and obviously wrecked, but the vital question was whether or not any torpedo tube shutters had been damaged.

There Horst learned why the *Harder* had been misbehaving and that she was not to blame. It seems that in their excitement the torpedomen at the forward tubes had flooded in too much water in order to compensate for the weight of the expended torpedoes. This overweight, once the *Harder* nosed down for its dive, was too much for Lieut. Lynch to handle in his stride, especially when he did not know about it. On his way aft, Horst reported his findings in the control room. The only casualty he noted was that Thomason, in the galley, was standing ankle-deep in mashed potatoes garnished with a glittering sea of what had been steaks, gravy, and fried eggs. Being a thoughtful fellow, Jack had felt that all hands would have big appetites once the hunting was over. During the run to penetrate the picket line, the regular evening meal had been just a quickly grabbed cold snack.

Even for a young, athletic man, the climb up to the *Harder's* after torpedo room was not an easy one. Engine rooms and maneuvering room seemed to be doing fine, except that all hands were bursting with curiosity. "Did we hit 'em?" "Where are we?" "When do we eat?" "Are we stuck?" "Are we leading?" and other inquiries along similar lines of vital statistics.

All of these Horst tried to answer as best he could while he ran, out of breath, ducking through doors with low clearances overhead and high thresholds.

At last he came to the after torpedo room door. He tried to open it. And he had a heck of a time. Built to withstand heavy pressure, this contraption weighs about 200 pounds and, with the sub nosing down, the door was leaning against the direction in which it opened. At long last, almost worn to a frazzle, Horst was able to push it open enough for him to wriggle through. What spurred him on and gave him almost superhuman strength was a weird, high pitched whistling that neither stopped nor changed in tempo. Horst did not know what to make of it. Inside he saw the torpedomen standing in a tight little group well back from the closed tube doors. There was no talking. They were silent, serious, and well they might be, at a moment like that, in a situation such as the *Harder* was in—up tilted from the bottom. Rocking gently, or not so gently, whenever a depth charge exploded a little closer than its companions—it was easy for men to allow their apprehensive imaginations free play.

The only person in the room who seemed cool and cheerful was Adolph Balevicz of North Arlington, Mass., one of the ablest Torpedomen First Class. He had been hand-picked by Frank Lynch at New London. Being in charge of the stern tubes, Al always felt that the after torpedoes were neglected and the bow torps preferred.

"Got any idea what that trouble is?" asked Horst.

"Yes, sir. The whistling comes from an air leak at one of the air line joints on Number 8 tube."

"Is it serious? I mean, can it do any damage?"

"No, sir. In fact, if I had a piece of chewing gum, I think I could stop it." Balevicz looked steadily at Don's jaws. They were chomping on a piece of gum.

"Oh," said Horst. "Here." He removed the lump and held it out. "What'll we do with it?"

"Just put it right there—on that flange," answered the torpedoman, pointing. Horst executed the mission. The wad was placed on the joint. To the surprise and amusement of the group, the noise stopped. Either Don had a way with 100-pound air leaks or the gum dispersed the air in such a way that the whistling ended. And that, for the moment, was that!

The ashcan dropping on the *Harder* ended about 0230 when the thirteenth depth charge exploded. None were dangerously close. All of them were set too high, thus confirming Sam's earlier estimate of Jap procedure. But the precision of the operation showed that the attackers were not "bush leaguers," as Sam expressed it. When no more cans came down, Sam concluded that the patrol boat had exhausted its stock at hand. But the fact that it stuck around, as evinced by the nearness of its propeller beat, indicated to Dealey that it was holding down the spot until reinforcements came along.

"I reckon that it is now or never," ran Sam's comment in the control room. "He knows we are here but he can't do anything about it. So what matter if we do kick up some noise and stir up some mud and bubbles in breaking free? So shoot the works, Frank, and let's get away from under before the second team comes up with enough cans to pave the way from here to Houston."

With Frank in charge, the job of working the *Harder* free began in earnest. To the Japs, looking and listening from above, it must have seemed that the sub they sat on was in its very death throes. Frank blew safety tanks and bow buoyancy tanks with much gargling of bottom ooze. Finally, after forty-five minutes of agonizing suspense, Lynch felt the ship lift free. Still, the heavy-nosed craft was loggy and unresponsive. It had barely swung free from the bottom when it hit another shelf. More time was wasted in giving the *Harder* a lift.

This was no silent, slinky getaway. The sub's trim pump, according to Sam, "sounded like a cement mixer." With dawn only ninety minutes away and one or more patrol craft perhaps even closer than that, Sam decided to forego satisfying his curiosity by taking a periscope peep. Instead, he headed south at fairly deep submergence. He was at a safe distance when two hours later he heard the second team announce its arrival by dropping depth charges at the place where the *Harder* had been.

Feeling fairly secure, he spent the early morning hours getting his ship back into trim. After that, he saw to it that all hands were fed and that the greatest possible number had a chance to rest. The balance of the day was uneventful. The sub sighted a brace of destroyers which did not come into range and heard some depth bombs go off at intervals throughout the afternoon. At 2047 the *Harder* arose after a submergence that had lasted twenty hours.

At 0418, under bright moonlight, a clear sky, and twinkling stars, a king-size radar pip forecast the presence of a large vessel. "The biggest pip I've ever seen on the screen," said Radarman Richard Berg of Houston to Hatfield, his boss.

With but half an hour to daylight, there was need for haste. As the sub dove to radar depth, the range was 16,500 yards. Sam concluded that his target had come up from the Truk-Saipan area and was heading for Nagoya. It had no escort—would probably pick up a plane at dawn. With the Jap making about 15 knots, the gap between the enemy and the sub was soon reduced to 5000 yards. At this time the *Harder* went to periscope depth. And, bit by bit, as if unseen hands were turning on invisible flood lights, sea, sky, and ship grew visibly brighter.

When the gap had closed to 2500 yards and the clock in the conning tower stood at 0447, flashes of gun fire showed from the deck of the oncoming steamer. The lookout had seen the *Harder's* periscope. These were not dull cargo sluggards.

Sam silently admired the alertness that brought discovery of the slim pencil of a periscope in the slithering mists of daybreak. He admired as well the marksmanship that sent shells and 20-mm bullets tearing right overhead. But this admiration did not stop him from ordering four torpex-headed torpedoes fired from the forward tubes. The target was, at the same moment, making a quick turn away from the telltale streaks of the ultra-high explosive fish. He dodged all but one. The first torpedo hit between bow and bridge after a run of one minute and forty seconds. From the volume of noise and the fact that the ship seemed to try to jump out of the water, Sam concluded that it had received a back-breaking hit under the keel. The wounded craft drew rapidly away from the sub and was making knots toward Daio Saki when Sam decided not to surface and pursue. For a sub to be caught on top in broad daylight and in shallow water was a sure way of inviting disaster. Besides, Sam felt that he had hit the ship hard enough to put it out of commission for a long time even if it should reach port. The long and widening oil slick that stretched in the merchantman's wake gave ground for belief that she had been seriously damaged.

The very close escape from being permanently stuck on the bottom gave Sam a lot to think about. The one factor that worried him most about the type of infighting the *Harder* had been engaged in was that if the sub were run aground or lost in shallow water and Japs were in a position to salvage her, the highly secret coding machine would be compromised. This was an alarming thought, and Sam concluded that a lot of submariners held back from going into full pursuit of the enemy in shoal waters because of that danger. In fact, patrol orders forbade taking such chances. He decided to recommend that sub skippers be permitted to leave them behind.

That afternoon, while sitting alone in his stateroom, Sam reviewed his first patrol to date. It had, he knew, been highly successful. And yet he had a surprisingly empty feeling about his victories. The exultation, the satisfaction he had expected to feel on taking the vengeance that he believed he had been thirsting to impose failed to appear.

This reaction is not surprising for a man with Sam's upbringing and religious background. His cheery disposition was not conditioned to bear a grudge. Besides, the destruction of a proud ship and all that she carried left Sam—as it did scores of his fellow skippers—with a distinct feeling of nausea. War, to him, had become a game, a grim game which he was determined to win, but one which could never supply the joyous thrills of a football match or a ring battle. The Bible, he thought, must be right when it says vengeance belongs to the Lord.

The night patrol passed without incident, but at 0614 on the morning of 24 June, smoke was sighted to westward. The sun was just above the horizon and the *Harder*, submerged, was well inside the 100-fathom curve west of

Daio Saki. The OOD headed for the smoke and stepped to the loud speaker. "Captain to the conning tower, Captain to the conning tower," squawked the repeaters below.

At 0643 a patrol boat was sighted under the smoke. Sam held his course toward it, not with the intention of expending a ten-thousand-dollar torpedo on a puffing little spit-kit, but to see whether it might be running interference for something better. Two minutes later three nice fat-looking AK's came into view on a course of about 060. The patrol boat was keeping station on the port quarter of the convoy. The three ships were almost abreast in slight echelon, with the third one straggling a bit astern.

"It's about time," said Sam to Jack Maurer, as the latter stood by his side in the role of assistant approach officer, "that we used the after tubes."

"After Torpedo Room," called Jack over the intercom, "make ready all tubes."

Just before the moment of firing, the three vessels made a zig that placed the center AK and the AK closest to the shore almost in line with the *Harder's* tubes.

"Commence firing," ordered Sam. As the last torpedo left the tube, his 'scope went up and he saw the white trails of four fish streak toward the center vessel. With dismay, Sam also saw that all four torps would pass astern of the AK. He did not wait to see them miss. Instead, he showed a brief glimpse of the genius for swift action that was his. With no time to cry over spilled milk, he ordered what a taxicab driver would call a tight U-turn: "Right full rudder. Make ready three tubes forward."

With an angle of 66 degrees on the gyro settings, three fish were ejected from three forward tubes. The sub had now almost completely reversed her course. One hit near the bow of the center AK in seventy seconds after a run of 1750 yards. The two others ran ahead of the stricken vessel and, it was believed aboard the *Harder*, hit the inshore target amidships and toward the stern.

But no one aboard the *Harder* saw this happen. When the torpex head hit the middle and nearest AK, the explosion was so loud and sounded so near that Sam, without giving the matter a second thought, concluded that an aerial bomb had fallen close aboard.

"Take her down. Deep submergence and rig for depth charge." On this order, the *Harder* coasted down smoothly to safer depths than a mere 100 feet.

As the sub descended, Maurer held a stop watch. He was listening for the remaining two torpedoes to explode. One was heard at 117 seconds and the other in 137 seconds.

"I'd certainly call those possible hits!" offered Maurer. "They came much too soon for end-of-run explosions. They must have been the real thing."

Now sound reported two ships were passing overhead. After giving the screw count close attention, it was concluded they were the third AK and the patrol boat. The latter evidently did not carry depth charges; anyway, it did not drop any.

"Say," chortled Sam with a hearty laugh, "we did not have to go to the deep south this time at all. That explosion! I thought it was an aircraft bomb. So help me, Hannah, it was our own fish hitting the middle AK with a terrific punch. That was a lot of work, but a good way to start the day," observed Sam as he headed down the conning tower hatch. "I have a feeling it is time to grab some breakfast.

The cause of the four misses from the stern tubes was a matter of immediate concern to Dealey and Torpedo Officer Sam Logan. The torpedo gang and the electricians put on a quick investigation and found that the gyro setting dials in the C.T. and in the after torpedo room (ATR) were ten degrees out of phase. The cause was obscure—possibly a weak phase in the Selsyn system or a poor contact—and would require further investigation on return to base. However, the cure was simple—merely turning the switch off; then on again.

"We'll try to maneuver for stern tube shots next attack, Ramrod," he told Logan, "and watch that repeater like a hawk. Those lads in the afterroom feel awful low about those misses—lower than a snake's belly in a well."

So that was the plan at 1520 on 25 June when the

periscope watch sighted smoke. On this day the *Harder* had made her morning dive southwest of Shiono Misaki Light and was working northward. Five minutes later, with Dealey at the 'scope, the jigsaw pieces of an approaching convoy had fallen into place. Dealey grinned when he saw a patrol boat lay down foaming wakes as it dashed at full speed back and forth across the head of a column of three cargo ships, all smoking heavily.

Evidently the Nips had learned from the *Harder's* recent operations that an escort on the flank of a convoy was very ineffective protection. Furthermore, they had sent out as a protector, not the usual refugee from a scrapheap, but a new-looking PC boat which proudly flew a king-sized Japanese man-of-war flag.

As Battle Stations, Submerged, sounded, men tumbled out of their bunks on the double and in a matter of seconds all stations were reported ready. Vernard Sloggett, Chief of the Boat and the most experienced torpedoman in the ship, turned over his job at the flood and vent station in the control room to Chief Machinist's Mate Carl Finney and headed for the A.T.R. He wanted to give Torpedoman Al Balevicz a hand and keep an eagle eye on that errant Selsyn repeater.

As Maurer jockeyed for position during the approach phase, it became clear that the chances were just about perfect for easy stern tube shots. Orders went out as Sam took over at periscope depth. "After Torpedo Room: Stand by to fire all four."

At the torpedo data computer, Sam Logan fed in the ranges, bearings, and speeds as they came to him from the Skipper by way of Jack Maurer, the attack 'scope, and Keith Phillips and Max Kerns at the plotting board. McMasters, whose battle station submerged was recorder in the conning tower, was at his place. In the control room below, Frank Lynch was the Diving Officer.

Half an hour ticked by. During that time, between observations, Sam gave all hands a verbal look at his battle plan. This was a very vital morale factor and probably the most appreciated thing that Sam did for his crew. His play-by-play accounts always had an attentive audience.

"The way I see it," came the voice of the Old Man to all stations in the boat, "we'll have an excellent chance to give this convoy a real quick one-two.

"The P.C. boat is well out in front of the convoy, dashing back and forth ahead of AK Number One. In column astern of the leader are two more fat AK's. They are really pouring on the coal, to judge by the smoke they're making."

Sam paused and signalled the periscope jockey for "Up 'scope." After a ten-second sweep of the scene up topsides, he motioned the 'scope down and, with an excited look on his expressive face, returned to his battle plan: "By the time AK Number Two swings into target position, the escort should be about 5000 yards away, ahead of us. As I figure it, that is plenty of room to let us sock the AK with our stern tubes and make a 180-degree turn that should put us in position to hit the third AK with fish from our bow tubes. That is all."

As the mike clicked off, enthusiasm swept through the sub. Here was a real fighting ship—the *Harder!* Here was a real fighting skipper—Old Man Dealey!

As planned—so executed. At 1603, Logan, on the command to fire, smacked the big firing button with the palm of his hand. At eight-second intervals, he sped four torpex-loaded torps on their way from the stern tubes. One hit; two went astern; one exploded just short of the target. Sam thought this countermined—set off by the explosion of the torpedo ahead of it; however, it might have been a premature.

With a fine, full-speed swing that bore no resemblance to the Chinese turns of the old S-20, the *Harder's* bow swung left until her tubes bore on the third AK. Fire! Out of three torpedoes, one was believed to be a definite hit. The other two were misses. That all was not well aboard the two targets was revealed when both of them turned with right rudder for the beach some two miles away. Both were blowing their whistles wildly, as shown by the streamers of white steam that plumed from their whistle pipes. When last seen, the first target was sinking fast, stern first. The second target, while not visibly hurt, was still plowing toward the beach. As for the first AK on the line of three—it was holding its course and speeding away from the scene as fast as it could. But the escort, with a bone in her teeth, was racing for the *Harder's* position.

At 1625 the patrol boat was too close for comfort and Sam went deep. He had barely gotten rigged for silent running and depth charging before the PC boat's first calling card arrived. It whoomed off some 200 yards away; the next was at the same distance; the third was at 100 yards. This was poor shooting. They came at two-minute intervals which indicated the Jap skipper was trying to relocate the sub after each drop. Sam thanked his Irish luck for that baffling Kuroshio Current which he had damned a few days before. Its thermoclines were good.

After the third, nothing happened. Minutes went by. It could be all over. In his notebook, the Quartermaster wrote: "At deep submergence. Steering 180. Evading the enemy (I hope)."

But it was not to be as easy as that. Starting at 1639, three more ashcans exploded at two-minute intervals, but at distances that grew from 200 to 300 and 500 yards. The closing period came almost a full hour later when Depth Charge #7 went off some 2000 yards away. The *Harder* had made another successful evasion.

With only two shots left in his six-shootin' bow tubes, the Torpedo Totin' Texan hoped to make each one count. To be sure, he had nothing to complain about. In five days, he estimated that he had sunk or damaged no less than six fair-sized vessels with a total displacement of about 30,000 tons.

The next five days—from the sinking on the afternoon of 25 June to the forenoon of 29 June—gave the *Harder* men a chance to realize how dull an inactive submarine patrol can be. The only break was a rather negative encounter with two DD's. It came at the end of a long day when she had already been submerged fifteen and a half hours. The sub's batteries were running low and the air in the boat was none too good. So Sam went deep, ran silent, and made a strategic withdrawal to the southward.

As the *Harder* sought some relief from the pressures of her very hot area—Sam remarked in his log that he felt they had worn out their welcome—by heading out to sea, all hands were pretty well beaten down. Dealey noted that he felt short of breath and that the men operating the diving planes and steering were also panting with any exertion. He called on Chief Pharmacist's Mate "Doc" Everett Bradshaw for a test of the air as to oxygen content and as to the presence of the deadly carbon dioxide. Three per cent of the latter was considered the limit of safety.

The report of the Doc was startling: $CO_2$ had reached a dangerous $3\frac{1}{2}$ per cent. This caused a flurry of excitement while $CO_2$ absorbent was distributed throughout the compartments and oxygen released from the reserve supply.

In a very few minutes the beneficial effects of these measures were apparent and men who had been drooping like tired Easter lilies perked up. Sam expected any minute to see some Tarzan begin beating his chest.

"Man, oh, man," said the irrepressible Max Kerns, "this hundred-proof fresh air tastes good. It's sure been scarce on this job."

"Careful what you say, Max," rejoined Frank Lynch, "first thing you know, they will slap a luxury tax on it."

Submerged and running close to the 100-fathom curve, at 0800 on 29 June the 'scope watch saw the masts of a three-ship convoy standing up from the west and moving along the coast toward Omai Saki. Unfortunately, however, the sub was too far from the convoy's track to make interception possible, but Sam continued on, hoping to get into position before the next one came along. At 1135 the Officer of the Watch sighted a large ship, toward the coast, at a range of seven miles. The plot, to recoin a phrase, was thickening.

To Sam's request for speed and range of the last sighted vessel, Logan, who was working the TDC, replied: "She's heading east and the range is about 15,000 yards, but she's stopped, Captain. She bears 315 true."

"Come left to course 315," ordered the Skipper. "Let's have a look at her."

As the sub nosed toward its newest sighting, Sam took several peeps and soon concluded that the vessel, which was lying broadside to the beach, was the big passenger freighter he had hit coming up from the Truk-Saipan run a few days earlier. She was obviously aground with her masts and kingposts still showing, but her deck was evidently just under water. She was a valuable ship and presented a fairly simple salvage problem.

"Better slip her another pickle, Jack," said Sam to the Exec. "Keep the fathometer going as we stand in and get our last two torps ready forward."

"Aye, aye, sir," replied Maurer, and set about the business.

With the passage of every minute, the *Harder* ran closer toward the coast and shoal waters. In the control room, Frank Lynch turned to Don Horst, his assistant engineering officer, and remarked: "If we stay much longer on this course, the Old Man'll take us up some sewer into Nagoya."

"That's okay by me," chuckled the ever cheerful Horst. "Hope we surface right in the middle of a geisha house."

Meanwhile, in the conning tower, Sam watched carefully to determine the set and drift of inshore currents. The range had dropped to 10,000 yards. Some inner voice compelled him to take a last look around—a voice of admonition that seldom, if ever, went unheeded. He thumbed Up 'scope. As he walked the Number Two 'scope around the compass, half-crouching so as not to have too much stick exposure, this is what he saw: On his left, a three-ship convoy coming up the coast. Dead ahead, the stranded left-over from the 23 June shooting and, latest and last addition to the scene, an unescorted freighter coming down the coast from Tokyo.

Sam waved the 'scope down with a motion of exasperation. "Well, now, wouldn't that blow a man down," he

gloomed, "an ocean full of targets and us caught with our
torpedoes down."

In his log, he later made this comment: "They were
moving right into our lap. Here was choice of targets with
plenty to spare. Two torpedoes left and five good targets
practically begging for them! What a three-ring circus.
Decided that grounded target was not going anywhere for
a long time and no use risking the run into shallow water
with such a set-up where I was. Shifted attack to center
ship of the convoy and started approach."

The range to the ship that made the best target—the
large AK with a smaller AO (tanker) on each side—was
about 700–800 yards when Sam sent his last two fish on
the way. Because the run was short, he had no fear of
target evasion. And since no patrol boats with their racks
of depth charges were in sight, Sam kept the 'scope up as
the last two presents to Tojo ran their courses.

"They are running nice and straight," he monologued in
a muttering tone that was loud enough for all in the
conning tower to hear. "Our target, the center AK and the
left-flank OA, are nearest the coast—are practically in
line. I can barely see the tanker's bow. The range to our
second target I should say is about 1900 yards—well,
maybe only 1895 (a low chuckle)—anyhow maybe one has
slowed up or the other has speeded up—say, maybe they
are racing for the nearest saki shop. Almost any moment
now . . ."

WHAM! . . . All aboard the *Harder* heard the torpedo
explode.

"Smack between the foremast and the bow," continued
Sam's soft, slow voice. "He's already taken a down angle
by the nose. And he's stopped cold in his tracks. Yes,
sirree—and he stopped just soon enough—why, bless your
little heart—to let the second torpedo run right smack
ahead of him."

Breathless and motionless, the men within earshot froze
at their stations. In the control room those who could,
crowded close to the hatch for first-hand information.

"The AO is now overlapping our first target." In his

normal conning tower tone, he continued, "Full left rudder—I have a hunch a fly boy is going to bomb us." Then, remembering that he had fired his last two torpedoes, he grinned and gave the traditional end of combat order for submarines in the western Pacific: "Course zero nine zero."

A ragged cheer ran through the compartments. That order headed them for home. Again Dealey shot his periscope up for a quick look.

As the *Harder* swung eastward, the sinking AK and the shoreward AO just beyond it were blacked out by the third and lagging AO which was now coming up between the *Harder* and its victims.

Sam waved the 'scope down and intently watched Maurer, who, stopwatch in hand, was clocking the departure and explosions of the torpedoes. Maurer's record showed that the AK had been hit by the torpedo at twenty-seven seconds—a run of 700 yards. Now came a second torpedo explosion at seventy seconds—a run of 1875 yards.

"Gosh," said Sam with mock embarrassment, "I missed my guess by twenty yards!"

Then he blushed from the rim of his hairline to the base of his throat. He had not meant to brag. Only to wisecrack at his own expense. He need not have worried. No one aboard the *Harder* ever felt that their Old Man was a single millimeter short of perfection.

"Pure, unadulterated luck on that second shot, but a sure hit," records the log. "Since no surface escort was around, I reasoned that an air escort would be present. It was. I ordered deep submergence and rigged for depth charges. As we passed 100 feet, an aerial bomb exploded close to the starboard quarter. Men in the after part of the ship said that this was the closest one of the patrol. No damage."

Cheers, yells, and hoorays rang throughout the vessel as Sam, at the mike speaker reported in a voice that reflected his pride and satisfaction in the performance of his ship and his crew: "Two ships sunk by our last two torpedoes."

The first patrol was over. The *Harder* had come of age

and now could take her stand among the veterans of the Pacific. Her torpedo tubes and racks were empty, but her efforts were crowned with glory.

Shortly after surfacing at 2200 on 29 June, the sub's Number One main engine went out of commission to remain inactive on the entire homeward journey. On 30 June, at 0500, Hachijo Jima was once more in sight. Throughout that morning and until late in the afternoon, while the *Harder* fishtailed submerged, Sam kept steady count on the course of a patrol boat that covered the bottleneck between Hachijo Jima and Mikura Jima, sixty miles to the north. Meanwhile the Quartermaster's gang was already starting to make the "sinking sun" flags that would flutter in a rainbow from the hoisted periscopes as the *Harder* entered Pearl—one flag to denote each victory scored.

# "Take Her Down—Take Her Deep"

The usual colorful, loud, and musical reception that welcomed all subs coming in from combat patrols greeted the *Harder* as she slipped alongside Pier 4 at the submarine base at Pearl Harbor. With the operational members of my staff—Capt. Sunshine Murray, Comdr. Dick Voge, and Lieut. Comdr. Sparky Woodruff among them—I was on hand to extend well-deserved congratulations and to take a look at the sub and its crew while sipping a cup of coffee in the wardroom.

I knew at first glance from the dock that the *Harder* was not only a taut ship but a happy ship. Her officers and men had that look—a combination of pride, confidence, and well-being—that always marks an efficient, spirited fighting ship's personnel.

The patrol just past—her maiden patrol—had, we knew, been a grueling one. Ducking in and out of shoal waters off an enemy coast is not a sedative for even the steadiest nerves. In spite of this tough initiation into the game of war, Dealey—who, of course, bore the brunt of the stress and strain—had not allowed his ship to grow slack on the way home. On the contrary, he had held a full-scale Captain's inspection of the *Harder* on the run in from Midway and she was—to lapse into New England vernacular —slick as a greased kitty's ear.

Dealey himself was quiet, smiling, completely unperturbed by his experiences, and entirely modest about his ship's success. Luck, he called it—luck and a damn fine team.

With the milk, ice cream, fruit, and music for the *Harder's* men came mail and transportation to take all hands to the Royal Hawaiian Hotel, where reservations had been arranged for them at no expense to anyone beyond a small charge for laundry. The entire staff was Navy, from the cooks to the Officer in Charge.

One submarine command policy that bothered Sam more than any other was the policy that required personnel changes aboard all submarines at the end of each patrol. This served two purposes: to supply trained nucleus crews to new construction and to give experience to men from the schools. On the *Harder's* return to Pearl Harbor, Sam had informed all hands at morning quarters that any man who desired transfer from his ship could have one without prejudice of any sort. Not one crew member had asked for such a transfer. So, when orders arrived that about 25 per cent of the crew were to be taken off the *Harder* and sent back to the States, Sam almost hit the ceiling. To him this was a deep personal loss. On top of that came another blow when he discovered that he would lose Don Horst. His smart young officer, who had had four hectic war patrols on another sub, had to report back to stateside for new construction. Sam came straight to Comsubpac's office and asked me to cancel Don's orders. I had to tell him, of course, that the orders came from the Navy Department and were part and parcel of a program which we must support. Sam felt somewhat reconciled when I told him that he could keep Max Kerns, even though Tom Buckner, whose place he filled, would be discharged from the hospital before the *Harder* left.

Sam was enough of a Texas horse trader to drive a hard bargain. Before this conversation ended, he had virtually swept the board. In addition to Ensign Buckner, he had corralled Ensign William F. Beebe. Also he had won promotion to Warrant Officer for Chief Torpedoman Vernard

Sloggett. Elmo Mays, it had already been decided, would succeed Sloggett as Chief of the Boat.

"Look, Dealey," said I, trying to keep my face straight, "you have almost enough names on your officer's roster for your next sailing to man a battlewagon. What you need now is a ship-stretcher to make room for them."

"Well, Admiral," he replied with that wide grin of his, "this old pigboat of mine may not be a wagon, but she sure can do battle! And when it comes to needing able hands, heck, you've almost got to be a Cal Tech man to know how to operate the head aboard a sub."

In filling vacancies in the enlisted personnel, the CPO'S or leading petty officers of the various departments, in consultation with the Chief of the Boat, made their pick of the waiting list. If there were no waiting list, the Base Detail officer would have to exercise his own best judgment in assigning replacements. The *Harder*, however, always had plenty of applicants to choose from. Success breeds success, 'tis said, and certainly that is true in military organizations. Successful outfits attract the best recruits.

Chief Torpedoman Elmo Mays, Sloggett's successor as Chief of the Boat, was young in years for the importance of his job but was nonetheless a salty soul with wide submarine experience. His word would carry plenty of weight. Also his was the sort of personality that fitted him for this key position. Warrant Officer Sloggett's new job was a sort of overall supervision of bow and stern torpedo rooms before, during, and after moments of action—a responsible job thought up as a new phase of combat control on subs.

Tom Buckner came aboard a few days before the second patrol got underway. At the time he arrived from the hospital, Tom was wondering why all his old wardroom pals maintained such mysterious airs. But when he entered the wardroom, he found the answer. No longer did Dinah Shore's photo monopolize the bulkheads. From every point of the compass smiled the perfect dentures, the lovely lips, and the beautiful eyes of more than a score of Hollywood's reigning queens from the frames of large

Navy Cross

photos; on the big white matrix of each was written, above the star's million-dollar signature, the legend: "From the *Harder's* Guardian Angel. . . ."

"Well, well," exclaimed the pop-eyed, slack-jawed Tom from Ten-o-see, "if you all don't clean mah shovel—I'll mow ye douwn!"

All who had crowded into the tiny room joined Tom in the rip-roaring laughter that swept the wardroom.

Toward the end of the waiting period, Sam was so tired of relaxing that he holed in on the base and seldom left his ship except to go with his gang to the Officers' Club for a beer or two. Since he always sat with his wardroom gang and visited the Skippers' Bar very rarely, the *Harder* table would grow to gargantuan proportions in the course of each evening, as others joined the party. Here Sam always talked shop. But he did more listening than talking. He had told his officers and chiefs to learn as much as they could from other pigboatmen about combat tricks. And Sam set a good example by listening.

A piece of news that reached Sam during those lengthening days of waiting to return to the shooting country was that the Submarine Force Awards Board, headed by Captain E. W. Grenfell, had recommended him for the Navy Cross, the Navy's highest award, since the Congressional Medal of Honor is awarded only by the President with the consent of the Congress. Sam's reaction to this news was characteristic. He would rather have recognition bestowed upon the *Harder's* officers and men.

And, actually, this had been done. Recognizing the fact that in submarines, usually only the skipper makes the attack, his award is considered first. However, Boards of Awards also realize that a successful skipper is the top man of a smart team which also deserves great credit, and so the outstanding members of that team are included in their recommendations. The reports of our Subpac Board went up to Fleet Admiral Nimitz's Cincpac Board of Awards—and, in case a Medal of Honor was under consideration—on to the Department.

The *Harder's* entire crew was awarded the newly authorized combat award—a submarine silhouette pin given in recognition of a successful patrol on which damage was inflicted on the enemy.

Well past the middle of August, plans for the *Harder's* next patrol were ready and Comdr. Dealey was called to my closely guarded Operations Room by Comdr. Dick Voge of my staff.

"Look, Sam," said Voge, admitting him to the inner sanctorum, "the Boss says to give you another shot at that Empire Circuit. You found a lot of meat there last time and salted some of it down. By the time you get there, Areas 4 and 5 both will be vacant; hence we will give you carte blanche to patrol either of them—wherever you find the best shooting."

"That is quite a stretch of coastline to cover," said Sam, stepping it off with dividers on the huge wall chart. "Area 4 starts here at Nojima Saki Light, the eastern point of the entrance to Tokyo Bay, runs through O Shima Island, south of Tokyo Bay, then down the coast to Omai Zaki Light."

"That's about ninety miles as the crow flies—if they have crows out there," observed Voge.

"Okay, Commander," he grinned at Dick, "I sure want to have a crack at that Tokyo Bay traffic. So that's where I'll probably start. If that gets too hot for me, I can always beat a strategic retreat to Area 5 where I patrolled last time. I know every rock on the bottom of that area—I've hit most of them! Even lost my sonar head."

"You did a fine job," countered Voge. "For the size of the bag you brought in we can afford to write off a few sonar heads. Don't worry about that; just keep on beating them out of the bushes."

Sam blushed modestly—and then blushed some more because he was embarrassed about blushing.

The *Harder's* final polishing-up exercises were supervised by Comdr. Freddy Warder. In that pair we had a couple of fighting men that any Force could be proud of, and it would be hard to say which was training whom.

A day or so later, on 24 August, the *Harder* again

backed away from the Sub Base, and again she pointed her bow westward for the long trek to Tojo land.

Once past Midway, drills were renewed aboard the *Harder* to train new men and to take the harbor barnacles off veterans. Despite his pleas, Sam's personnel losses had been quite distressing. Among the men lost were nearly all of Maurer's hand-picked lookouts. New men had to be selected and trained. Not only did they have to have the quick eyes—with excellent night vision—sound judgment, and reporting ability necessary for lookouts but, when the diving alarm sounded, they had to become bow and stern plane operators, which jobs they automatically assumed. These were key operational jobs of the first order.

Among the men selected to stand watch as reserve lookouts was Bob Moore. Before Alabama went topside to stand lookout the first time, he was alone with the Old Man in the wardroom.

"Don't take this extra duty lightly, Alabama," admonished Sam.

"No, Captain, indeed I won't."

"There are many reasons why you must take it very seriously," continued the Skipper. "First, there's the ship. It cost Uncle Sam seven and a half million dollars."

Bob nodded in agreement.

"Then there are your shipmates. If you fail to keep a sharp lookout, they may die."

Again Bob nodded his understanding. Then, as Sam seemed to have reached the end of his point by point review, Alabama added: "But, Cap'n, there is one more!"

"Yeah?" asked Sam. "Who?"

"There's me," explained Alabama.

Bob shone as a shipmate of unfailing good cheer in the wardroom pantry and as a salad maker in the galley. But where he shone in his fullest splendor was during gun action or drill with the three-incher on the *Harder's* foredeck.

In order to serve this three-inch gun with shells, a human chain of men had to be formed from the magazine below the messroom to the gun position on deck forward of the bridge superstructure. This meant an unbroken string of men from the crew's messroom forward into the control room, to a man poised on the ladder to the conning tower, across the latter to the short ladder to the bridge, from there down to the deck, and, finally, to the loaders at the gun. This sounds like a slow sort of an assembly line, but actually it could be organized and set into swift motion in a jiffy. Meanwhile, in the bridge structure were enough shells in a pressure-proof box to give the gunners a start. Lieut. Logan, as gunnery officer, supervised those drills, and he had a mighty efficient team. The *Harder* had only one gunner's mate to care for her three-incher as well as her 50-caliber machine guns and 20-mm cannon. Therefore crew members had to be trained in gunnery and the operation of these weapons. And one of the best among these was Commissary Steward John Thomason. In fact, on the second patrol, he was to become gun captain, a post of which he was justifiably proud.

But Jack's pride in being gun captain was no greater than Alabama's pride in being the keystone in the ammunition passing team. The most difficult and man-killing job in this line-up was held by him who stood in the conning tower beneath the bridge hatch. Although less than the control room to conning tower distance, it was well over seven feet to the bridge. To get the shells up required a tall man with muscles—a tough job that needed plenty of stamina. That job was Alabama's. This six-foot-plus giant was ideal for standing in the conning tower and passing three-inch shells or ammo for the 20-mm cannon up through the opening above him. Alabama was proud of his strength, proud of his endurance, proud of his job—and well he might be.

When a submarine went into gun action, there was usually an element of surprise—a very necessary factor in getting the jump on the enemy and registering hits to stampede his gun crews. Therefore the speed with which the *Harder's* three-inch gun could be brought into play was a matter of split-second training.

One trick the *Harder* men developed in gun drills to a fine point—on surfacing for make-believe gun action—was to pack the gun captain, the trainer, and the sight setter into the forward escape trunk just a few moments before the sub was to surface. The officer at the periscope would pass the word to the forward torpedo room the instant he saw the *Harder's* bull nose and the foredeck—just a little more up-tilted than usual—broach the surface. Since the escape hatch was built for two and not three occupants, the space was a bit crowded during the few seconds of occupation.

On getting word from the conning tower that the foredeck was surfaced, the Chief Torpedoman in the forward room would hit the lower hatch of the escape trunk with a hammer or some similar tool. On this signal, the top man on the totem pole of gunners in the escape chamber would open the hatch to the deck; out would pour the gunners, as the receding waters still lapped against the bridge structure, and make the three-incher ready for action. Being the last men out from the conning tower, the two loaders would make a beeline for the pressure-proof cylinder in the bridge structure for shells with which to start firing while the shell brigade got going. By the time the surfacing had been completed, and in far less than a minute, the gun would be trained, sighted, and ready to pour out a stream of projectiles.

But Sam had more serious and exacting training problems than just gunnery. The impending transfer of Jack Maurer to a command of his own, endorsed as it was by Sam himself, left promotion problems within the *Harder* to be considered. Frank Lynch, in line to become Second-in-Command, had to get the hang of household jobs handled by the Executive in addition to those of Assistant Approach Officer and Navigator. The station of Diving Officer, vacated by Lynch, was to be filled by highly competent Sam Logan. He, in turn, if all went as planned, would probably be succeeded at the Torpedo Data Computer —and also as Gunnery Officer—by Tom Buckner. Even this early in the patrol, the Nashville youth was revealing exceptional adaptability. And so it went, down the line, the cumulative effect of one single change at the top. Young Beebe, the newlywed Ensign who never made Submarine School, was assigned as Assistant Communications Officer.

"Ramrod" Logan—who was addicted to the reflective chewing of a toothpick after meals, and whose fondest wish at that time was to see a picture of the baby his wife had given birth to during his first patrol—took to the Diving Officer job like a penguin to an open ocean ice floe. His swift, mathematical mind found pleasure in figuring out and meeting the many incidental problems involved in the operations called for when the klaxon squawked twice and the call came, "Dive! Dive!" while on surface; or for the possibly less frantic "Take her down" when the *Harder* had to descend from periscope depth to lower levels.

As his sub approached enemy waters, Sam and his wardroom gang were listening late one night to the news summary out of San Francisco. They learned that a major U.S. Task Force had smashed Marcus Island on the morning of 1 September.

"If this means that our ships have been plastering Hirohito's," said Sam, "we may look for his disabled ships to be limping home to Yokosuka for repairs. And we should be in nice position to intercept."

This prospect tickled Skipper Dealey to the core. Having free play to strike anywhere in two large areas pleased him mightily. "With good luck," he recorded in his log, "we hope to convince the Japs that there are *no* empty submarine areas off southern Honshu."

On that early September night, Sam, after a moment's reflection, said: "We'll start in Area Four in the neighborhood of Tokyo. It may not have as much shipping as we found last patrol in Area Five—but the man-o'-war traffic in or out from Yokohama should be considerable in view of the Marcus Island developments. It sure would be nice to bag a big fat carrier."

"Yes, sir," agreed Jack Maurer. "Besides, Area Four is also the nearest."

"Right, Jack. We'd save fuel by hitting Area Four first and then going on to Area Five from there."

A day or two later the *Harder*, still three hundred miles from Tokyo, sighted patrol vessels and night-flying aircraft. Yes, indeed, Jap resistance to submarines had truly stiffened since Sam's previous visit. He passed Hachijo Jima. There, as he had planned, he swung north toward Tokyo and Area Four, with frequent sighting of day and night patrol planes.

Sam's first real enemy encounter on his second patrol came in the pre-dawn hours of 9 September. As ever, Sam had firm faith in his fathometer and in his J-Factor—the latter meaning the trust our fighting submariners have always had in the power to save of Him who died on the Cross for the salvation of mankind. This phrase, the J-Factor, was used without intention of irreverence; on the contrary, with deep veneration.

At 0142 on 9 September, the *Harder* picked up on her radar a freighter and its escort. The sub was then only three miles off the Honshu coast near Nojima Saki, at the entrance to Sagami Sea. The latter is Tokyo's outer portal and well nigh as sacred to Japanese possessive pride as is the moat that encircles the Mikado's Palace.

To get into firing position—and out again—that close to the Japanese homeland required much help from the *Harder's* rabbit foot.

The skyline of Japan, at the point where the waters of Sagami Nada join those that roll around the promontory where stands Nojima Saki Light, is rolling rather than rugged. But the hills rise high enough from the shoreline to furnish a background of shadows sufficiently dark to hide a sub like the *Harder*. At this point, too, the 100-fathom curve swings so close toward shore that well within the circle of Nojima beacon's warning white and red flashing beams, there is enough water for a daring sub skipper to take a chance on the surface.

On the dark bridge of the *Harder* were the Skipper and the regular bridge watch and lookouts. Below, in the conning tower, Lieut. Maurer called data to Phillips and

Buckner at the plotboard. Sam Logan was at the Torpedo
Data Computer ready to feed into it target data at the
proper moment. Brostrom, usually at the helm for Battle
Stations, was at his post and passed the word on fathometer readings as it came up from the control room where
Lieut. Lynch, Diving Officer, and Elmo Mays, Chief of
the Boat, stood ready to slip to radar or to periscope depth
the moment Maurer gave orders to pull the plug. To build
up Maurer's experience against the soon-to-come day when
he would skipper his own sub, Sam had Maurer conduct
all the approach phases.

There was no chatter in the conning tower. Again the
sign of a taut, well-organized ship. The small, dimly lit
space was wrapped in a silence vibrant with anticipation.
Below, in the control room, the two seats before the slim
spoked wheels at the bow and stern plane stations stood
empty until the lookout should tumble down from the
periscope shears.

"Thirty fathoms," came the voice of Fatty, the quartermaster operating the fathometer. On the bridge, Sam saw
what little was to be seen in the dark of the night.

At the moment, the sub was considerably ahead and to
shoreward of the coast-hugging freighter. On the latter's
seaward quarter and astern steamed the patrol boat.

Sam maintained position ahead until Maurer determined
that the target's base course was 020 degrees, true, and its
speed 9 knots. Then with a quickly executed full left turn
he brought the *Harder* into position on the port bow of
the intended victim. The setup looked perfect except for a
scanty 23 fathoms under the sub's keel—far too little water
for successful evasive tactics submerged in case she had to
duck.

"Jack."

"Yes, sir."

"Coach the helmsman on to the attack course. What is
it?"

"Zero eight zero, sir."

"Okay, stand by to fire three fish."

"Standing by, Cap'n."

"Fire one!"

Then occurred one of those sudden and unpredictable shifts in the fortunes of submarine war that can change victory into defeat or vice versa: the target zigged sharply away. Perhaps it was a routine zig; possibly she had sighted the sub. In any case, the three torpex-loaded fish streaked harmlessly across the freighter's bow. One torpedo broached and leaped clear of the water with a roar of racing propellers as though to express its anger and frustration.

Silent—or not so silent—curses came from all hands on topsides except Sam Dealey. He had no time to curse even if he had been a profane man, which he was not. That zig of the fat Jap freighter put the *Harder* in a situation which Ben Franklin might have described as "tight as that of a fish between two cats." With shallow water under his keel, the coastline blocking off retreat to westward, and an alerted enemy escort between him and deep water, Dealey was really in a vise. One perfectly good attack, planned and executed with all of the *Harder's* customary daring and dispatch, had turned into what might be a death trap for the attacker.

On the freighter, Sam could see a stabbing signal light, undoubtedly sending the alarm to the escort.

Up the hatch came Maurer's voice: "Radio reports someone close aboard is pounding out a message on 450 kilocycles, sir."

"Twenty-four fathoms," came the fathometer report.

Dealey took swift action: "Right full rudder. All ahead flank!"

The roar of her Diesels increased and, flinging the choppy seas high above her bow, the *Harder* swung to the reverse course of the convoy, hoping to slip unseen astern of the trailing escort, which, so far, had been seen only on radar.

Suddenly the lookout sighted the enemy escort sharp on the port bow, 2000 yards ahead. Now the situation, already critical, was desperate. Nothing for it but to bluff, and that Dealey did.

"Right full rudder; clear the bridge; stand by all tubes."

Down tumbled lookouts, bridge watch, and all; so that in one-fourth of a minute, Sam stood all alone on the bridge of the *Harder*. Below, sealed off in steel-walled compartments, were men whose lives were suspended on the slim thread of one man's capacity to reach a proper solution—and one man's luck. It was as thin as that—one man's J-Factor. It was as close to eternity as that.

This change of course slanted the submarine back toward the coast and shoal water, but there was no help for it. Sam was determined not to dive until he had more water under the keel, and he counted on the bluff to get his ship clear. Almost immediately the skipper reversed the rudder to full left and brought his ship to an opposite but parallel course with the enemy escort.

To the seventy-nine men shut up in the steel hull of the *Harder* the tenseness of these moments of waiting and uncertainty must have been agonizingly acute. They knew the *Harder* was in a trap. Would she be able to pull out before the jaws of doom crushed out their lives?

Dealey intuitively sensing their thoughts—which probably paralleled his own—spoke quietly into the bridge mike—as quietly as though recounting some everyday occurrence: "Well, men, it looks like the good Lord is still with us. The escort hasn't opened fire yet and when he does, the 30-knot deflection of our combined speeds may worry his gunners. Keep your chins up and stand by to dive, fire torpedoes, or ram. That is all."

Sam may have sounded steady as a rock, but waiting for the flicker of heavy gunfire from an enemy vessel, while keeping one thumb on the diving alarm, can test the nerve of the bravest.

Later, under a comforting blanket of 200 feet of the Japan Current, Dealey recorded the story in his log: "Counted on the element of surprise, high speed (with 30 knots relative movement), and our 'rabbit's foot' to get by on the surface, but one thumb on the diving alarm while waiting for the first Jap salvo. It never came. Either the bridge watch on the Japanese escort was asleep at the switch or the O.O.D. was too surprised to act. The escort held course and speed, did not open fire or attempt to challenge."

In spite of this high-pressure start before sun-up, the day did not live up to its promise, except that, at 1620, the *Harder* came upon a vessel that acted too coy to be true. After an approach that brought the ship within 6500 yards of the *Harder's* tubes, Sam broke off and sneaked away after executing a hard-right-rudder. His hunch was that the target was one of those mysterious "Q" ships that other American submarines had reported. She probably carried a concealed battery and might be towing a submerged submarine. Better give her a wide berth.

The patrol continued into the next day—and that following—but there was nothing to report except increased Jap air and sea patrols. In the late afternoon of 10 September, a big merchantman was sighted, but the sub could not close to stage an attack before nightfall. After sunset, bright moonlight made it necessary for Dealey to maintain a distance of 8000 yards between the sub and its victim to avoid discovery, while he made an end run to get into torpedo position ahead. While the Jap had a P.C. boat as escort, it hung back on the quarter in usual Japanese fashion and did not give Sam any trouble.

At 0045 of 11 September, with the target's speed and zigzag plan all "taped" as our British cousins say, Sam dived to radar depth in a position which would put the target in the moon streak. As one reads the *Harder's* patrol reports, he is amazed at the expertness of Dealey's attacks. He never missed an opportunity to seize an advantage which would give his ship a better chance of destroying the enemy—and of surviving.

He commented that Jack Maurer did an excellent job in plotting and charting the target's zigzag plan.

About this time a second P.C. boat arrived on the scene, probably from a nearby anti-submarine base as a relief for the P.C. which had escorted the cargo ship out of Tokyo Bay. Both ships searched the depths with continuous pinging, but as the *Harder* might have said, "They never touched me." The sharp temperature gradient in the Kuroshio stream worked greatly in favor of our submarines.

The remainder of the attack went off according to Sam's well-laid plans and this time at 0120, with a range of 1000 yards, he fired three fish from the stern tubes. His chase of nearly eight hours was ended. At the correct time for Number One torpedo to strike the target, a dull thud was heard—undoubtedly from a dud hit. Number Two torpedo, however, hit and exploded between the stack and stern of the doomed ship. Flames shot up 200 feet in the air and the freighter, with her back broken, sank. The sound operator reported the now familiar crunching sounds of a ship breaking up in her death agony. Instead of waiting to see the pyrotechnics, Sam went deep and away. However, the Jap escorts dropped nine depth charges. All of them were triggered above the *Harder's* level and were on the light side—only about 300 pounds, Sam estimated. The closest DC (depth charge) came within about 100 yards.

This sinking really aroused a nest full of yellow jackets afloat and a-wing. Now the *Harder* had a real glimpse of the Jap resistance he had sensed but not really felt up to this time. Over the radio, Tokyo Rose shouted tirades of hate against the fleet of American submarines that had invaded Japanese waters and the horrible fate that awaited all the piratical Yankee submariners. Meanwhile, minor convoys came into Sam's sights on 11 and 12 September, but opportunities for sinkings were zero.

"The moonlight, all night long now," said Sam in his log for the early hours of 13 September, "is as unpleasantly brilliant as we have ever seen. Islands from thirty to forty miles away stand out clearly in vision without benefit of binoculars."

That afternoon, the sea's surface as slick as glass, found the *Harder* well inside the 100-fathom curve, about two miles off the beach and still closing the shore. Her aim was to sink one or both of a two-ship AK convoy that was coming into focus and guarded by a single escort boat. The TDC was clicking into place for a stern shot as Logan fed the information on the machine—the Fruit Machine as

British submariners aptly named it—as swiftly as he got it. The Old Man and Maurer worked the periscope, taking very quick, short peeks. This because even the slightest periscope feather was a dead give-away under such glassy sea conditions.

Captain Dealey was waiting to reach the proper attack distance when Logan, watching his TDC brains do their mechanical thinking, said: "Torpedo run dial predicts 700 yards!" In accord with previous orders, the men in the after torpedo room made the fish ready in tubes #7 and #8 for firing at ten-second intervals.

Sam ran the periscope up for one final bearing and observed, almost dreamily: "Why, if that isn't the prettiest little red airplane I've ever seen. He's about 500 yards away and only about 50 feet above the surface." Then, realizing what a dangerous threat this was to the *Harder*, he almost shouted: "Down 'scope!"

After thirty seconds, Sam shot the lens up again for another final sighting and in the hope the plane had not seen his previous observation. The target had zigged; the range was now 1400 yards. Given the new range and bearing, Logan was ready.

"Fire," said Sam.

Just as the torpedoes sped away from the *Harder*, an airplane bomb fell close aboard the submerged pigboat from the pretty little red airplane. Thanks to a timely zig, the AK escaped the missiles; thanks to poor marksmanship, the alert airplane pilot missed the *Harder*. So it was a stand-off. Sam took his vessel deep and rigged for silent running. Six minutes later came the first of nine depth charges. In the course of the next eight hours the sub was exposed to a tenacious, if futile, search by airplanes as well as patrol boats. That afternoon, thanks to previous preparations by Bill Bryson, the sub's new baker, Sam's birthday (13 September) was celebrated in wardroom and messroom by frosted, decorated birthday cakes, cut by Sam to ringing cheers and the singing of "Happy Birthday, Skipper Dealey . . ." with more enthusiasm than harmony.

At 1952 the sub came up to change air and charge

batteries. The latter were fairly low. Forty-five minutes later, at two miles, an aircraft was sighted. Down went the sub. During the next two hours, there was another gentle shower of nine airplane bombs. The *Harder* ran too deep to be greatly worried.

Even at midnight the moon made the night as bright as day. About 0300 on 14 September Sam brought the sub up to periscope depth. He hummed gently as he thumbed the 'scope up and took a look. Ten miles away, on a bearing of 30 degrees, true, he saw the beams of Iro Saki.

So far as he could see, the sky was clear of enemy planes and the sea was empty. After twenty-three minutes of careful reconnoitering, Sam surfaced. This time he hoped the *Harder* would have at least six to eight hours undisturbed —the time needed to jam her batteries full.

Congratulating himself on getting a chance to charge his sadly depleted batteries, Sam was just about to go below when Maurer shouted up the hatch: "Radar contact! Aircraft at four miles. Bearing dead ahead. It seems to be closing on us."

"Clear the bridge! Dive, dive!" cried the OOD without waiting for a confirmatory nod from the Old Man. The orders aboard the *Harder* were that any operation not actually connected with an attack phase was executed by the officer who had the direct responsibility under the Navy Regulations.

"I saw him just as I ducked under the cowling," said acting quartermaster Brostrom, one of the last to leave the bridge, "at about two miles. His running lights were on."

Once again the sub was diving without having had a chance to fill the "can." Daylight was drawing near. When would she get another chance?

Watching the depth gauge, Frank heard the skipper's voice from the conning tower above: "Take her to 100 feet, Frank!"

Down she went; past radar level; past periscope level. Just as she passed 85 feet, which was 15 feet above the ordered cruising depth, an aircraft bomb smacked on the surface and exploded rather close aboard.

"Take her deep, Frank," came the Old Man's voice again, as always, calm and assured.

While he acknowledged the order, Frank shut off the shallow depth gauge and shifted his gaze to the much smaller deep gauge dial, placed in the middle of the diving gauge board between the seats occupied by the planesmen. As the sub reached the required depth, power was cut to one-third. Quickly the *Harder's* trim was adjusted and Lynch sang out, "Trim completed."

Although no listening devices were involved in the airborne attack now in progress, the sub was slowed to creeping speed. This to husband her much reduced battery potential.

One thing really baffled Sam—why did Jap pilots leave their navigation lights on at night and thus reduce the element of surprise in their attacks? He did not object. In fact, he applauded the idea.

That the plane had seen the sub was proven by the bombs that followed her on the way down.

"Looks like they're trying to pin us down; force us to run our batteries dry and, in time, make us come up for air," observed Sam as he leaned on the chart table in the control room. "It would not surprise me if we might get sporadic DC's or bombings during the rest of the night."

Sam's unhappy expectations in that regard were realized. Haphazard aerial bombings lasted from long before dawn until late into the forenoon. Then the *Harder*—as a change in diet—received another dose of depth chargings. At a slowly measured pace, twenty-four DC's were dropped within a span of two hours.

"It was too close for promiscuous bombing," logged Sam, "and too close for comfort."

"Man, oh man," moaned Alabama to Tom Buckner, his Commissary Officer, during the protracted bombings at deep submergence, "we gits sighted, we gits submerged, we gits poked around, isn't it 'bout time Captain Sam begins to git to do some sinkings?"

At 1946 of 14 September, the skipper ordered, "Stand by to surface!" Prior to that he had been joined by Phillips and Buckner, who would stand Officer of the Deck watch, and Brostrom, always Dealey's favorite quartermaster in ticklish situations. All the ship's electronic eyes and ears were fully manned and Maurer stood watch at the periscope.

So that the ship would have quick warning to slide below again if enemies were lurking in the uncertain light of the moonstreak, Brostrom stood beneath the conning tower hatch, ready to open it on order of the Captain.

"Okay, Brostrom, sound the surfacing signal."

Brostrom gave the klaxon a swift triple touch. As the sub responded to the manipulations of the men at its diving planes under the watchful eyes of Frank Lynch, the sub picked up speed and nosed upward on an easy slope by shifting plane angles and by blowing of the bow buoyancy tank. The depth gauges, already shifted from deep to shallow, recorded the sub's upward progress. Finally she was up and awash, deck barely above sea level. Before Frank could sing out that the sub was surfaced, Sam knew it by reading the helmsman's depth gauge.

From Maurer, on the periscope: "All clear here."

From men on radar and sonar, "All clear!"

On Sam's order: "Open the hatch," Brostrom twirled the wheel that undogged it and pulled the lanyard trigger that released the lid. As it sprang open, Sam popped through like a jack-in-the-box. "All clear," he shouted after he had made a quick round-the-horizon sweep.

Now the Quartermaster and Officers of the Deck came quickly to the bridge. Phillips, as Senior Officer of the Deck, took the starboard side of the bridge; Buckner, as Junior Officer of the Deck, headed for his portside station. Brostrom had made a streak for the cigarette deck. The Quartermaster covered the after half of the ship and supervised the lookouts as well.

"All clear," came in quick succession from each of the trio.

"Set the section watch," shouted the OOD through the C.T. hatch that opened directly in front of his station.

As the lookouts swarmed toward their lofty perches, those on deck heard the hiss of the hydraulic ram as the main air induction valve opened. The ship automatically shifted from batteries to Diesels, and immediately the silence of the night was broken by the snortings of the four main engines as they blew water out of their mufflers and began their rhythmic purr. To expedite pouring amperes into the batteries, whose specific gravity was down to 1145, two engines were put on the charge.

By and large, it makes little difference to crews of submarines whether they are on the surface or submerged. Under most combat conditions, they feel a bit more secure when submerged, because a submarine is terribly vulnerable when on the surface—vulnerable to shell fire, vulnerable to aircraft bombs or machine-gunning, vulnerable to ramming or collision. One hole in a submarine's pressure hull is assumed to be fatal, although there have been notable exceptions to this assumption. Nevertheless, there was no better morale builder than a well-fought gun action. The thrill of passing ammo, serving the gun, and seeing the shells land—in all of which a number of men participate—will never fade. There were those in high places who said our submarines used their guns too much— took too many chances. I was not among those critics. The guns were tremendously useful for targets not worth a torpedo.

And so, as we said in the beginning, to the submariners there was not much choice between surface and submerged action. The experience which is really grueling to the spirits of a submarine crew—officers and men alike—is one such as they sweated out on 14 September. We have just related the principal events of that harrowing day and the night before, during which the *Harder* was forced to dive time after time without a proper opportunity to replenish the dangerously low reserve of ampere hours remaining in her storage batteries.

When a sub runs deep for hour after endless hour to escape listeners who follow in tenacious pursuit, the situation assumes the worst features of deadly monotony and deadly danger. When a sub runs at its utmost capacity for silence, it has, truly, the silence of the grave. When the smooth, almost inaudible master gyro has been stopped and the electrically driven propellers revolve at fish-tailing pace, the sharpest hydrophone can hear no sound. Add to that the precautions taken with respect to human noises—no clatter from tools, voices lowered to bare whispers, even shoes removed as men walk about in socks or barefooted. Silence of that kind, when it piles up, can tower like a house of cards; can build up to total collapse because of the threat of explosive emotional tensions.

At such times, the paternal power of the captain's leadership asserts itself more than ever. That is when a skipper who holds the confidence of his men works wonders by his mere presence. Sam was that kind of a skipper. By being as normal and as natural in what he said and did during long submerged and silent runs, he acted as a highly efficient safety valve for his people. It was not just a matter of being fearless. To disregard danger—to sweep it under the rug, as it were—is just another form of courage, and submariners have to have plenty of that. To be without fear—to be a completely blithe spirit—was what the hour demanded, and Sam was so completely confident that his submarine and his submariners were superior to anything the enemy could muster that he never gave thought to such secondary dangers as DC's that went off above his head.

Sam, too, was a stickler for the nicer normalcies of life even when the *Harder* ran silently deep and the galley could provide only sandwiches.

The wardroom table was, as usual, immaculate at suppertime on 14 September. There had been just one DC after the solid two-hour barrage ended about 1120; that one can had exploded quite a distance aft at 1622. Nothing since then—but one never knew.

As the wardroom gang was seated around the small but well-set table, Rufino and Alabama kept the platters heaped high with cheese or Spam sandwiches and cups of coffee. As usual, there was the general lively table conversation. That was where Frank Lynch shone as the topic pitcher and Tom Buckner as an all-around conversational batter who would slug away at any subject.

Soon after supper that evening of 14 September, Jack Maurer came into Captain Dealey's stateroom. Seating himself on the edge of the bunk, Sam told Jack to take the only chair in the cubicle.

"The battery gravity," Maurer said, "is way down. The situation can really become critical if Jap night fighters should be able to hold us down one more night!"

"Well," said Sam, "I think that last night we were a little gun-shy—inclined to duck too soon. Let's take a look-see."

At periscope depth, all looked well. At radar depth, there were no telltale pips.

When the *Harder* broke out on the surface at 1946, all was clear and charging of the batteries began immediately. Sixty seconds later radar reported aircraft at a distance of seven miles.

"Keep a close watch on him," ordered Sam. "But we'll not take a powder unless he comes closer—or until he comes closer."

Seconds later, radar reported aircraft at six and a half miles. Sam thoughtfully listened to the music of the sub's engines. Every second of drumming exhaust rumblings meant life-giving juice to the sub and a better chance for survival to all hands.

"Aircraft at six miles," reported radar. "Looks like a group of several planes. The pip seems to break into smaller parts." A brief pause. Then from a lookout: "Four airplanes with their running lights on."

Sam raised his night glasses. The lights aloft sped like swiftly scooting stars. The planes were high overhead. Even if they sighted the submarine, it would take them some time to circle back and attack. He kept them in sight until they had vanished to southward.

"That ought to please the Chief Engineer," remarked Sam, "but it's a little tough on the nerves of us deckhands."

Once again the sea was flooded with bright-as-day moonlight. Running on surface on such a night was almost foolhardy, considering the possibility of lurking Jap subs, but there was no other alternative. And so the charging engines purred on.

An hour before noon, on 15 September, the *Harder* sighted a minesweeper. In the belief that it would rile the Japs no end if he sank any kind of a man-o'-war, Sam decided to have a go at it.

Unhappily, the plot failed. As Sam wrote in his report: "1104—Sighted enemy warship; believed to be minesweeper. Maneuvered for bow shot and 70 degrees port track, but as firing bearing was reached (range of 700 yards), gyros were moving too fast to be matched. Swung hard left and came in astern the target.

"Track now 180 gyros zero, torpedo run 1600 yards. Fired two torpedoes without spread; depth set at ten feet. Torpedoes were observed to pass under the target and several dozen Japs suddenly ran to the stern and pointed at tracks. No hits. It is believed that the torpedoes were set too deep."

This was very bad luck. First, when the *Harder* was in good position, she had to swing so fast to keep up with the speed of the target across the bow that the Selsyn repeaters which set the gyro angles simply could not keep pace. Refusing to accept defeat, Sam then swung in astern of his intended victim and fired "up the kilt," as the British say. This is a difficult shot at a narrow beamed target—a shot which was ideal for a reliable magnetic exploder, if such had existed. Lieut. Phillips—who was also the ship's combat photographer—was busily taking some periscope photographs of the disappearing minesweeper at 1233, when down came an airplane bomb; down came the periscope; down careened the sub to deep submergence and down came two more depth bombs. At 1237 the *Harder* took another solid going over by DC's. Within one hour, twenty-four deecees were dropped. While most of them were quite close, the saving fact was that they were all set too shallow.

"The depth gauges really jumped when these went off," noted Sam's log.

Although there were no pings from echo ranging, only listening, the sound operators on the attackers were really good. The *Harder's* sonarmen thought they heard the fast screws of a destroyer—as well as other patrol craft—overhead.

"The *Harder* really had the enemy surrounded on this attack," wrote Sam with his usual sense of humor going at full blast, "but was unable to attain good firing position for anything but shots from the signal gun—and no shots were fired." The signal gun mentioned fires nothing more lethal than recognition signals—another touch of the Dealey humor.

The *Harder* rose to periscope depth at 1920 that same evening. Sam was inclined to go surfacing, but he changed his mind on sighting three destroyers at a range of eight miles. Following another two-hour wait, broken by frequent cautious 'scope looks, the sub rose to the surface at 2100. This time the coast was clear and it remained that way through the night, except for a fleet of sampans which was easily avoided. This welcome break was well earned by all hands aboard the *Harder*. Prior to its surfacing, the sub had been submerged 56 out of 66 hours and had been the target of 59 DC's or aerial bombs.

"And we muffed a fine up-the-kilt shot by setting the fish too deep," muttered Sam to young Phillips. "Oh, well—you can't get them all."

During the days that followed, the *Harder* sighted more planes and surface vessels, even a destroyer, on evident antisubmarine missions. But finding no adequate targets, she bided her time. The moonlight was still an overwhelming menace during hours that should bring darkness. A new cause for apprehension arose forty minutes past midnight, on 18 September, when a night flier dropped a green flare about one mile on the sub's port bow.

"Dive, dive!" shouted the Officer of the Deck as soon as he got the bridge cleared.

Chief Hatfield and his skipper were convinced that the enemy planes were using the *Harder's* SD radar beam to "home" on the submarine. This had been suspected for some time in the Submarine Force, and the standard practice was to use the SD very sparingly. Dealey decided to discontinue its use and depend entirely on his bridge watch and lookouts.

At midday on 18 September the weather took a turn for

the worse and typhoon indications made their appearance. This change, after the long siege of most unwelcome moonlight which they had endured, was greeted with enthusiasm by the *Harder*. Not only would bad weather blot out the moon, but it would keep pestilential night fliers on the ground.

Hourly it grew worse until, by the early morning of 19 September, the seas were so high that it was difficult to maintain control at periscope depth. In mid-afternoon, as he was working his way submerged southwesterly along the coast, Sam came upon a freighter and its escort. As he figured his chances of getting into range—and decided they were not good—Sam discovered a tanker coming his way—better game and a better target. The solution this time was so simple that after but one observation, from which all necessary data was fed into Logan's TDC, three torpedoes rasped out of the sub's forward tubes at seven-second intervals. Despite the heavy seas, they kept their courses at depth settings of ten feet. The results were, as in the previous sinking, one dud, one hit, and one miss. The single fish that hit, however, blew the tanker's entire bow into bits.

The target sank rapidly; in twenty seconds after being hit, its stern slid vertically beneath the sea. Sam turned the sub hard away from the beach—now only about one mile away—and streaked for deeper water. And every fathom of depth the *Harder* won, it needed. Within five minutes, the escort had started leaving his calling cards, dropping a total of eight in a thirty-minute barrage. The lad's aim was good.

"Paint was knocked off the bulkhead and the depth gauges jumped radically with each concussion," noted Sam's patrol report. "A respite for fifty minutes; then two more explosions."

An hour and a half after this show of aggression began, sound reported fast propellers overhead. The *Harder* remained tightly buttoned up downstairs—one might say in the basement—but Sam wanted to get into the subbasement. Again those aboard the *Harder* revealed the value of their thorough training. As a result of the beatings it had taken by many much-too-close-aboard bombs and DC's, some of its gear was getting rather noisy. This included the pumps and the diving planes.

"We'll oscillate her down," said Frank Lynch to Mays, Chief of the Boat. "First, we'll go down by the bow. Send ten men from aft up to the forward torpedo room and keep them there until we have enough of a down angle. When I sing out, move them aft through the ship to the after torpedo room. First we want to bring her into balance. After that, we'll push her down astern, and so on. It will take some running back and forth but it should be fairly easy to bring her down where the Captain wants her by making a few shifts of weight first one way—and then the other."

And that was how the *Harder* was brought out of a threatening situation without making any give-away sounds for the benefit of alert listeners on the surface.

The next day offered seas so high that Sam doubted if any torpedoes fired would perform properly. Most of the day, he ran at 80 feet. Whenever he tried periscope observation, the *Harder* broached and slammed down upon the rearing, heaving waves like a tank speeding over a corduroy road.

The ensuing twenty-four hours were uneventful, as were those of the morning and forenoon of 22 September. Sam and all hands were getting a bit bored with the lack of action when, at 1648, a tanker and a cargo vessel were sighted in the vicinity of Daio Saki. Sam had to make full speed submerged to get a shot at the tanker, and even then her range was a long 2000 yards. He fired three bow torpedoes, but got no hits. Dealey suspected that some might have been duds. At the time the 'scope sightings were made, there had been no sign of sea or air escort. But, just as the *Harder* lowered her periscope after the attack, an airplane dropped a series of five bombs.

The first of these was well placed. Had it gone off a few feet deeper, or had the sub been just a few feet closer to the surface, the saga of the *Harder* could have ended then and there. As it was, that first bomb was a denture loosener.

Later inspection showed that the forward 20-mm gun had been knocked into a jammed position and the bridge talkback system flooded out. Several light bulbs were smashed in the compartments.

"Secure the conning tower. Lay below into the control room!"

As Sam's order was obeyed, he was the last to slide down the control room ladder and slam the connecting hatch shut. Turning to Frank Lynch, the Diving Officer, he found that no orders were required. The ship was already clawing for depth. "It won't be long, I think," said Sam. "It's only one plane."

Nevertheless four more bombs followed. None was as close as the first one. "That son of Nippon has one very bad habit," observed Kerns to Buckner.

"Yeah," flashed the latter, "if you'd ask me, I'd say he was a real son of habituay!" Thoroughly satisfied with his pun, Tom smiled broadly as he headed toward the wardroom for an off-duty cup of coffee. He smiled even broader as he entered the compartment with a few of his brother officers at his heels. "Look!" he shouted. "Look what's happened! All is well and justice is triumphant!"

To Tom's great joy, all around the room lay pictures of movie stars—fallen Guardian Angels of the *Harder*. But proudly in its place on the bulkhead was the photograph of the basic Guardian Angel—Miss Dinah Shore! "Give that picture a reading boys!" said Tom with glowing pride. "When I put them up, they stay up."

Meanwhile the sub retired to the southeast and remained deep until dusk when she surfaced at 2004. The moon—reduced to less than half size—rose about 0100, and some two hours later the radar picked up a two-ship convoy at 18,000 yards. Shortly, at 16,000 yards, the radar pips had grown so that they were half an inch high. Later, the radarman said that they were the largest pips he had ever seen.

Battle Stations, submerged, were ordered, and at 0355 on 23 September, Sam and Lieut. Commander Maurer tackled the job of conducting the approach phase at radar and periscope levels. Sam identified his targets as large ships, probably 7000-ton freighters of the Lyons Maru class as shown in the *Harder's* O.N.I. booklet. They evidently had neither night airborne escorts nor surface escorts. Probably their daytime escorts were to pick them up at dawn.

At 0555, three bow torpedoes sped over a range of 800 yards. Score: one hit and one Lyons Maru sunk. At 0557, three fish left the stern tubes. Score: one hit and a second Lyons Maru sunk. When last seen, the first freighter was gurgling toward the bottom with the bow sticking fifty feet straight up from the sea. The other blew skyward a moment after the *Harder* had turned away to look for safer quarters.

When search planes reached the area some two and a half hours later, they put on a fine face-saving show. Of course, they had no way of knowing where the *Harder* would be. One hundred and fifty minutes is a lot of time for a sub to get lost in. But what the planes—no one on the sub knew how many took part in the show—lacked in accuracy, they more than made up for in the intensity of their bombing. The missiles they let drop were, according to the *Harder* men, regular block-busters. Had one of those giants been the first near-miss that was dropped by Tom Buckner's Son of Habituay, the *Harder* might have been flattened like a pancake or forced deep, out of control.

Wrote Sam in his log: "Their noise and pressure waves were far more intense than any depth charges or other aerial bombs that we have heard. Fifteen of these big ones were dropped, each making a distinct slap on striking the water before the explosion took place."

It should not be difficult, at this point, to visualize the irate character of the conferences that took place in the headquarters of the Imperial Japanese Navy's High Command —as well as those at even higher levels. Despite all precautions, such as more and better patrol and picket line vessels and radar-equipped night-flying planes, the sinkings of Jap shipping in Empire waters by the despised Yankee submarines continued.

Worst of it was that these depredations did not take place away out to sea where the Navy commands controlled the news, but close inshore where thousands of home-loving Japs could see the ruins of their ships in the form of pillars of smoke by day and towers of flame by night. Therefore the specious lies of the Tokyo radio announcers had little impact on the audience. People knew better, and news by word of mouth—the ancient grapevine telegraph—travels fast.

While the brains of the Imperial Japanese Navy at Tokyo and Yokusuka were figuring how to rid themselves of the Yankee subs which were raising merry Hell in their own front yard, the cause of all the furore, the USS *Harder,* was taking a well-earned breather. The hands needed a bit of sack time, and several items required repairs.

For some time the *Harder* had been hunting close inshore in Area Four, where her last kill, a double, had been made. And, since the *Harder* had only two torpedoes left—both in her forward tubes, Sam decided to be a bit choosy about his targets and do the greatest possible damage before he turned homeward. The vigilant and ever-present patrol boats, most of them equipped with listening devices, were an increasing menace as, day by day, the sounds of the *Harder* in the silence of the sea grew louder and louder. The damage she had suffered in repeated depth chargings would soon make itself heard to eavesdropping electronic ears. In addition, her equipment was breaking down. In fact, the *Harder* was proof of the reality that submarines can have multitudes of pains and yet do amazingly fine sea duty.

The same applied to the *Harder's* men. Submariners can be exposed to amazing nervous and mental pressures and yet keep swinging along. Sam, as the patrol grew older, kept close watch for psychological disturbances, but found none. All hands bore the nervous and mental strain of severe and persistent depth chargings remarkably well. Sam had by now concluded that the worst agony a submariner can suffer is from the boredom of inactivity. The general health was good. In fact, Chief Pharmacist's Mate Everett Bradshaw did not even have the usual run of common colds to contend with. A germ-killing ray installed in the *Harder's* ventilation system during that delaying New London overhaul conducted constant war on cold-inducing bugs.

In mess and torpedo rooms, during off-duty hours, men played games, read, chewed the rag, or sang. In the wardroom much the same took place, except for an emphasis on songfests at night. Not only were the new officers, much to Sam's delight, good singers, but some had had barbershop quartet training. Tom Buckner enlivened the cruise by posting occasional cartoons, personal but not biting. He also used his artistic ability to design the *Harder's* battle flag, which was to become very, very famous. This banner showed a green dolphin on a white background, lined with red and cornered by stars, one star for each patrol. In the center, poised on its tail, stood the dolphin, the emblem of the silent service. On its head was a white sailor's cap at a rakish angle. In its mouth was a long cigar with a sportive up-tilt. On its right extended flipper was a foaming glass of beer; under its left arm was tucked a black torpedo with a red warhead. And above the figure was the fighting slogan that was to ring from Pearl to Perth—"Hit 'em Harder!" This flag, with the Stars and Stripes and a meat-ball pennant for every Jap ship sunk, was to fly above the *Harder* on all its future homecomings.

But it was not until an early sun-up hour of 28 September that the *Harder* was to find a target Sam thought worthy of her last two fish. At 0523, standing inshore off Miki Saki, whose flashing beams still revolved ghost-like in the gray light of the early day, the *Harder* saw a five-ship convoy coming up the coast. It was escorted by two patrol boats that came up to seaward. At 2500 yards, Sam let both torpedoes go. About ninety seconds later, those in the conning tower heard the dull but sure impact of a dud hitting the side of a vessel. The other torpedo, running either nine seconds before or behind its impotent partner, was never heard from. Two torpedoes. No explosions. No more torpedoes. No more sinkings this time!

"Turn away and take her down," ordered Sam as he left the conning tower. Two deecees saluted his departure. "Jack, while I think of it, lay course for Hachijo Jima and home," he grinned at Maurer just as his head poked above the control room hatch combing. This last sentence ran through the ship like a song. Bright faces and enlivened chatter indicated that the order was a popular one.

The next noon, as the *Harder* was steaming on the surface at three-engine speed, a two-engine bomber streaked at her low out of the sun. Luckily the lookout spotted the would-be assassin and a quick dive took the sub below damage depth from two small aircraft bombs.

It was noted in the patrol log that this brought the total of explosive missiles aimed at the *Harder* on its second patrol to 102.

"We haven't too much to show for it this time," said Sam to Jack Maurer.

"Well, I don't know," mused the latter. "After all, besides the damage to Japanese morale on sea and on land, three juicy freighters and a fully loaded tanker is—I believe—first-team performance in anybody's league. And let's not forget that air umbrella they put up, and the glassy seas, and a possible six dud hits."

"You've really got something there, Jack," agreed Dealey with a wry smile. "We sure were robbed by them. Wonder what Uncle Charlie (nickname for Comsubpac) will do to whip the dud problem?"

A welcome diversion to all hands occurred toward sunset on 30 September when two armed trawlers were sighted at a distance of ten miles. While she changed course so as to bring the Jap ships into the western glow, Sam ordered his gun crews to be ready for a little shooting bee. There was no need of having gunners explode on deck by way of the forward escape hatch. The *Harder* was not running submerged in those relatively safe waters.

The three-inch gun was made ready and the shell brigade was formed with Alabama standing in the key position under the bridge hatch. The firing began at 1740 and ended at 1912 when all three-inch ammunition had been expended. Some damage was done to one of the enemy ships, but both got away. Most of the time, the *Harder* remained beyond her foes' 3000 yard range. But a couple of times she was close enough to hear shells whine overhead and drop into the sea 50 yards beyond her or 100 yards short. It was all very exciting and good diversion for the crew—which was the one and only purpose of the engagement, aside from giving all gunners a bit of practical experience.

As the *Harder* returned to her eastward course, Sam came upon Bob Moore in the pantry. "Tell me, Alabama," he asked, "got any idea how many shells we fired?"

"Yes, sir, yes, indeed, sir," answered the man who had hoisted every one of them high above his head, one by one, up onto the bridge. "One hundred and forty rounds of high-explosive shells. And sixty rounds of armor-piercing shells. And one magazine of 20-mm stuff."

Without batting an eye, Robert Moore's powerful arms had hoisted perhaps half a ton of sudden death in some two hundred installments. And he had not even been breathing hard when he sang his private battle song: "Praise the Lord and Pass the Ammunition!"

On 8 October, the *Harder*—victory, battle, and other flags aflutter—docked at the submarine base at Pearl Harbor. She had completed her second patrol and Sam figured that she had left more than 25,000 tons of Japanese shipping beneath the seas behind her. This, added to the ships claimed sunk and/or damaged during her first patrol, made a total of 67,000 tons.

En route home, Sam learned by radio of his promotion to full Commander. News that their Old Man was now a regular Brass Hat was well received by all hands.

Once again we are scourin' the seas for the Jappies,
To smack 'em and sink 'em where e'er they may be,
When the Red Sun looms up in front of the Skipper,
He gets mad and he hollers "Get set—fire three."
—*Harder Hymn*

★★★★★★★★★★★★★★★★★★★★★★★★★★★★★★★★★★★★★★★★★★★★★ **13**

# Hunting with Warder's Wolves

Torpedoes, both steam-propelled and electric-propelled, were arriving in quantity at Pearl when the *Harder* pulled in from her excellent second patrol. New submarines were arriving in substantial numbers from the veteran building yards at Portsmouth, New London, and Mare Island. Last, but not least, came boats from a new recruit to the submarine building game—Manitowoc, Wisconsin—a thousand miles from the salt water of the Gulf of Mexico into which they found their way via the Mississippi.

This boost to our numbers and consequent coverage throughout the entire Pacific Ocean Areas permitted us to turn our attention to a matter which had been under consideration for some time now: Coordinated Attack Groups, better known as wolf packs. The size of Japanese convoys—frequently twelve or more ships—was such that a single submarine could not cope with so many targets. Hence, we desired to patrol the main shipping arteries with wolf packs of three or four boats under direction of a pack commander who was a division commander or the senior submarine skipper of the group.

The situation was ripe for these operations and on 1 October, 1943, the first wolf pack, consisting of *Cero*, *Shad*, and *Grayback*, left Midway under command of the redoubtable Captain C. B. "Swede" Momsen—destination the East China Sea. Captain F. B. "Fearless Freddie" Warder, of *Seawolf* fame, was next in line and, at the time of the *Harder's* arrival on 8 October, Freddie was busily working on his plans for the second pack, although all members of his team had not yet been selected. This group was intended to strike a heavy blow at shipping lanes near the Marianas Islands for the purpose of disrupting supply lines to those Japanese bastions and, at the same time, shutting off reenforcements to the Gilbert Islands where Makin and Tarawa were marked for assault in mid-November.

In the course of our conference with Comdr. Dealey on the day of his arrival, my staff and I had an excellent opportunity to study this newcomer who in his first two patrols had won for himself a place in the front rank of our submarine team.

At this meeting, Sam asked to be assigned to Warder's Wolfpack. I told him that I would take the request under consideration. Privately, I thought it was a good idea. I knew from Warder that Sam stood high in his book. "The most important thing right now," I continued, "is to get yourself and your people settled at the Royal Hawaiian and give all of you a full recuperation period."

With a cheery "Aye, aye, sir," and a broad smile, Sam was on his way.

Later in the day, just as Sam was ready to leave his sub for the Royal Hawaiian, W/O Sloggett entered his stateroom. "I've got some bad news," said Sloggett slowly. "The scuttlebutt is that I'll not be aboard the *Harder* on its next patrol. Why—I don't know. I also heard that Ensign Beebe will be transferred."

"Holy jumping catfish," contributed Sam with real fear, "don't tell me that Mister Maurer is leaving the boat, too."

"No, sir—but the talk is that he'll be getting new construction after his next cruise."

How they know all they know—and where they get their usually accurate knowledge, those old chiefs of the

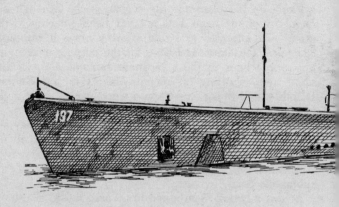

**U.S.S. Seawolf**

old Navy, is a question that only Neptune himself can answer. But the fact is that whether you wear a warrant officer's broken stripe or three vice admiral's stars, your chiefs know as much, if not more, about what is going on than you. And in thirty-nine years of active Navy service, in submarines and out, I have never known one single chief who abused that knowledge.

A snappy seaman messenger took Sam to his quarters in the hotel and opened the door. Sam whistled with amazement as his eyes took in the elegant corner apartment. "Ye gods!" he exclaimed, "they've given me the Bridal Suite."

"No, sir," cut in the messenger. "The last guest here was Mrs. Eleanor Roosevelt."

This time, after Bud returned to Kauai, Sam did not have the empty hours of leisure on his hands that had characterized his previous lay-over. By this time he had learned that the *Harder* would be designated as the third

vessel in Warder's Wolfpack. Hence, he spent most of his time on the sub at the tender *Griffin,* where it was being overhauled.

Other *Harder* men were on hand, including such members of its electronics department as the newly arrived Lieut. Evert Levin, Chief Electrician Hatfield, and Radio Technician Richard Berg. The latter hailed from Houston, Texas. They were adjusting and installing new radar equipment with the aim of improving their sub's SJ radar range. They were the sort of eager beavers who would never settle for anything less than the best and who thought nothing of long work hours.

"Wait until we get this thing rigged, Cap'n," Chief Hatfield would promise, "then this old boat will pick up pips all the way from Hawaii to Hong Kong.—That Mr. Levin is a wizard at electronics."

I recall vividly another occasion during the *Harder's*

refit period. Cincpac's Awards Board had approved a number of decorations for submarine personnel, and among them was Dealey's Navy Cross for his First War Patrol. And so, on 19 October, 1943, I had the pleasure of pinning Sam's first Navy Cross on his chest—they grew to become quite a collection as the patrols rolled up. He was as shy and uncomfortable as a shotgun groom at his first wedding. He stood stock-still, but the blood flowed furiously through his veins and his face was rosy with blushing embarrassment.

The three-ship Coordinated Attack Group—made up of the *Snook*, commanded by Comdr. Treibel; the *Pargo*, commanded by Lieut. Comdr. Eddy; and the *Harder*, skippered by Comdr. Sam Dealey; with Comdr. Warder flying his Division pennant in the *Pargo*—was the second of its kind organized in Pearl. The small but effective flotilla left Pearl Harbor about noon on 30 October by way of Midway. From there, after the *Harder* got a light gray paint camouflage more suitable for tropic seas, the subs laid a course for an area northeast of the Marianas. Their tracks would take them within easy bombing range of enemy-held Wake and Marcus islands. It was important that the Pack should not be sighted because that would result in the re-routing of enemy shipping.

The thirteen-day run from Pearl to the area was made to order for skippers who, like Sam, believed in training their men as close to the point of perfection as possible.

With three submarines to participate in such a program, Comdr. Warder established training schedules that included the use of all electronic devices—locating and tracking and getting the range on targets. Swift identification, radar approaches for torpedo attacks, as well as simulated torpedo firings, were included.

Aboard the *Harder*, no opportunity for training was missed. As radar operators learned how to be expert fingermen in putting their victims on the spot for the torpedo shooters, so Sam had his sonar crews trained to listen for screws of the targets and to estimate their ranges. Experienced men improved their effectiveness. Inexperienced men learned a lot. What with sixteen new men, plus the loss of two good officers, W/O Sloggett and Ensign Beebe, the *Harder* had suffered a great personnel loss, especially in the torpedo department where Sloggett was a past master at the art of putting final adjustments on a wayward fish.

But, as Sam well knew, in the Navy game, one plays the cards as they are dealt. He was fortunate in being able to hang on to as many of his plank owning chiefs as he did. All of them, especially those in the Engineering Department, were wizards at making the *Harder's* cranky engines deliver the goods. Frank Majuri, an electrician's mate, was rising into Wayne Brostrom's class as a pinch hitter at conning tower and bridge key posts, and as a machine gunner, he had a keen shooting eye. As a lookout he was like Sam himself. Frank Majuri had almost perfect night vision. Dick Berg, the Houston lad who had helped a fellow Scandinavian, Lieut. Levin, and Chief Hatfield to install the new SJ radar, developed into a very clever operator. Like Hatfield, he was a plank owner and the *Harder* could do no wrong in his eyes.

In the morning watch of 10 November, Sam got a pleasant surprise. He was called to the conning tower at 0400 by the OOD, Lieut. Kerns. The radar operator, Berg, had picked up a pip dead ahead at a range of 17,000 yards. Of course, the *Pargo* was up there somewhere ahead, but the usual range at which they had been able to pick up a submarine was 14,000 yards. The pip looked like it might be a sub—but whose sub? Jap-owned Marcus Island lay only about one hundred miles to northward. Sam and Chief Hatfield did a little tracking with the TDC, feeding the radar ranges into it, and soon determined that the craft, whatever it might be, was on the same course and at about the same speed as the *Harder*. Sam decided it was the *Pargo*, and so it proved to be. Before he headed back for his bunk, he took occasion to compliment Hatfield and his gang and made an entry in the log regarding the good work which had been done toward improving their often temperamental set.

In Lieut. (jg) Levin, the ship's Communication Officer, Sam had acquired "a gem of purest ray serene," as the poet might have said. Perhaps he recognized this fact, for he dubbed Levin "Ray" as soon as he reported aboard.

"What's your first name? What do folks call you?" Sam had inquired.

"Evert, sir," replied the newcomer.

Sam looked him up and down. He saw a tall, slim youth who, despite his Swedish-Finnish ancestry, was as dark as a Latin.

"Evert? Evert?" He seemed to smack his lips as if he were tasting it. "Won't do," he shortly observed. "Too complicated," he continued. "Everyone aboard here is Tom, Jack, Frank, Max, or Sam. All short, quick, and easy names to remember and to use. Tell you what. How'd you like to be called Ray? You've got a bright smile—so it seems to fit you."

So Ray it was and Ray it remained for Lieut. Levin in the Navy until he left it and submarines, only a few years ago, on account of family obligations. Aboard the *Harder*, Ray—because of his electronic studies at Minnesota University—was made Communications and Electronics Officer.

Just before midnight, on the night of 11–12 November when the *Harder* was making 15 knots on the surface, word was flashed by the Task Group Commander to increase speed to 17 knots.

Two hours later, at 0015 of 12 November, a heavy vibration ran through the *Harder*, set up by the number-four main engine. In a matter of seconds, Joe Sauvagean, who had the duty, shut the engine down. Soon he was joined by Chief Finney, a light sleeper, who made a swift race for the engine room. By the time he arrived, Motor Machinist's Mate Clarence Clark of Chehalis, Washington, and Victor Mount of Dallas, Texas, were making a rapid examination of the blower drive gears. Several teeth had broken off the idler and nearly wrecked the whole gear train. The engine was out of commission for the duration except in extreme emergency.

Four hours after she reached her station at noon on 12 November, the sub's high periscope watch reported a vessel about ten miles away, bearing north. After broadcasting a contact report on the Pack frequency and receiving one from the *Pargo*, Sam maneuvered on the surface to get station ahead of the target. At 1454 the sub dived and began the approach with Lieut. Comdr. Maurer in charge of that phase of the operation. As the *Harder* came closer to its prey, it found that there were three vessels, not one. The ship first seen was a patrol boat. The next to be identified was a cargo vessel, and the third, a large, well-armed trawler of the class Sam and his men knew so well.

During the approach, the trawler kept its station on the port quarter of the cargo vessel. But the patrol boat, by dashing hither and yon, made quite a nuisance of herself. Jack had to be careful lest his periscope be sighted.

As the approach phase ended, Sam took over and, at 800 yards, fired three torpedoes. One hit forward and the other aft of the cargo ship's smokestack. The third was never heard from. To the watching skipper it seemed as if he had never seen greater destruction in so concentrated a space. The forward half of the ship disintegrated and many large and small fragments of the enemy ship were hurled aloft. There were loud slaps as they struck the water. The stern section sank, tail high, in less than ten seconds.

"Right full rudder—and take her deep," ordered the Skipper. As they passed 100 feet, two depth charges were dropped rather close aboard. Then a more distant, flatter explosion. Then: nothing.

Having done his job—fired his torpedoes, sunk his target, and brought his ship and his crew into a position of relative safety, Sam's job was done. He stepped back from the scope with a grin full of half-hidden mischief on his lean-cheeked face. Was it due to a quick sinking, to impotent depth charges, to a run for safety well accomplished? No one in the *Harder* at that time knew. But later, when the Wolfpack returned to Pearl, it was learned that Comdr. Eddy and his *Pargo* were about to fire a salvo of torpedoes at the same ship when, suddenly, it blew up in their faces. Could it be that Sam had a hunch that he had beaten the *Pargo* to the draw?

After almost an hour's wait, the sub rose to periscope depth. Taking a sneak-peek, Sam saw through the 'scope that the trawler escort was lying dead in the water, her stern blown off and with a 20-degree list to starboard.

"Take a look, Jack, and tell me what you think," invited Sam to his Number One.

"I think he blew his own tail off with one of his own ashcans," replied Maurer after a quick look. The Old Man nodded reflectively. "Or it might have been our third torpedo," he speculated. As for the other patrol craft, his screws were heard as he circled the vicinity of the stricken trawler, probably picking up survivors.

Dealey had considered surfacing and putting a boarding party on the wreck to look for papers and other things of interest, but the presence of the patrol boat made that impracticable. Too, Jap planes on Maug Island were only eighty miles away. They might already have been alerted. So Sam decided to wait until the approach of darkness, then surface and finish the wreck off with gun fire.

And that was how it worked out. At 1857, the *Harder* surfaced and, with a lot of not too well-placed shots—the sea was choppy, the night shutting down and the target small—finally set fire to the ship and sank her. During this bit of target practice, the sub's radar kept watch on the other patrol boat. The latter remained at a distance of 4200 yards and took no part in the show—nor did any planes show up from nearby Maug.

One thing the gun practice proved to the conviction of Sam and others concerned was that a three-inch gun does not have the punch it takes to do deadly damage to a well-constructed steel vessel.

"What do you say, Captain," asked Lieut. Logan, the gunnery officer, "that we try to get a gun of heavier caliber at the first opportunity?"

"Right," answered Sam, "that's just what I'll try."

The next few days for the *Harder* were uneventful

except for sightings or radar contacts with her two Wolfpack companions. Also her SJ radar took this opportunity to show what it really could do by picking up Pajaros Island, the northernmost of the Marianas Group, on 12 November at 40,500 yards. The next day Asuncion Island was picked up at 80,000 yards! Its range and bearing checked nicely with the *Harder's* dead-reckoning position on the chart. Lieut. Levin and his radar gang were all smiles.

The weather en route to the *Harder's* station had been perfect for surface patrolling: flat seas and high visibility; and most of the time spent in her patrol area was equally pleasant. Of course, with the Equator only twenty degrees to the south, the boat did warm up in the middle of the day. However, the air-conditioning system functioned well and the warm sun encouraged many men to volunteer for lookout duty. Watches on the lookout stands were cut to one hour so as to give more of our submarine moles a chance to acquire a real tan, as opposed to the synthetic tans they could acquire from the sunlamps in the engine rooms.

Since there was little or no air opposition, the *Harder* remained on surface most of the time. In fact, from 12 November to 20 November—the actual period spent in her patrol area—she ran submerged only forty-eight miles. Of course, while running on surface, the *Harder* used the most difficult types of zig-zag patterns to foil enemy submarines.—We lost, so we believe, a possible five or six submarines to Japanese torpedoes launched from subs. The threat posed by enemy undersea craft was not an idle one.

Nevertheless, the *Harder's* personnel were restive from lack of action. They were a thoroughly attack-minded crew and tended to grow restless when targets were hard to find. Friendly arguments became more heated as boredom increased and food, of course, came in for a share of the gripes.

Tom Buckner was Commissary Officer mainly because he loved it by virtue of his interest in food and in cooking. One day in the wardroom, he got into a chow discussion with Frank Lynch.

"Tell you what I think," Frank chided, "the food is not as good on this boat now as it was when we started out."

With that, Tom exploded and Levin with him.

"Okay, okay," soothed Frank, "if you two guys are so good at cooking, why don't you give Thomason and Dugan a breathing spell and cook us a real dinner."

"Betcha we will—betcha," thundered Tom. "Come along, Ray, we'll just show him that there's real chow on the *Harder*.

That was how Tom Buckner and Ray Levin came to cook up a meat ball dinner with spaghetti and gravy that long was the talk of the ship. But the two master chefs readily agreed that what really put that meal over to all hands were the salads prepared by Alabama Moore.

Chief Pharmacist Mate Bradshaw distributed a lot of soda mints and alka seltzer that night to sailormen who had taken too much gastronomic cargo aboard—and that's well nigh impossible for a sailor.

There were songfests at night in the wardroom and in other parts of the ship. Among serious subjects brought up in the former place was the hope that, one of these days— and soon—the closed season on Jap destroyers would come to an end. The edict that torpedoes were too scarce and too valuable to be expended on DD's, because cargo destruction would mean greater loss to the enemy, still stood, even though torpedoes were now plentiful.

Sam always maintained that if he ever had a real opportunity to try the theories he had worked out with Tex Edwards aboard the *Reuben James* and in the old S-20, he would demonstrate that DD's had more cause to fear subs than the other way around.

"They are supposed to be our mortal enemies and the main threat to submarine survival," Sam would say, "but I don't see it that way. All a sub has to do is to stand up to the DD, provided, of course, that the circumstances are favorable. Just remember that, once you hit it, a DD is a dead duck."

During those hot nights, Tom Buckner and Ray Levin had appropriated the smooth metal deck space in the conning tower along the bulkheads, and separated by the periscope well, as their bunk place. It was, they claimed, the coolest spot in the ship when at night it ran on the surface and cool breezes swung down from aloft by way of the bridge hatch. Here they would sleep or talk, talk, talk on the subjects young men barely out of college talk about when they discuss the many perplexing aspects of a world that is not as they found it depicted in their text books.

Of course, there would be nights when one or the other had the duty. Then whoever of the twain had no watch to stand would draw Alabama into conversation whenever he returned from the bridge after having delivered fresh supplies of coffee.

One very hot night, when the whole ship seemed to be crushed by oppressive heat, Alabama, cool and cheerful as usual, slid down the bridge hatch ladder and, turning toward the outstretched but sleepless Tom Buckner, said in his deliberate reach for his comedy role: "Lawdy, Mister Buckner, sir—I wish I was a-lying down the way youall is a-laying down!"

"Well, Alabama," replied Tom dutifully in his allotted role of the Straight Man, "why ain't youall a-layin' down?"

"Because, sir, because, Ah'm just too weary to lay down!"

Bob Moore disappeared chuckling down through the control room hatch. John Glave, of Bayonne, N.J., Quartermaster (2c) who had the helm—and helmsmen are supposed to hear nothing, see nothing, and do nothing that is not related to steering the ship—joined Tom in raucous guffaws.

The long days of inaction, and the even longer nights, dragged by in dull procession. Then at 0200, when 19 November was still young, came this report from radar: "Contact on three large ships. Range, 27,000 yards. Bearing, 044."

"Captain to the bridge; Captain to the bridge," was the instant call on the squawk box. Cap on his head, sandals on his feet, pajamas on his well-muscled, medium frame, Sam barged out of his stateroom. Again, he was diverted to the radar screen. With eyes quickly cleared of sleep and mouth slightly agape, he looked at the three solidly out-lined radar pips.

"You say—27,000 yards," and there was a note of disbe-lief in his voice. "Why that's the best ship contact yet on our radar—" Facing the operator, Galvin Bull of Spring-field, Nebraska, squarely, he asked: "You sure you're read-ing this right, Galvin?"

"Yes, sir," answered the youth with thinly suppressed pride. Radio Technician Berg had gotten him aboard the *Harder* and he knew the job that had gone into making her new powerful SJ equipment. No sub in the fleet had one like it. Of that, he was sure.

"Call the Communications Officer," said the Skipper. On Ray Levin's arrival, Sam ordered: "We want to send contact messages to the *Snook* and the *Pargo*."

The information for those ships went out at 0210. The *Snook* receipted. When nothing was heard from *Pargo*, Levin repeated several times. No word from *Pargo*. At 0225, the *Harder* called *Pargo urgent*. No reply. Sam was getting worried and exasperated. Had the *Pargo* been lost? There ought to be some better way for subs to communicate in enemy waters.

Here he had three enemy ships in his 'scope, thanks to a souped-up SJ radar. But what good did it do to have teammates if you could not communicate with them? (Later we put radio phones on all submarines.) Also, Sam's com-petitive instinct and fear that the targets might get away goaded him into laying claim to the three Jap ducks in his part of the pond. At 0254, a full half-hour after his *urgent* signal, Sam, now on the bridge and fully clad in skivy shirt, shorts, cap, and sandals, lost patience. By now the *Harder* had been in contact with the enemy for almost an hour. As he drew closer to the three Jap vessels—which evidently were heading for the homeland—the further use of radio became a dangerous giveaway. Still, Sam played on a team.

Aubrey Givens, of Evansville, Indiana, the youngest man in the boat, who had joined the *Harder* at New London and who was now RM2c,—and proud of it—sent a message to the *Snook* and *Pargo* giving target course and speed. Again receipt had come in from the *Snook*. Still no word from *Pargo*. Any chance of further communication was broken by an angry buzzing in the receiver.

"Can't get through, sir," said the boy to Levin, who was standing back of him in the radio shack. "The Japs are jamming us out. They're on our frequency and sitting smack on the key."

On reporting this to the Old Man, Ray was told to stop all transmissions.

Long before it was time to call Battle Stations, Sam summoned his officers to the control room. There, as they gathered around the chart table over the master gyro compass, he spread out a chart and proceeded to give them all the picture. "We," he said, pointing with the rubber end of a pencil on the chart, "we are down here—northeast of Asuncion Island. Three large ships, AK's or AP's, are zigging on a base course of 320 at a speed of 10 knots." Sam chewed thoughtfully on his empty pipe, as his eyes took in the young, tense faces that circled the chart table, and continued: "We are making 17 knots and standing northwest so as to make an end run. At present, we are on their port quarter. I want to keep at least 15,000 yards from them in order to keep out of sight—to gain position ahead for an attack. That clear?"

When nods and excited murmurs signified understanding by all present, Sam continued: "As for other vessels, this is the situation: the convoy has three escorts. It looks as if one patrol boat—we do not know what type—is 5000 to 2000 yards ahead of the three ships. They are steaming abreast. Two additional patrol boats are guarding the convoy's port and starboard flanks.

"According to my figuring, the *Snook* should be forty or more miles away. If she attacks, I believe that she will be on the target's starboard flank. The *Pargo*? I have no idea where she is, but she should be near that convoy. It'll be a matter of a couple of hours before we shall be ready to submerge—let's say 0445, or thereabouts."

Turning to Tom Buckner, he added: "Call the cooks, so

all hands will have had breakfast before we call Battle Stations. It may be quite a while before this hand is played out."

"Yes, sir," snapped Tom. As the meeting broke up, he headed for the galley. He had not mentioned this to the Old Man, but Tom had anticipated the order and summoned Thomason and Dugan to their pots and pans as well as Bill Bryson, the *Harder's* excellent baker. When it came to turning out breads and rolls—as well as cakes— Bill was a real treasure. With a will, the galley crew turned out a real pre-battle breakfast—iced fruit juices, ham and eggs, fluffy hot rolls, and gallons of authoritative black and aromatic coffee.

"Wonder what the Japs will be having," mused Bob Moore. Because of his ministerial calling, he could not help but reflect that, for many of those luckless Jap sailors, it would probably be their last meal—if they had time to get one. It was Bob's habit, whenever the *Harder* had scored a victory, to offer a silent prayer for the men— enemies though they were—whose lives had been snuffed out in combat.

Ray Levin, having inherited some of the deep introspectiveness of his Scandinavian forebears, knew just what Bob ment. There were times, especially when the *Harder* men celebrated victory with steak-'n-egg, when it seemed to Ray as if the newly dead, with silent voices and sightless eyes, beat their hands on the *Harder's* hull for re-admission to the world of the living they had so suddenly and violently departed. In fact, it was one of the subjects he and Tom used to talk about during their conning tower nights— what happened after death?

At 0456, with daylight threatening to break, Sam took the *Harder* under. She was then 15,000 yards ahead of the convoy. Although she had only three of her four engines in operation, the sub had found no difficulty in maintaining an even 17-knot speed. Ships of the *Harder* class did not drive their propeller shafts directly from their engines. Instead, their Diesel engines drove generators which provided juice for the motors that drove the shafts. The

*Harder's* three engines could provide ample juice for her ordinary requirements. However, on occasion, when the storage batteries might be really power hungry, she would cruise on two engines while using her third for jamming juice into her depleted "can."

With Jack Maurer at the periscope, the sub nosed under and began its approach run at radar depth for Number Two Periscope. When within 10,000 yards of the slowly approaching three-ship, three-patrol convoy, Jack took the sub deeper and swung to his Number One or attack 'scope.

Although the *Harder* had heard no pingings or other signs of probing Japanese radar fingers, and although Jack had kept his 'scope exposures away below the usual ten-second maximum, it seemed that the leading DD was getting suspicious. It had been determined by this time that all the escorts were destroyers—which indicated an important convoy. When the convoy range from the sub was reduced to 8000 yards, the leading DD dropped back from its position of 5000 yards in the van of its charges, to only 2000 yards. . . . Why?

The hydro-phone operator reported sound conditions good. He said that the DD's screws—drumming faster than the sluggish, swish, swish, swish of the props of its charges—had been heard steadily until the range to it was 6000 yards. Then they stopped. Listened. Started again. Stopped. Listened. And started again. The Japs were good at that listening game and Sam—standing during the approach run in the small space under the bridge hatch—was happy that the *Harder* had cut its submerged speed to a creeping pace long before the DD began to show its suspicions.

"Echo ranging from the starboard bow," came the report from the sonar man.

"Swing right to bring it dead ahead," directed Dealey. In this position the *Harder* would present a narrow target to echo-ranging beams that reached out at supersonic speed from the Jap DD and reported back any contact they made.

With the approach phase ended, Sam took over, dropped down to periscope depth, and stepped up to the Number One 'Scope to launch the attack. As the sub made little headway while the convoy crept closer at 10-knot speed, the somewhat faster escort cut the range from 5000 to 4000 to 3000 to 2000 to 1000 yards—to 500 yards. And with each approaching yard its pingings were more audible to observers aboard the *Harder*.

"What do you think?" asked Sam of Jack Maurer.

"He's got us located," the latter said.

"Must have!" agreed the sonar operator. "Those pings are bouncing off our hull like rain on a tin roof!"

Turning to Sam Logan at the Torpedo Data Computer, Sam asked: "What's the TDC dope?"

"Twenty-five hundred yards, sir, on the biggest cargo vessel."

Up-'scoping quickly, Sam stole a look. It revealed the pinging DD rushing along the starboard side of the *Harder* at a distance of some 400 yards and on an opposite course.

"Left full rudder; all ahead two-thirds," he ordered as the 'scope slid down into its well. This restored the sub's position as a slim pinging target and, at the same time, swung the bow tubes into firing position for the northwest-bound AK on the convoy's starboard flank. "Looks like a photo finish between our torpedoes and the DC's from the DD," said Sam between the clenched teeth of the fighting grin.

As Sam waited for his ship to come into the firing bearing, he tried not to think about the detonations of the exploding ashcans he expected to hear at almost any moment. At periscope depth the *Harder* would be easy pickings. Dawn was only moments away and the keen nosed destroyer was just as close.

Between periscope looks, Sam glanced around his CT. He noted Buckner and Phillips at the plotting board doing swift calculations. And stout-hearted Jack Maurer—his right-hand man—stood as solidly and unconcerned at his post as if this were just an exercise off Fishers Island in faraway Long Island Sound.

The dials of the TDC moved in absolute silence. The louder rumble of the *Harder's* own screws could be heard through the hull. Outside, a destroyer was searching. Not very well, Sam hoped. But eagerly. All it needed was some of the same luck those aboard the *Harder* were praying for. At times such as this, there are prayers, indeed, silent and individual—from bow to stern of a sub—prayers for survival by men who wait.

Outside, three important targets, steaming almost abreast, were bearing down upon the *Harder*. By now, Sam calculated, he should have crossed the bow of the freighter on the convoy's port flank. He probably was in the path of the on-plodding ship in the convoy's center. As for the two trailing DD's—where were they? And what had they found out about the *Harder*?

"Only one way to find out," thought Sam, and then, almost in a whisper, he ordered, "Up 'scope."

At this precise moment, the three targets zigged 30 degrees to their right. The center and starboard flank AK's were presenting perfect shots. The port flanker, the nearest AK, was headed straight for the submarine.

"Stand by to fire," said Sam. The muscles of his face were tense.

At 0537 Dealey fired three torpedoes from the bow tubes at the right flank AK, at a range of 2700 yards. Then, with a new, swiftly generated TDC set-up, he dispatched the three fish remaining in the forward tube nest to meet the center AK at a point-blank range of 600 yards.

The action in this encounter is almost too swift for the mind to follow, and the *Harder's* position at this time, as well as her life expectancy, might optimistically be described as most insecure. There she was, with torpedo hits being registered from the six torpedoes she had just fired, in mortal peril of being rammed by the flank AK or blown to bits by the depth charges of a vengeful destroyer. Swift action was required, and that was Sam Dealey's first, last, and middle name. His patrol log, from this point onward, reads as follows:

"0538—Swung hard right to prevent being rammed by

left flank AK." (He heard two hits on first target, three on second.)

"0540—As he went by, fired one stern tube shot at him, but range was too close and the gyro too large, 136°. Continued swinging right and shifted back to the center AK. He had turned left and again presented a perfect target at 1500 yards.

"0542—Fired three stern tube shots; track angle 120 port; TWO hits! (A total of five hits in this one.) (All torpedoes set to run at 8 feet, divergent spreads used, and gyro angles near zero.) This had been a dream come true. The *Harder* was in the middle of an enemy convoy and I felt like a 'possum in a hen house, but the destroyer escorts were uninvited participants. . . . Dawn was breaking at this time and though all enemy ships were clearly visible, it is not believed that our periscope was sighted. The reconstructed melee is only an approximation at best: Screw noises in every direction, torpedo explosions, a near collision, and then the destroyers started dropping depth charges! They let these go in patterns of two, three, or four, and though none were close, they were loud. Ordered deep submergence, silent running, and went to 300 feet."

There, luckily, the *Harder* found a perfect "layer" —negative temperature gradient on the bathythermograph —at 210 feet and had no trouble in evading the DD's as long as she remained under its protection. But every time she ventured above it, Whoom! Whoom! came the DC's. Sixty-four of these unwelcome calling cards were dropped in the *Harder*'s vicinity in the next five hours before she found an opportunity to return to periscope depth.

When the *Harder* did slip back to periscope depth at 1125, Sam sighted heavy smoke on the northwestern horizon. That, he concluded, had to come from whatever ships of the convoy remained afloat. He therefore set a course of 318 degrees and gave chase while reloading torpedo tubes forward and aft. Not a single fish remained in the *Harder*'s ten torpedo tubes.

In five terrific, action-packed minutes, the *Harder* had

fired ten torpedoes at three different targets and obtained seven hits. One ship sank with five hits in her; one limped away, suffering from two hits; and the third still had a whole skin. None of the three destroyers had been attacked and therefore remained as dangerous opponents as ever, except that they had sixty-four fewer DC's than before.

It may be asked why the *Harder* had not reloaded her tubes during those five long hours after the attack. The answer is: noise. Reloading is not a silent operation with from sixteen to twenty men working furiously in the two end compartments. Noisy chainfalls, the hum of the loading motors, the clatter of tools accidentally dropped on the steel decks were detectable sonic risks which the *Harder* could not afford to take.

At noon that day, around the mess tables in the dinette, conversation ran riot. The nerve-racking strains and stresses of that long, danger-packed morning, the saturation of their senses, the feeling of emotional exhaustion which follows the terrific tension of great peril—all were wearing off. Now elation, the heady wine of triumph, and, above all, confidence were surging through their veins.

"Boy, did we wallop those b - - ds!"

"What a Skipper!—And can he sling torpedoes!"

"Let's go get one of those stinking tincans."

Here and there might be seen a man who sat silent, the deadly crash of depth charges still ringing in his ears. Perhaps he was realizing for the first time the narrow margin between life and death—wondering how the *Harder* would have looked lying crushed and mangled on the bottom of the ocean, if even one of those depth charges had registered. Perhaps he recalled a line from the Bible: "In the midst of life, there is death."

In the wardroom, elation was mixed with questioning. How had that cripple managed to get away with two torpedo hits in him? Had it really required five hits to sink that center AK? Were our torpedoes losing their punch? Or were these new, well-compartmented ships? . . . Probably the latter.

For about two hours after lunch, while all hands who could be spared had a chance to relax, the *Harder* pursued her prey at periscope depth. At 1409, with the convoy still far ahead and their tops barely in sight above the horizon, Sam surfaced, set a high periscope observer, and sent his best lookouts and the bridge watch topside. Their orders were to make an end run and keep the tips of the Jap's masts in sight. Also, Sam sent contact messages with all necessary information to the *Snook* and *Pargo*. This time, to Sam's relief, the *Pargo* answered. His unvoiced fears that something had happened to her had not been justified. The *Snook*, however, was silent. The message had barely cleared when approaching aircraft called for a swift dive.

Not until 1805 did the *Harder* reappear on the surface. Increasing darkness, with no moon until 2300, enabled Sam to track the runaways at ranges from 15,000 to 24,000 yards. Careful reconnaissance showed that one of the three AKs had vanished. Of the two remaining, one was proceeding under tow by a destroyer at about 5 knots. A second destroyer was cruising in protective circles about the pair. The other, evidently unharmed, merchantman—the one that had been missed by the single tail-shot that Sam fired around the corner—was standing by not far from its crippled companion. As for the third DD, it was not in sight. Those aboard the *Harder* wondered where it could be—and what it could be up to.

Two hours later, when the sub—at a safe distance—had forged 24,000 yards ahead of the convoy, radar lost all its convoy pips but one. Those in the *Harder's* conning tower assumed that the towing DD was having trouble with his cripple and that the still undamaged AK had been sent on ahead. The TDC soon determined that this target's speed was 10 knots on a base course of 330.

At 2229, even as the first faint loom from the light of the soon-to-rise moon was seen on the horizon, Sam dove and gave Jack Maurer a chance to make an unhurried, elementary approach. Up to now, the *Harder's* plan of attack on this convoy, from first sighting by her ultra-long-range SJ radar, had been beautifully conceived and brilliantly executed. It was technical know-how seasoned by imaginative skill and alert anticipation.

"I will try for a bow tube shot with a 90-degree starboard track at about 1000 yards," said Sam as he took over and went from radar to periscope depth. "We'll fire four with a one-degree divergent spread, depth settings of 12 feet."

"All set, sir," replied Ramrod Logan as he adjusted his TDC dials.

"Fire!"

Away went four bow torpedoes. But there were no explosions. Sam could see that their bubble trails passed under the target. Long past the time when the first or the last torpedo should have smacked into the target—nothing. Later, far off and at well-spaced intervals, were heard the booming of end-of-run explosions.

"Those fish were evidently set too deep," Sam observed. "These ships must be heading home very light—in ballast."

There being no destroyers around to hinder the quick execution of another end run by the sub to get ahead of its victim for another shot, the *Harder* surfaced in the increasing moonlight. Naturally, the target was wary by now. He altered his base course fully 70 degrees to the left and zigged with the radical zags. Also, he boosted his speed to 11 knots. The *Harder* got ahead of her target after a run of an hour and a half. Sam dove at a range of 12,000 yards ahead and made a regular radar-periscope approach.

This time Dealey attacked from the port side at a range of 1000 yards. He ordered the torpedoes set for an 8-foot depth and, at 0041 of 20 November, fired three fish.

Two of them hit, one amidships and the other near the stern. The target started settling down aft and inside of five minutes his after deck was well nigh awash.

Here was a good chance for Sam to let his crew—the men who did the spade work but never saw the end result of their labors—take a look at their sinking enemy ship. The word was passed via the public address system and, for ten minutes, men from torpedo rooms, engine rooms,

U.S.S. Tang

and other compartments pressed their sweaty brows against the rubber eye guard of the periscope to stare with wide grins at the clearly defined Jap ship. By now the night was bright with moonlight.

When Sam noticed Pappy Lonas step back from the scope—a baffled expression on his hard-bitten visage— Sam asked what was troubling him.

"You sure, sir, that that Jap is sinking?" Lonas inquired.

"He sure ought to be," Sam replied.

"It just don't look that way to me, sir!" came Pappy's totally unexpected reply. Taking a swift turn at the scope, Sam looked and found that he was 'way off the beam. The target was not only rising by the stern, but streams of water—at least ten heavy hoses—were dumping water over the side.

Watching closely, the *Harder* pulled within 300-yard range at periscope depth, and Sam observed what he

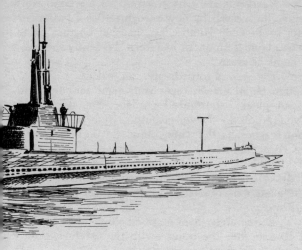

described later as a truly efficient damage control party at work. Through a miracle of efficient seamanship and damage control, which he watched with undisguised admiration, Sam saw the enemy's stern brought up to normal level and observed that the ship lost its list to port. It no longer looked like a wounded creature of the sea but had, to all intents and purposes, the appearance of a seaworthy vessel.

Sam was almost sorrowful as he ordered the *Harder* to get into a position for a single stern shot at a range of 600 yards. The torpedo was set for a 10-foot depth.

"Fire!"

The sound man, instead of his usual singsong report on a torpedo run—hot, straight, and normal—said: "That fish isn't running straight—she's hot all right, but she's angling off to the left."

No hit.

As the *Harder* made a fresh set-up for a second stern tube shot, the vessel, by now recognized as a passenger-freighter of the 6550 Hitati Class, had her engines going. Water was boiling up under her stern. Presently she had a 1 to 2 knots headway.

"Fire!" The second torpedo also ran erratic.

"Captain Hitati, or whatever your name may be, I admire your pluck," murmured Dealey. "You don't know when you're licked.—Never give up.—Unfortunately, Uncle Sam teaches us the same thing. So here is another dose of Torpex for you."

But skillful hands at the AK's helm managed to twist the crippled ship so that its bow pointed toward the 'scope. Thus he made a narrow target for the *Harder's* torpedoes. The fish was a miss.

Slowly, deliberately, Sam emptied stern tubes Number 9 and 10 one after the other—with the careful aim of a hunter administering the coup de grace.

Number 9 ran erratic on relative bearing of 140 instead of 180. A miss.

Number 10 started out on 210 degrees and then circled.

There was considerable worry and tension in the conning tower as the high whine of the runaway torpedo was tracked by the sonarman as it recurved and came closer to the *Harder*. Up to that time, in World War II, no American submarine was known to have been lost because of a circular run by its own torpedo. We were to learn after the war that the *Tullibee* went down with all but one of her personnel because of a circular run. Also that many of those aboard the *Tang*\* were killed when one of her own fish made a turn-around and hit home. The loss of those two fine submarines occurred after this incident on the *Harder*. In each of those cases the submarines were on the surface and thus unable to go deep and evade the circling missile.

---

\*For a full account of *Tang's* wartime battle action and of her loss read CLEAR THE BRIDGE by Rear Admiral Richard H. O'Kane, Ret. Another volume in the Bantam War Book Series.

Even though a circling torpedo gives all aboard a sub a hair-raising scare, the danger aboard the *Harder* was minimized by the fact that the runaway torpedo was set at 8 feet, while the sub was running at 60 feet.

"It is getting louder—coming closer," reported the sonarman.

"Take her down deep," ordered Sam. And, since the *Harder's* bow pointed away from the AK, its only known obstacle, the Skipper continued: "All ahead, full!"

Within minutes, the sonarman, listening with rapt attention, let go a great sigh of relief. "I can still hear it. But not so close," he reported.

Just then the "boom-a-run," as Alabama called it, staged an end-of-run explosion that was near enough to give the *Harder* a bit of tooth rattling. "Uncomfortably close," was Sam's log comment.

In a matter of eighteen minutes from the time the batch of erratic torps had been sent on their cockeyed courses, the sub had opened the distance from the Jap vessel to 4000 yards.

"Surface!" came the order.

Quickly the submarine rose to the surface of the moonlit ocean under the guidance of Frank Lynch's able hands. Bridge watch and lookouts were stationed. Leaning on the bridge cowling, Sam put his glasses on the indestructible Jap and its indomitable skipper.

"What now?" he asked himself. With all torpedoes expended, what course should he take to sink the Jap? Gunfire from his three-incher?

The Jap, seemingly anticipating his thought, at that moment sent a brace of shells toward the *Harder.* Two, of four- or five-inch caliber, splashed much too close. Good gunnery, too. "That guy's got everything! Too bad he isn't on our team," he remarked to Max Kerns, the OOD.

"Looks like he's got us out-gunned, too, Captain," said Max, "coming that close to us at this range."

"Yes," replied Sam, "I reckon he's too hot to handle with our three-inch pop-gun. . . . Maybe he won't get home," he concluded more cheerfully. (And, according to post-war reports, Sam was right, for the *Nikko Maru* of 5949 tons is listed as having been sunk by the *Harder* on 20 November, 1943.)

"It was a bitter disappointment not to finish this ship off, but he was a worthy opponent," wrote Sam in his log. "He won our grudging admiration for his fight, efficiency, and unwillingness to give up.

"Because of the efficiency of the crew in righting the ship and effecting repairs, and because of the accuracy of their gunfire, it is believed that these three ships were operated as naval auxiliaries. It was a surprise and a disappointment to leave two such fine ships after they had absorbed so much punishment."

At that time, as he headed toward the point of rendezvous with the *Snook* and *Pargo*, Sam considered his score for the patrol as two vessels sunk and two damaged. But the next night, when heavy weather blew in from east-southeast, Sam changed his mind. Two vessels, damaged as badly as were both his surviving targets, could not, he believed, possibly weather the storm that was rushing down upon them. Therefore he marked both of them down as sunk. Total *Harder* patrol score: Four vessels and one trawler—24,825 tons.

With all torpedoes expended, Dealey reported by dispatch to Comdr. Freddie Warder and to Comsubpac. He was released by the Pack Commander and ordered by Comsubpac to return direct to Pearl.

On 25 November, the day before the *Harder* crossed the International Date Line, Levin reported that he had decoded a total of 358 messages since the *Harder* left Pearl Harbor on 30 October. Fully two-thirds of these, he said, had come in at night. The average decoding time was some ten minutes.

"Pretty tough," agreed the Old Man, "we'll just have to try as hard as we can to get someone to help you on decoding. Anyway, you can be damn proud that, but for you and Hatfield and Berg and your radar work, three big and brand-new Jap vessels might now be steaming toward a safe anchorage instead of being in the port of missing ships."

En route home, the boys of the juice gang, officially known as electricians mates, wrote the basic part of a victory song that became known as "The Harder Hymn." Chief E. M. Lloyd Weidman, another plank owner, who hailed from Vallejo, California, inspired the effort. Set to the tune of a long-popular hill-billy melody, it had seven verses and a chorus, which described the valor of the *Harder* and the fighting skills of her Skipper, Jack Maurer, Frank Lynch, and Sam Logan. The basic seven verses eventually grew into more than thirty. Some stanzas have been used as chapter headings in this book. Here are a few samples:

As we were a'cruisin' one morning for pleasure,
Jack spied three tincans a'tearin' along,
Their sound heads were pingin', their depth charges ringin'
And as we submerged we were singin' this song.

(*Chorus*)
Take her down, take her deep,
Don't stay near the surface,
For something about this appears to be wrong,
Take her down, take her deep,
Oh! Frankie, my Wonder,
Or 'Davey Jones' locker will be our new home.

Then we were submerged, torpedoes all ready,
The Captain was giving the bearings to Sam,
Frankie asked what was the dope on the tincans,
The Captain said "All clear" and then came a WHAM!

There was, however, more than versifying to demand the attention of the *Harder's* crew. Homeward-bound on three engines, the sub ran into more trouble when, because of excessive vibration, one cylinder of its Number Three Main Engine, broke a piston rod which wrecked that cylinder. This meant that Number Three limped home on only eight cylinders, and that only because of the skill of Chief Finney and his able grease monkeys, many of whom were inspired technicians.

Although the *Snook, Pargo,* and *Harder* did not pull into Pearl Harbor in company, the trio displayed victory flags that told of no less than nine sinkings, which represented a total loss of 55,000 tons of shipping to Hirohito. The *Harder* claimed five ships for a total score of almost 25,000 tons.

Much good news awaited the *Harder* on her return to Pearl. Sam received the good tidings that he had been awarded a second Navy Cross as a result of his highly productive second patrol. In addition, he was informed that he would be recommended for a third Navy Cross based on the results of his just-completed venture in Pacific waters.

But, above and beyond that, orders were issued for Sam and his sub to proceed about 5 December to Mare Island, California, where the sub was to receive new engines and undergo a major overhaul.

Home for Christmas!

Alas, good news is frequently seasoned with news that is not so cheering. In Sam's case, it was the not-unexpected information that Jack Maurer would be detached from the *Harder* on her arrival at San Francisco. In the States he was to take command—a well-earned promotion—of a brand-new submarine, the *Atule.* For the sake of the record let it be known that, in the course of three patrols, the *Atule* deprived the Japs of six ships totaling 33,379 tons. Jack, now Captain Maurer, U.S.N., is, at this writing, back in the Submarine Service and in command of a topnotch squadron.

As we were a'wending our peaceful way homeward,
With sinkin's chalked up to our wonderful score,
All hands looking forward to the Royal Hawaiian,
Then back to the *Harder* and out for some more.
—Harder Hymn

★★★★★★★★★★★★★★★★★★★★★★★★★★★★★★★★★★★★★★★★★★★★ **14**

# Through Hell and Deep Water

With Sam's usual capacity for making every man under his command do his own individual thinking, Sam had enlisted the ingenuity of all hands for opinions and ideas with respect to necessary or desirable improvements as the *Harder* pushed eastward over the 2100-mile route to the Golden Gate.

Barely had the cloud-crowned Paradise of the Pacific sunk low on the horizon on 5 December, the day of departure, before Sam called his entire wardroom outfit into a huddle and, without preamble, put his plan for a new deal in submarine combat equipment on the table: "During our first three patrols," he told his eager and enthusiastic audience, as Bob Moore made the rounds with a well-filled coffee pot, "we have all learned a lot and developed new ideas of one sort or another for doing things better than we, at first, thought they could be done. I welcome all your ideas for improvements or changes in equipment."

As several of the officers leaned forward, ready to take the floor, Sam laughed and held up a silencing hand as he continued: "No, let's not talk about it. Verbal ideas are N.G. If you have any suggestions, put them on paper. Better yet, if you can, make a drawing, as well, to illustrate what you are proposing. The same thing goes for the chiefs and ratings in your respective departments. Ask for their ideas. Tell them to put them down and to make drawings if they can."

After pausing briefly to let this very sensible and clever plan sink in, he reached for the final point: "The main thought is," he said, "for me to be able to make the powers that be at Mare Island not only understand what we want done with respect to the suggestions we may have to offer, but also make them so clear and so convincing that they will be accepted and put into effect."

During the next seven days, as the *Harder* ate up mileage, so many hands aboard the sub were busy drawing plans and making sketches that its various compartments looked like classes in a submarine engineering school. Every department in the ship had members with one or more ideas to offer.

As the *Harder* entered into her hard-earned overhaul period, there were eagerly awaited leaves to be granted to combat-weary and work-worn men. However, since the main engine replacement was a long job, there was no difficulty in giving each officer and man a month's leave and still retaining a maintenance crew of about one-third on board. . . . And the yarns those lads could tell to their home folks would certainly do a lot toward perking up the national morale which, by that time, was beginning to come out from under the bed where it had been driven by prophets of doom and gloom during our earlier reverses.

Another thought that held front place in Sam's mind was that at long last the slim bridge of letters between his loved ones in Santa Monica and Dallas and himself would be replaced by actual contacts. To Sam's happy surprise, Edwina and the children, Joan, David, and tiny Barbara Lee, awaited him at the Mare Island docks when the *Harder*, a proud 23-knot bone in her teeth, swooped down upon her pier. Knowing Sam and his attitude toward his ship, Wena realized that he would not dream of leaving his vessel until repairs were well under way. So she had found a cottage at Vallejo for the family. Later, they went to Dallas for family reunions with Mother Dealey and the extensive Dallas clan. All told, it was a wonderful

Jeep

Christmas for the spreading Dealey family of which Mrs. Samuel David Dealey, Sr., was the proud, happy, and beloved matriarch.

Upon arrival at Mare Island, Maurer was detached and Frank Lynch took over as the Executive Officer. While he was not the kind of a new broom that had to sweep clean on the first swoop—and actually, there were few leftover sweepings that required the broom—Frank was a different type of second-in-command than Jack Maurer had been. No two exec.'s are ever identical, and this Navy Yard period was ideal for letting Frank work his own ideas into the ship's organization. Lieut. Lynch, towering more than six feet and tipping the scales at a good two hundred pounds, had the physique and bounce of a trained, fast-thinking, hard-hitting athlete. It was often said in the Navy that no exec. is doing his job unless the crew thinks he is an SOB. That was not true in "Tiny" Lynch's case.

He had the personality and the commanding bearing to be a splendid leader, for it is human nature for men to want a big man, physically as well as mentally, to lead in any walk of life.

And yet, for all his bearlike size, Lynch had the sensitivity of understanding to realize that his Skipper was a rare type of man who needed more from his exec. than just a watchful and capable senior officer. He knew, as Maurer had known, that the Old Man occasionally needed a restraining hand to prevent him from barging into waters where even angels with waterwings would fear to cruise. The Achilles heel in Sam Dealey's makeup, if it could be called that, was his inborn incapacity to fear danger from the hands of his enemies, plus his steadily increasing disdain for their ability to inflict damage upon him.

Lieut. Lynch, being an observant fellow, had noticed how, time and again, Maurer's little nudge to Sam to "let's get to hell out of here" had been effective and complied with. He hoped that he, too, might earn his Skipper's confidence to an extent where he might serve as a brake on Sam's instinctive desire to follow—regardless of odds— the Navy's time-honored tradition to seek the enemy out and destroy him.

Still, driver though he was, Frank was not the sort who believed in all work and no play. This was revealed fairly early at Mare Island. One of his first official acts was to waylay a jeep from some obscure source in the Navy Yard, and, with that to save time, Frank would seem to be in a dozen places at once, looking after and expediting the work on the *Harder*. One day he drove up to the dock where the *Harder* was moored, yelled for Ray Levin, and told him with great glee: "Well, boy, I got 'em—now it's up to you to get them aboard and get 'em working!"

"But what've you got, Frank?" asked the somewhat bemused Ray.

"A juke box with a couple of hundred records and a small refrigerator to keep our snacks cool in the messroom. Out in the shooting country they'll both be worth their weight in sunken Nip ships."

Ray had to agree without hesitation that Frank was right on the beam. Borrowing the jeep, he drove to the second-hand shop where Frank had "promoted" his bargain. The refrigerator was no problem at all; but the juke box, a veritable monster of its kind, was a horse of another color. Ray had a devil of a time transporting the huge rainbow-hued, glass and chrome affair to the dock and then to the deck of the *Harder*. There he discovered that not a single hatch—not even those for loading torpedoes—was large enough to admit the juke box. All hands welcomed the music-maker with open arms and, as a final recourse, Ray and a couple of electricians mates dismantled the machine —a very dirty job because pounds of carbon dust, scraped off recordings by the tone-arm needles, had gathered in every nook and cranny of the inside. At last, under the master-minding of Frank Majuri, an electrician with a gift for improvising, the entire machine was reduced to separate parts, cleaned, polished, and reassembled in the crew's messroom. To replace the coin slot, a trigger was installed. The turntable was loaded with as many records as it could hold—and there was music. Not only in the dinette, but, via the ventilation piping, the music was heard all over the vessel from conning tower to both torpedo rooms and points in between.

The juke box was a welcome addition, but also a disappointment: the tone arm would not stay in place when the *Harder* rode on the usually choppy seas. However, when she ran submerged, the box worked its musical charms.

Another morale sustainer which the *Harder* obtained at Mare Island was an electric ice cream freezer. It may seem a small thing, but the effect of a dish of ice cream on tired, shut-in men, in a ship whose air conditioning and ventilation systems might be shut down for hours during silent running for evasion of the enemy, was remarkable. It was just another of the items which make submariners boast that their chow is the best in any of the Armed Services. . . . Not a bad spirit to encourage.

After more than two solid months of around-the-clock

work on the *Harder*, the veteran submarine was ready to leave Mare Island for Pearl Harbor and its fourth patrol.

The *Harder* that left Mare Island—after extensive alterations and a complete overhaul—on 19 February, 1944, was nowhere near the same submarine that had arrived in San Francisco Bay from Hawaii on 12 December. The Navy Yard had, as we say, "jacked up the whistle and built a new boat under it." That, of course, is a considerable exaggeration, but they had put into her all the minor alterations and improvements which had been developed during the first two years of the war.

In addition, her limping, man-killing main engines—of an experimental type which, unfortunately, had been installed in about a dozen boats—were ripped out by the roots and a brand-new set of trusty Wintons (General Motors 16–278A) installed in their place.

One alteration which delighted Sam was the replacement of his pea-shooting three-inch gun with a business-like four-inch weapon taken from one of the obsolescent S-boats.

"Oh, boy," chortled Sam Logan, "those damn Jap trawlers better stand from under now!"

Even more important to Sam was the addition of four whole feet to his conning tower. This gave him room in which to install a proper plotting table and a dead-reckoning tracer—the latter a valuable aid to his navigation when held down for long periods by enemy opposition. Various improvements were made also to radar, sonar, and periscopes. The *Harder* was really, as Frank expressed it, "the cat's meow."

Not only did these changes add to the confidence of her people in their ship, but the fact that each had contributed something toward their accomplishment gave all hands a feeling that they owned a part of that submarine. The resultant effect upon the esprit de corps of the *Harder* was excellent.

One factor which added tremendously to the morale of the ship was the home leave which each officer and man had enjoyed. The opportunity to visit once more wife, mother, sweetheart; to spin salty yarns to home-town buddies; to take "late hammocks" every morning with no bonging gongs or squawk boxes to awaken him; to bask in the envious glances of the neighborhood kids; to see the look of pride in his father's eyes—those are intangibles that have a very vital influence on every man's self-confidence and fighting resolution. They are intangibles which cannot be discounted or disregarded.

Of course, there were new faces here and there around the mess tables—some of the old-timers had gone to break in and train new crews on new ships—but the backbone of any submarine crew, the chief petty officers, were there almost to a man.

Around the wardroom table there had been changes also. Gone was Lieut. Kerns, transferred to another submarine. Absent, too, was Warrant Officer Sloggett. But those sturdy old-timers—Lieutenants Keith Phillips, Ray Levin, Sam Logan, and Tom Buckner—remained to serve as the right and left bowers of Dealey and Lynch. New officers aboard were Ensigns Phil Sampson, of Mound, Minn., and Clarence Brock, of Washington, D.C. Also in the wardroom was ex-Chief Carl Finney, who had been promoted to the rank of Warrant Machinist. Carl was the second *Harder* chief to be welcomed into Officer Country. A third, Chief Radioman Hatfield, was soon to make a similar journey. Promotions of this kind were very popular among crewmen. They drew attention to the close relationship which exists between officers and enlisted men in a submarine and made every man feel that he, too, had the same chance. That this feeling was well founded is shown by the fact that at the close of the fourth patrol no less than twenty-eight of Sam's seventy men had secured advancement in rating.

On returning to Pearl Harbor and after a short period of training exercises, during which six practice torpedoes were fired, Captain Dealey and his submarine were ready for their next contacts with the enemy.

On 16 March, 1944, the *Harder* left Pearl Harbor at 1100 with secret orders not to be opened until the ship had departed from Johnston Island, some seven hundred miles to the southwest, where she was to stop for refueling. As usual, Dealey was heading for a very hot area, but this time far removed from the fragrant shores of Honshu where he had made his first two patrols.

At this stage of the war, Tarawa, Makin, Apamama, and the entire Gilbert Islands group were in the bag. The *Harder* had unknowingly celebrated the storming of these enemy strongholds by sinking three Jap freighters on 19–20 November.

Then on 29 January, 1944, began the softening up of the Marshall Islands by Admiral Spruance's Fifth Fleet preparatory to assaults by Army and Marine divisions. This was the largest amphibious operation yet undertaken, and into its plans had been integrated the lessons learned at Bloody Tarawa.*

The taking of the Kwajalein Atoll—and beautiful Majuro, which was found abandoned—plus Eniwetok, captured on 20 February, gave the Fleet three excellent anchorages from which to operate. We of the Submarine Force immediately moved into Majuro Lagoon with two tenders and a floating drydock. The by-passed Japanese air bases at Milli, Wotje and Jaluit still constituted a threat in that area, but almost daily training runs by our bombers were rapidly hammering them into impotence.

So much for the background and stage setting.

The immediate operation with which the *Harder* was concerned was a corollary to the impending strike by the Fifth Fleet—and, in particular, the carriers thereof, Task Force 58—on the Western Caroline Islands. The purpose of this strike was to destroy the enemy air potential at Palau, Yap, and Woleai in preparation for General MacArthur's advance up the northeast New Guinea coast.

The *Harder's* station was at Woleai as one of our recently organized Lifeguard League whose mission was to

*For the classic account of this battle read TARAWA: The Story of the Battle by Robert Sherrod. Another volume in the Bantam War Book Series.

rescue aviators—zoomies, we called them—who might be shot down or otherwise forced to land in the sea. As will be seen, the interpretation of his exact area of operations was a matter for decision by the Lifeguard's Skipper and one which led many a boat into divers thrilling adventures.

The date set for her arrival at Woleai was 30 March; hence, to preserve the security of the Fifth Fleet's projected operation, it was necessary to give the *Harder*, when she sailed in mid-March, sealed orders not to be opened until she had severed her last physical contact with shore activities. In company with Sam was the *Seahorse*, another submarine with an enviable record of sinkings, under the command of Comdr. Slade Cutter, one of the Navy's all-time football greats.

As it happened, transfers out of the *Harder* had left the sub hard hit in several departments, especially those that dealt with communications and electronics. Virtually all Sam's radar, sonar, and sound operators were green as living sea grass. But, thanks to the presence of the *Seahorse*, Sam decided to change the inexperience of these men into experience. Fortunately, Slade Cutter was in a cooperative frame of mind. He, too, liked to whet the keenness of his operators to the sharpest possible point. So, during the two days and two nights it took the subs to reach Johnston Island, the two vessels staged almost continuous radar trackings with each other. Simultaneously, Sam trained his two fire control teams—combat and reserve—a new high in submarine fighting efficiency.

At Johnston Island the *Harder* filled all its fuel tanks to overflowing. What with a lengthy patrol ahead, to be followed by the long, long run to way down under, the *Harder* needed plenty of fuel. To this end its Number 4 main ballast tank had been converted into a fuel-ballast tank.

In Frank Lynch's book, coming into and going out of the Johnston Island lagoon will always remain a hair-raising experience. The Seabees had blasted a channel out of a solid wall of coral that almost reached the surface of the sea, but they had cut it so narrow that two men with hemp fenders had to be posted in the bow of the *Harder* and two more on each quarter to make sure the submarine's tender outer hull would not be gashed by the razor-edged outjuttings of coral chunks. The sun was sinking low in the west before the two subs had been fully serviced, and Frank was in a cold sweat for fear he would have to make a night departure. He knew that the *Harder's* schedule was so tight that she could not afford to risk a night's layover. Fortunately, the boats had plenty of daylight left and both emerged from the narrow green channel out of Johnston's lagoon without a scratch.

At 1830, soon after her Johnston Island aircraft escort had departed, Sam opened his orders and read them to all concerned.

These orders, as related previously, required coopera-tion with the Fifth Fleet to the extent of performing lifeguard duty at Woleai. Other than that, they assigned the *Harder* a certain lane to be patrolled to her station. After being released from lifeguard duty, she was in-structed to guard approaches to Woleai until fuel ran low and then proceed toward the Celebes Sea—south of the Philippines.

Upon crossing the 130th Meridian, East Longitude, the *Harder* would pass from my command, as Comsubpac, to the command of Comsubsowespac—Rear Admiral Ralph Christie—and report to that officer by dispatch for duty in his areas. Her eventual base would be Fremantle, on the southwest coast of Australia.

"Well," commented Frank Lynch as the reading was completed, "looks like the name of this operation was taken smack out of the *Harder's* own hymn."

"And what title is that, sir?" inquired young Ensign Sampson.

"Through Hell and Deep Water," replied Lynch with a broad grin.

"Could be," agreed Sam, "but let me tell you all this: unless we really spend every moment we have until we reach the area, getting as sharp at the game as we can, we'll probably catch a lot of hell and get into deeper water than we can get out of." Turning to Frank, he asked: "When do you think we will reach Woleai?"

After a quick look at the chart spread on the table, on which he had laid down his courses, Frank replied: "All conditions remaining normal, we should be there on the morning of 29 March.

"That gives us roughly eleven days," commented Sam. "Of those we will have the *Seahorse* in company until about sunset on 26 March—eight days. Eight invaluable days for double training of two submarine crews. After dark, we'll pull alongside the *Seahorse* and I'll try to work up a program with Captain Cutter."

As planned, so done; again Sam found Slade Cutter an enthusiastic training colleague. As the days went by, training schedules were carried on with such good effect that, on 26 March, after the two subs had parted to go their separate ways, Sam wrote in his log:

"1900—Parted company with the *Seahorse* and proceeded independently to station. The mutual advantages which resulted from proceeding in company with another sub cannot be overestimated.

"On both subs:—The fire control parties have had continuous and realistic drills. The radar plotting and tracking parties have had a real target to work with. The radar operators have always had a target (day and night) to work on and have developed a self-confidence and efficiency in their bearings and ranges. All lookouts have had the chance to see periscopes at various ranges and know what to look for. Lookouts have had the chance to study the appearance of another darkened ship at night, at different ranges, different angles on the bow, and under varying degrees of visibility.

"Both subs had the advantage of the other's lookouts and radar operators in detecting approach of planes.

"Psychologically, the presence of another sub lessened the usual monotony of a normal cruise to station.—Many mentioned that it didn't seem as if the patrol had really started until the other sub took departure."

In very short order, Sam was to see his driving urge for

Zero Fighter

technical perfection pay off in life-sized dividends. On 26 March, two enemy planes were sighted and avoided by means of swiftly executed dives. Virtually every day thereafter—and quite a few nights—presented aircraft contacts with types of Jap planes ranging from Zero fighters to Betty bombers. At first, these contacts were interesting and exciting. But as they became commonplace and repetitious, the shout: "Aircraft sighted. Dive. Dive," became a burdensome bore. The weather was hot; the water was hot. Despite the air conditioning, the air in the submarine while running submerged became humid and stale.

On 29 March, as planned, the high periscope lookout sighted Woleai at 0715, distant fifteen miles. At 0815, the submarine dived to avoid an airplane. Then she ran within two miles of the coast and began a day-long search of the islands of the atoll which lies in mid-Pacific almost halfway between Guam and Palau. The main island of this reeflike group that surrounds a rather large lagoon rests on the atoll's southern tip. Like most other Pacific tropical sand dabs, it was covered by heavy jungle growth that would make a fine hiding place for an airstrip. This, assuredly, it did, and it was up to the *Harder* to spot it and report its exact location to Comsubpac. Throughout the morning and afternoon, Sam conducted his periscope search, interrupted now and then by the flight of Jap planes, mostly medium bombers. Not until 1445, when he had worked his way from the north coast of the island to its southern shores by way of its eastern fringe, did the periscope watch locate the airstrip. With great satisfaction, Sam told Levin to encode a message to Pearl describing what they had located. While there was no shipping in the lagoon, which was entered from the atoll's southern approaches, the periscope watchers saw evidence of several construction jobs in progress. Cincpac, as well as Comsubpac, had good reason to be curious about Woleai and what was going on there. Not only was it an important staging point for bases south and east, but lying as it did only about six or seven hundred miles from the New Guinea coast, it could offer serious interference to General MacArthur's planned operations.

According to Sam's information, Woleai was to get a working-over by carrier planes of Vice Admiral Pete Mitscher's Task Force 58, supported by Admiral Spruance's Fifth Fleet on the mornings of 31 March and 1 April. The first attack, staged in four waves by small numbers of carrier-based bombers began at 0105 of the first date. Ten minutes earlier, the sub's radar had picked up the approaching planes at 30,000 yards to the southwestward. The first wave took the Japs so much by surprise that no ack-ack shells rose to repel the aerial invaders. The next wave, at 0112, met with fairly heavy but rather ineffective AA fire. At any rate, there were no zoomie casualties for the *Harder* to rescue from the Jap devils or the deep blue sea. Similar negative rescue requirements followed the third and fourth waves.

Sam remained on the surface until driven down at 0820

by enemy planes. About an hour and a half later, just as he was housing his periscope after an observation, an aircraft bomb landed close aboard. The bridge talk-back was knocked out of order, several light bulbs were shattered, and the ship was well shaken up; but no serious damage was done. After that, Dealey remained at 80-foot depth with periodical ascents to periscope depth. Finally, at 1545, he closed in to within one-half mile of the lagoon entrance. That the runway had not been put out of commission and the bombers on the island were still flyable, was evident. Sam saw planes on the runway and taking off. To him it seemed as if the night's harassing raid had served only to set the hornets in this Nip nest a-buzzing, but he was much elated by the excellent performance of his SJ radar. Ranges on bombers had been obtained up to 40,000 yards.

At 0351, 1 April, the *Harder* was cruising on the surface preliminary to the expected air strike. She had reached her preassigned rescue spot close under the southern shores of Woleai when a hostile plane was picked up by radar at 19,000 yards. Tense eyes watched the radar screen as the plane's pip indicated that it was moving straight toward the sub. Another dive? Sam, leaning on the bridge cowling, stood pat. Then, at a range of 14,000 yards, the plane changed course and flew off. The *Harder* continued its figure-eight zigzag at its assigned station, unperturbed, wide open to enemy eyes and ready to save aviators. If and when they came. But where were they?

Hours went by. The sun rose. Fortunately, no Jap flyboys rose with it. Three hours. Four hours. Where were our zoomies? Five hours. Then, at 0825, just when Sam and Frank were speculating if the first of April strike would turn into an April fool joke, radar reported: "Solid cluster of pips, large flights of planes at 36,000 yards and coming in fast from the southwest." The stage was set. The show was on—and what a show it turned out to be!

Soon after the pips appeared on the radar screen, the bridge watch and lookouts on the shears saw and heard the rush and roar of a man-made hurricane of carrier planes—fighters, bombers, and heavy torpedo bombers with giant bombs in their bellies.

Like a long-tailed cyclone they came in a heavy black line from the western horizon—scores, hundreds of them. Soon the din of their engines and the whine of their props filled the air, for most of them came in rather low. In fact, the fighters, because of the then prevailing overcast over Woleai, were almost at deck level. Even before their machine guns began to hose the airstrip and surrounding areas with lead to drive the ack-ack crews from their guns, Sam heard the angry bark of the AA guns—this time the Japs were ready.

As the planes approached, the *Harder's* radio men, under the direction of Ray Levin, established voice communication with a flight leader. And, no sooner had that contact been established than a frantic voice broke in: "Fighter plane, burning, falling into the drink. The pilot chuted out. He is now in the water—about five miles to the north of the second island west of Woleai."

The *Harder* waited for no more. A quick glance at the chart showed that the shortest course to the downed zoomie lay around the northeast point of Woleai. The OOD rang for full speed and Sam set a course by nautical eye while Frank cut in the ship's position by periscope bearings. The race to save a life was on.

Subsequent calls from the aviator's squadron leader, who was evidently sticking by him, reported that the zoomie was drifting with the wind toward the reef-bordered island mentioned before.

Studying the chart he had brought to the bridge, Sam saw that the downed flyer must be drifting toward the island of Tagaulap, an uninhabited strip of sand and coral covered by dense jungle vegetation. Further checking the chart, he found that fairly deep water, 20 fathoms or better, reached almost to the reef that skirted the shoreline five hundred yards off shore. If the man survived until Sam could reach him, there might be a good chance of picking him up—provided, of course, Jap opposition did not make it impossible for the sub to stay on surface.

Naturally, in-shore work could be highly dangerous if the *Harder* were caught in shallow water by enemy planes. It could be the end for the sub and all hands. But, if such thoughts passed through the Skipper's mind, he kept them well concealed. He probably calculated his risks, as he always did, and figured that the Jap planes would have other problems to worry about. It would take all of three hours to make the run, even at full speed, around the east coast of Woleai to the spot where the aviator was reported down. But let us turn to the *Harder's* log for Sam's own highly interesting story of the incident:

"0840—Made full speed on four engines. From here on, the picture in the skies looked like a gigantic Cleveland Air Show. With dozens of fighters forming a comfortable umbrella above us, we watched a show that made the Hollywood Colossals seem tame. We rounded the southeast coast of Woleai one to two miles off the beach and had the perfect ringside seat.

"The plastering that the airmen gave this Jap base was terrific! Bombs of all sizes rained on every structure on the island. Several buildings seemed to be lifted and thrown high in the air. Causeways between the various islands were bombed. Oil or gasoline storage tanks blew up, covering the islands with heavy clouds of black smoke. The runway on the island was hit time and again with large and small bombs. It was hard to believe that anything could be left on the islands after the first waves of planes had gone over, and yet some bursts of AA fire continued to meet the planes on each attack.

"The bombers hit Woleai from the south, waited for the smoke to clear, reformed, and then gave it the works from east-west courses! Fighters seemed to hit the place from all directions, peeling off from high above and diving straight into the AA fire that still persisted. Many looked as if they would go right on thru the blanket of smoke and crash on the islands, but all managed to pull out just above the trees. Fires blazed intermittently on Woleai and most of its adjacent islands, and gradually the AA defense was reduced to a few sporadic bursts.

"Fighters now zoomed the *Harder* one mile off the NE corner of Woleai and guided us toward the downed pilot.

"1145—He was finally sighted on the NW tip of the second island to the west of Woleai. Battle surface stations were manned, the ship flooded down and maneuvered into a spot about 1500 yards off the beach. White water was breaking over the shoals only 20 yards in front of the ship and the fathometer had ceased to record. Planes now advised us that if rescue looked too difficult from here (and it *did*), a better approach might be made from another direction.

"Backed off to make approach from another angle. The aviator had been standing on the beach and was now observed to fall and lie there outstretched on the sand. His collapse was undoubtedly due mainly to physical exhaustion, but also to the disappointment in seeing his chances of rescue fade away. We were then advised by the plane that further air reconnaissance showed the first approach best after all. Reversed course and headed back at full speed.

"Made ready the rubber boat (no paddles were aboard), selected Lieutenant Sam Logan, J. W. Thomason, SC1c, and Francis X. Ryan, MoMM1c, from a large group of volunteers and maneuvered the ship in for a second attempt at rescue. Moved in again until the forward torpedo room reported, 'Bottom scraping forward' (soundings at zero fathoms) and worked both screws to keep the bow against the reef while preventing the ship from getting broadside to the waves.

"1200—The three volunteers dove over the side and commenced pushing and towing their rubber boat toward the beach about 1200 yards away. A line was payed out from the sub to the rubber raft in order to pull it back from the beach. Meanwhile one of the planes had dropped another rubber boat to the stranded aviator who got in and commenced feebly paddling it to sea against the tide. When the rescue party reached a spot where they could stand up, Thomason was directed to remain with the rubber boat while Logan and Ryan waded on through the surf toward the aviator. Both were in the breakers now most of the time and their feet and legs were badly cut by the coral reefs. After about half an hour, Logan and Ryan, alternately swimming and wading, reached the aviator whose raft had meanwhile drifted farther away. By this time he was thoroughly exhausted.

"They put him in the raft and by alternately pushing and swimming headed back toward their rubber boat from which a line led to the submarine about 500 yards away. Meanwhile a float plane (also attempting the rescue) taxied over the line to the raft and it parted! . . . The entire rescue party was now stranded. Thomason was then recalled and managed to swim back to the sub after a hard battle against the tide.

"Another volunteer swimmer, Freeman Paquet, Jr., GM1c, then dove over the side and finally managed to swim a line to the three men standing just in-shore of the heavy breakers. This line was made fast to the raft and, little by little, the four men were pulled through the breakers and brought back to the ship.

"Throughout the entire rescue, the cooperation of the aviators was superb. They kept up a continuous pounding of the islands by bombs and flew in low to strafe the Japs and divert their attention from the rescue. In spite of this, Jap snipers concealed in the trees along the beach commenced shooting at the ship and rescue party and bullets whined over the bridge, uncomfortably close. The rescue could never have been attempted without the protection afforded by the planes.

"Too much praise cannot be given to the officer and the three men who effected this rescue. Its daring execution, under the noses of the Japs and subject to sniper fire from the beach, can be classified as a truly courageous accomplishment, and the rescued aviator—Ensign John R. Galvin—though physically exhausted, showed a character that refused to admit defeat. It is a privilege to serve with men such as these.

"This account has been written in considerable detail, partly to portray the spectacular air smashing of a Jap base and partly in sheer pride of the volunteers who carried out the rescue."

There, in Captain Dealey's own rather too concise language, is the naked and unadorned story of which Admiral Chester W. Nimitz, a submariner from way back and the Navy's Big Boss in the Pacific, said: "The Commander-in-Chief, Pacific Fleet, considers the performance of the Commanding Officer, the Officers and Crew of the U.S.S. *Harder* one of the outstanding rescue feats accomplished to date in the Pacific area and in keeping with the high traditions of the entire submarine force.

"The cooperation between the attacking force and the rescue vessel is an example of a courageous fighting spirit and mutual support doctrine which will enable the Naval Service to overcome the greatest odds in successfully accomplishing its mission."

Neither Admiral Nimitz nor Comdr. Dealey took time out to interpret to the non-initiated what it means for a Captain to put his ship into dreadful jeopardy by placing its nose on a reef to hold it in position while all hands risk their lives to save the life of one single nameless flyer— and willingly. Nor do they relate the deadly dangers that could develop by sudden attack from land, sea, or air; nor the possibility that after a lapse of more than three hours, the real zoomie might have been caught by skulking Japs and a Jap put in his place to act as bait to draw the submarine and its rescue crew into potentially dangerous waters. So many things could have happened that it is nothing short of a miracle that none of them did.

Chief among those who lost a lot of cold sweat during this incident was Frank Lynch. With Logan, the *Harder's* diving and engineering officer, out on the reef directing the rescue of a helpless flier, Frank humbly offered multiple prayers for the safety of all concerned. Logan and his companions would be mighty hard men to replace. Of course, so far as working the screws so as to prevent the ship from being pushed broadside onto the reef by the breakers, Frank had cool and able Carl Finney to lean on. But even so, the outcome of the situation leaned pretty

Hellcat

much on how much of a J-factor the *Harder* had at its disposal. As things turned out, it had enough to bring the ordeal to a safe and happy ending for all concerned.

It is seldom that historians, who are also interested in the human aspects of their subject, find such a first-hand story of an incident as we discovered through the aid of the *Dallas Morning News*. It is reprinted here with permission of Mr. Ted Dealey, publisher of that newspaper. In a letter, sent about a year following the end of the war to Jack Krueger, City Editor of the paper of which Sam Dealey's uncle, George Bannerman Dealey, was a founder and long-time publisher, Lieut. John Galvin, USNR, the flier rescued by the *Harder*, gave a full account of a zoomie's view of the incident.

I was a member of Fighting Squadron Eight, based aboard the U.S.S. *Bunker Hill* and assigned to the first wave fighter sweep to go in and knock out all planes in the air and on the ground so that the dive bombers could go to work on the place.

Sixteen of the large carriers were to level everything on the island and I later found out there were no more targets after the first two hours.

A low cloud cover had forced us to make our strafing runs flat and consequently much slower. The four of us in our Hellcat division went sporting up the runway with all guns blazing indicating 25–50 feet off the concrete. I was firing at a plane when I was peppered with 20-mm. cannon shells. I heard the shells hit and immediately kicked the plane over and out to sea.

The engine was running smoothly, but smoke and then fire began to fill the cockpit so I had to bail out. Since both wing tanks were on fire I was afraid to roll it on its back, so out I went, head first. My excessive speed of 200 knots did not give me clearance time and the tail hit me in the back and all along the right side of my body.

That is all I remember until I suddenly found myself about to hit the water. I grabbed for the rip cord and it came free with no pull. At the same time I looked up and the chute was already open. Evidently, when I hit the tail, it tore the chute pack open because Lieut. Brown, the section leader, said the chute opened immediately after I left the plane.

While I was going down, Brown told Lieut. Harlan Gustafson that I had been shot down.

In the meantime I hit the water and after being dragged a good distance by the chute, I got out of the harness. I pulled the toggles for my life jacket only to have the air bubble up around me. It was torn from the impact and so was the rubber life boat!

There was only one thing left to do and that was swim for the line of trees visible on the crest of the waves. When I started to swim, I found that my back, right arm, and leg were hurt. By lying on my back and keeping my arms under water, I could keep swimming.

I got cramps several times but I was able to massage them off. There are periods of time I do not remember until I finally realized I was going head over heels on the bottom. After banging my head on a rock, I kicked free of the bottom to find myself in water only shoulder-high. Gus estimated that I went down about five miles from the island.

The water's edge was as far as I could go and I guess I collapsed. I had been in the water from zero eight-thirty to twelve-thirty. All this time, Lieut. Gustafson, along with Lieut. Brown and Lieut. Allen, were circling me and communicating with the submarine which was on the other side of the island. By repeated zooming they indicated my position to the submarine.

It was a welcome sight as the four men pushed me alongside the *Harder*. They helped me down through the hatches and into the Captain's cabin. From then on, for thirty-three days, I have never been treated so royally and kindly in my life.

Commander Dealey came in to welcome me aboard and to inspect my back and arm and leg. He broke out some medical brandy for me which was like swallowing a handful of needles after all that salt water. Then came a nice hot bath and I was told that was my last for the next ten days.

Lieut. Frank Lynch, the Executive Officer from Devon, Pa., gave up his bunk for me for the afternoon and evening. Then Ensign Sampson gave up his bunk for an army cot for the entire cruise.

Commander Dealey informed me later that he was not sure I was an American aviator. By then I had no helmet or life jacket, and my anti-blackout suit was wet and consequently looked black. Also my face was dark from sunburn . . . besides this, a native was squatting on the beach only a short distance from me, calmly watching the proceedings.

This naturally gave Commander Dealey every right to suspect some enemy trick. In fact, every gun on the sub was trained in my direction during the approach of the rescue party, just in case any false moves were made.

*        *        *

Through the entire rescue operation, Sam maintained the coolness of the proverbial cucumber—an apparent composure of mind which few, if any, of the *Harder's* complement shared. Least of all the four men—Logan, Thomason, Ryan, and Paquet—who had gone ashore to fetch Galvin aboard the sub. They knew—in fact the Skipper had told them before they went over the side with the rubber boat—that in event of trouble, the *Harder* would have no other course than to get into deeper water as soon as possible and leave them in the lurch.

Unhappiest man aboard was probably Frank Lynch. Although he, as Exec., had relinquished his duties as Chief Engineer and Diving Officer to Sam Logan, he felt a deep sense of personal responsibility toward the engines that were fishtailing the props ever so slowly to help the *Harder* keep her nose on the reef and avoid a beam-on stranding. Said Frank:

"Seems to me that I lost at least ten pounds during those sixty-four minutes we sat with our bow high on the reef while the stern whipped up white water as it banged up and down with each wave. It was sheer unadulterated agony. Sure, I'm glad we rescued Galvin; and I'd probably do it again—but I wouldn't like it."

When Galvin was aboard in the capable hands of Pharmacist's Mate Angelo Lo Cascio, and all who had no business on deck were properly below, the *Harder* reversed her motors, gently pulled her nose off its unorthodox resting place, and headed out to sea. All this while, Jap fliers had been kept grounded by the vigilant air umbrella provided by carrier planes. Not until 1630, about half an hour after the *Harder* had surfaced following a lengthy trim dive, did a Nip bomber appear. From a distance of nine miles, when he was picked up by radar, he closed quickly to six miles, whereupon the *Harder* executed a crash dive that took her to a 140-foot depth in record time. No bombs. On the heels of this experience—for Sam thought that the Woleai airstrip was surely beyond early use—Sam kept submerged until after evening chow was over at 2030. Soon after he sent his routine report to Comsubpac.

After the excitement of 1 April, the days stretched as uniformly dull as cheap pearls on a cotton string. No action. Only endless patrols across various traffic lanes—from Truk to the Marianas—from Rabaul to Saipan—from Saipan to Woleai. Nothing. For eleven solid days no sight on the seas but fish; no sight in the skies but seabirds and occasional enemy planes.

But the doldrums of inaction did not put an entirely paralyzing hand on those aboard the *Harder*. Where and when it could, the training course went on—particularly among the officers. When the second string plotting team was on duty, Sam Logan took Frank Lynch's place as Second in Command so one more officer other than Frank would know the procedure of approach and attack. Ramrod was a quick learner. So was Buckner in the former's post as Chief Engineer and Diving Officer. At such times, Finney or Levin worked the TDC.

Meanwhile, day by day, Frank Lynch got the hang of the job of CO because, as the patrols piled up, Sam more and more became the attack specialist whose job was to smack torpedoes into targets. Not that Sam did not conduct inspections—or roam the ship with eagle eyes for weak spots. But on those occasions when he noted anything wrong, he would not call the chief concerned to task. Instead he would stare at whatever troubled him a little longer than usual—and go on. But that was enough. Whatever Sam looked at was picked apart and put together until it was 100 per cent of what it should be.

He seldom issued orders that did not concern the strategic or tactical operation of the vessel. The effect of this attitude, born of his faith that all hands knew their jobs and would anticipate all requirements, gave the *Harder's* officers, chiefs, and men a strength and stamina of morale that is seldom found. Sam was always, day or night, cheerfully available for any kind of duty call ranging from reading the steady day-and-night trickle of messages to being summoned to the bridge, conning tower, or radar screens.

He was always cheerful and talkative at mealtime, and during normal night runs he would take part in the time-honored wardroom songfest. But the rest of the time he spent in his stateroom. In the daytime he would read books, re-read letters from Wena, the children, or the family in Dallas. Time and again he would look at his small but precious collection of snapshots from home. But, on patrols, he did not write letters. He evidently wanted to keep his mind free for the job at hand. At night there was no reading for Sam Dealey. He needed his eyes adjusted for night vision. Hence, he would lie on the bunk in his darkened stateroom. At such times, as his letters revealed, he would think with deep concentration of Wena, Joan, David, and Barbara Lee. He would actually walk down memory lane, year by year and month by month, re-living in his dark little cubby hole of a cabin the highlights of his years of happiness and love with Wena and their children; with his mother and the Dealey clan in Dallas. There was pain as well as pleasure in these journeys into yesterday, but with Sam they became an almost unbreakable habit. At night, on his narrow, solitary bunk, they were, for their brief durations, stimulating substitutes for reality. When the *Harder* ran on the surface, Sam would tune in on the ship's radio receiving wave. On this patrol, radio reception was truly wonderful—San Francisco, Tokyo, Moscow, Berlin, London, and occasionally, Paris came in at the touch of a knob. Sam's favorite broadcasts were music and news. To him, top newscaster on the air was William Winter in San Francisco.

While on patrol, Sam's favorite reading and writing were the patrol reports of other submarine captains and the writing of his own. As literature, submarine war patrols are in a class all their own. These concisely written but graphic documents record—or imply—virtually every combat action and thought of the skippers who write them. New tactical or strategic ideas are introduced in them and the results, when such ideas are tried out, furnish valuable practical information. Perusal of Sam's own logs produces ample evidence of his initiative and keen analytical talent. He seldom failed to get directly to the heart of a puzzling situation or an unusual attack set-up, and his handling of torpedo firing problems was nothing short of uncanny. This last talent, according to Frank Lynch, stemmed from his remarkable visual sense.

"He had the vision and mind of an artist," Frank told me. "His imagination pictured situations so vividly and scenes photographed themselves so clearly on the retina of his mind that he really did not need a TDC solution for making his attacks."

On combat submarines, time drags and spirits lag when day on day drifts slowly past without any of the sort of action that acts as adrenalin on the brave hearts of submariners. After a false chase on 12 April, when the heavily protected fox escaped the pursuing hounds, Sam wondered what he could do to restore the happy humors of his crewmen. Then, during the night of 12–13 April, Levin brought him a message from Comsubpac to the effect that Admiral King had lifted the ban against "wasting" torpedoes on destroyers. The time had come, among other things, to tear down the destroyer screens which the Japs were able to put around their fleet units.

Sam kept his own counsel on this, to him, good news and thought out a plan for action which he put into effect the following afternoon. At 1300, as the *Harder* was loafing along the Guam-Woleai route at two-engine speed on the surface, he posted his best lookouts—Brostrom, Majuri, Studstill, and Paquet—the latter three all gunners mates with good shooting eyes and therefore good lookouts. Equipped with high-power binoculars, each man was told to watch his sector of the sky without even blinking an eye and to report everything bigger than a seagull.

Keith Phillips was OOD with Carl Finney, who was one of the best bridge watchers aboard the *Harder*, as JOOD. Lloyd Sommershield, Signalman 1st class of Malvourne, Florida, was quartermaster. Below at the radar screens, Hi Hatfield himself was at the post with Ben Medley of Austin, Texas, at the dials. By virtue of special warning from the Skipper—but without knowing why—there was an air of almost electrified alertness throughout the *Harder;* an air of expectancy that had lifted the spirits of all hands to concert pitch. Sam himself went to the bridge the moment bridge watch and lookouts had been posted. His binoculars hung by their strap around his neck; his cap sat at its usual jaunty angle atop his closely cropped, dark hair.

Time went by as the *Harder*—a gray ship on a gray sea under a gray sky—nosed southward leaving a wide white wake on the mournful looking sea, much like a streamer at a Chinese funeral.

1330—Nothing happened.

1400—Nothing happened.

1430—Nothing happened.

The men of the *Harder* were just starting to wonder what sort of shenanigans, if any, their Old Man was up to. Of a lesser man, some of them might have thought that the heat and the boredom had temporarily softened his head. But not Sam, the Torpedo Totin' Texan.

1445—Hatfield reported: "SJ radar has pip on a plane; bearing—280 relative; distance, ten miles."

Sam acknowledged the information. Saw to it that the lookout concerned was watching in the proper direction. Made a similar check on the bridge watch. And went on pulling on his short-stemmed, dry-smoking pipe. No warning to the diving stations because of the plane. No sign of impending submergence. The *Harder* pushed on, its Diesels purring in rhythmic song. In a few moments the radar pip disappeared. On Sam's face was a strange expression of disappointment.

1446—Carl Finney sang out: "There's another plane, Captain. Bearing zero two zero, relative; distance, four miles."

Squint-eyed, Sam watched the plane. A smile curled around his pipestem when he saw the plane change course and head toward the sub. He waited to make sure that he was not wrong about this—that the plane had seen and was approaching the *Harder*. Being sure, he called out the command: "Clear the bridge," adding in a louder tone, "dive, dive."

He stood at the conning tower hatch as the klaxon

squawked its alarm and lookouts and bridge watch dropped below. White water was already washing the *Harder's* foredeck as Sam slid down the ladder and Sommershield pulled the hatch lanyard and spun the securing wheel.

"Give her hard right rudder. All ahead full. Take her to 100 feet," came Sam's order. To Frank Lynch, who had manned the conning tower—just in case—Sam nodded and said: "Come below with your gang down to the chart table. We'll have a little council of war."

When all concerned were gathered around the table on the main gyro top, Sam looked around the circle with eyes that had dancing highlights of sheer deviltry. In order that all hands might hear what he had to say, Sam had Ray Levin pass him the public address microphone. "We've been on a little fishing expedition this afternoon," he began. "The *Harder* was the hook and the bait. And the fish we were after was an airplane pilot who would sight us and radio back to his base for a destroyer to come and give us a dose of ashcans."

There were grins and understanding nods around the chart table. This prospect of relief from the monotony of inaction lifted spirits throughout the ship.

Sam continued: "There just aren't any worthwhile targets around here, so I aim to catch us a Jap tincan." The Dealey fighting grin was in full play as Sam looked around the circle of his immediate listeners. "Some of you may think that DD's are dangerous game and more deadly to subs than we are to them. Don't you believe it. An American sub can put a Nip DD down for the count any day. . . . And if youall don't believe me, I sure hope I'll have a chance to prove it."

Some of his control room audience looked a little dubious at this, but Dealey continued: "This is the plan. We know how the Japs work. They always comb the spot where a sub was last seen. So, to oblige them, we'll stick around, at slow speed and periscope depth, until Mr. Deedee shows up. Then we'll go on from there. Until that time, we'll have to play a waiting game. But one to ten across the board that Jap destroyer will be here in a couple of hours."

For a while sky and sea remained empty to the *Harder's* occasional periscope peeks. Then, at 1610, a land-type medium bomber arrived upon the scene and began circling the area in wide sweeps. Its distance from the submerged *Harder* was about two miles. Shortly, and to Sam's surprise, the aircraft headed north and out of sight.

Five minutes later—at a distance of some six miles from her diving point—the *Harder* sighted the masts of a destroyer.

"Battle Stations! Torpedoes!" came Sam's crisp order. Within seconds the *Harder's* first-string fire control team was at conning tower stations. Tom Buckner had succeeded at Sam Logan's old post at the TDC; Keith Phillips and Phil Sampson were at the plotting table. Frank Lynch, as Assistant Attack Officer, was at the periscope to handle the approach phase while Sam leaned against the bridge hatch ladder waiting for his entrance cue from Frank. In sinkings, Sam's role had become much like that of the toreador in the bullring. He did not step forward until the victim of the play was ready for the plunge of the sword into its heart.

By means of occasional periscope looks, it was established that the destroyer was no old, obsolete tincan such as the Nips ordinarily used for escort vessels. By means of the ONI Identification Book, Sam learned that his opponent was no less a foe than the brand-new 1850-ton *Inazuma* of the Fubuki class. (He missed his guess by only 100 tons; it was the 1950-ton *Ikazuchi*.)

Sam took over at the attack periscope; ordered one-third speed ahead, and, at frequent intervals, corrected his course to keep the *Harder's* nose toward the enemy so as to present the smallest target.

Throughout the approach, Sam kept a vigilant eye around the horizon for approaching aircraft. But, much to his surprise, none appeared. Evidently this destroyer was completely on its own, with no aircraft to guide or support it. Had a Jap plane been aloft, the chances are that it would have spotted the submarine's dark shadow in the clear tropic waters while running at periscope depth.

There being no need for worry on this score, Sam took his time for several reasons: sound conditions were excellent, so he did not want to risk detection by speeding up his props; he wanted to conserve battery power in case this should involve being held down most of the night; and, lastly, he desired to gain the advantage of low visibility conditions at twilight. He felt that the DD would make a determined effort to find the Yankee sub and would remain in the vicinity in the hope of catching him on surface at night.

Finally, at 1847, with the range down to 5000 yards, Sam ordered: "Make ready four tubes forward and four tubes aft!" He was taking no chances of losing this prize through misses or dud torpedoes.

Yard by yard—as the destroyer's pinging grew louder—the sub crept closer. At 3200 yards, it seemed that the Jap's echo ranging pings were bouncing off the sub's hull with deadly, maddening regularity. Wilbur Clark, of New Hampton, Missouri, who had developed into a skilled sound operator on this, his first cruise in the *Harder*, picked up a good turn count of the enemy's props at 2600 yards. "About 135 to 140 rpms—14 to 15 knots, Cap'n," he reported.

At this moment, the destroyer was zigging toward the *Harder* on a course that would take it from 800 to 1000 yards from the sub.

"Left full rudder," snapped Sam. A swift periscope sighting and Buckner's TDC data showed that the destroyer would pass the sub's bow at 900 yards in a matter of seconds.

During his last sightings, Sam found the low rays of the setting sun interfered with his vision. This called for the use of a sun-filter on the eyepiece, always a nuisance. Still, it did not interfere with Sam getting a good look at his target as the torpedoes raced forth from the *Harder's* tubes and white-trailed their way to the DD. Later, in one of his best descriptive moods, Sam made a colorful log entry on the climax of his attack:

"1859—Range now 900 yards. Commenced firing. Expended four torpedoes and one Jap destroyer! The four bow shots were fired at mean range of 900 yards, with a 2-degree diverging spread, track angle 80 port, mean gyro angle about 25 left, torpedo depth set at 6 feet.

"Just before the first torpedo hit, the Japs must have sighted the wakes, for they could be seen running in all directions. Forty seconds after the first shot, the first torpedo was heard and observed to hit—directly beneath the large raked stack. Seven seconds later the second torpedo hit. The target was immediately enveloped in a cloud of heavy black smoke and flame, its bow dropped rapidly, and the ship took a list of about 30 degrees to port.

"Ordered full right rudder and full speed to get clear of the destroyer before its depth charges started going off. At range of about 400 yards, slowed to two-thirds speed and started taking pictures through the periscope.

"About two minutes after being struck, the destroyer's bow dropped under, the tail came out, with both propellers fanning the air, and about two hundred Japs started clambering aft. No boats could have been launched. The tail now rose higher and higher, from 30 degrees to 60, then finally, as the angle got steeper, they began dropping into the water like so many ants. All officers in the conning tower and half a dozen of the crew observed these last minutes of the enemy ship.

"It disappeared from view just four minutes after it was hit. Now the Jap's own depth charges began to explode and it is doubted if any of its crew survived after this. The *Harder* was opening the range at about 500 yards when the depth charges started going off, but the blasts rocked us, shattered light bulbs, and threw loose gear around. Most of the crew were convinced that we were being bombed by aircraft, but no planes were in sight. Increased depth to 150 feet, made reload, and returned to periscope depth. Nothing in sight.

"Cleared the area at two-thirds speed and waited for darkness before coming up—in case the destroyer had been able to get off a distress signal, which is very unlikely."

For the first time after any sinking, Sam seemed really elated. "You see, Frank," he said to his Second-in-Command, "they really aren't invulnerable. They won't float with a couple of holes in their bottoms. . . . Well, there's one for the old *Reuben James*—and a down-payment for some of the bad times they gave us off Honshu."

But, for all Dealey's feeling of triumph and for all his hatred of Tojo's depth-charge-tossing tincans, when the *Ikazuchi* rolled on her side and hopeless Japanese sailors were desperately clinging to her slippery sides, Sam could watch no longer and walked away from the periscope.

Following this brilliant victory, spirits soared again in the *Harder*. Sam's dispatch to me that he had "expended four torpedoes and one Jap destroyer" roused plenty of enthusiasm at my Headquarters. Statistical reports showed that, up to this time, some sixty-four enemy DD's had been sunk. This left barely enough to screen the Jap Fleet's heavy ships. Further reductions would leave them none for convoy escort duty. Admiral Ernie King, Comdr.-in-Chief U.S. Fleets, figured that now was the time to concentrate on sinking destroyers and thus make enemy merchant ships—and major fleet units, as well—easier to attack.

At 0642 of 16 April the *Harder*, with her batteries chock-a-block, submerged for another day of patrolling. Another hot, empty day no doubt, within sight of the same old green and sun-blistered Woleai. Nothing to do but eat and watch the clock between chow times. And to heck with it!

But at 0825, as the *Harder* ran slightly north of the atoll, the periscope Watch Officer sounded a hurry call for "Captain to the conning tower."

On his arrival, Carl Finney, the OOD, reported to Sam that a medium AK, of about 3500 tons, was in sight coming out of the Woleai lagoon. This ship, which had been lying doggo within the lagoon's protecting reefs, had long been an eyesore to Sam and his men.

"Sure looks," he said to Lynch after a quick peep, "as if our long and none too patient waiting is about to be rewarded. Range about 6000 yards—angle on the bow, 35 degrees—looks quite promising, eh, Frank?"

The Exec. ran the 'scope up—and down again so quickly that the disk jockey almost pulled the operating lever out of its socket. "That AK," he whispered, "has company. Two blasted Fubuki class destroyers—one on its port and one on its starboard quarter!"

"Really," chuckled Sam. "Say, this is getting interesting. Those Fubuki destroyers are just our size. Maybe we can take another one."

"Yes, sir," answered Lynch with confidence which, however, became a bit dubious after another periscope peep. "But this time there's air cover, Captain. Moreover— moreover, whatever wind there was is dying down and the sea is getting glassy smooth."

"Hm!" Sam gave the situation a swift but thorough thinking over. Lynch was right. At this particular moment, chances were not favorable for an attack. As reflected by his log entry, these were the thoughts that ran through Sam's swiftly turning mental gears: "This picture stimulated the imagination. Here was a lightly loaded merchantman, heavily escorted by two large destroyers and provided with air coverage which was to remain until sunset! What made her valuable enough to justify such heavy protection? Or are the Japs just getting very, very short of cargo carriers? At any rate, our chances of getting another enemy combat ship looked good. Commenced trailing the targets at two-thirds speed and the chase was on!

"The convoy's first apparent base course was 270 (headed for Palau) and the AK was zigging radically, which gave her an advance of only 6 knots (she was making 10) along the base course. Our trailing speed of 4 knots enabled us to keep her in sight for a long time.

"1228—Smoke of the targets now just barely visible

through the periscope, and Woleai atoll could no longer be seen astern. Surfaced with two engines on propulsion and one on a battery charge (our fourth engine was out of commission) and continued pursuit of the smoke."

By the uninitiated, submarine actions against merchantmen are usually regarded as hit-and-sink affairs. While that is generally true, there are notable exceptions. Such an exception was the long-drawn chase staged by the *Harder* in pursuit of the AK protected by its sea and airborne escorts. Sam had a hunch that, come nightfall, his most formidable adversary, the medium bomber, would return to its base—Jap planes of that type seldom engaged in night flying. While this would leave two destroyers to deal with, Sam was willing to risk their depth charges.

For the rest of the morning of that 16 April, and throughout the afternoon, the sub trailed the three-ship procession either on surface or submerged, always close enough to keep the AK's plume of smoke in sight. Three times she had to dive to escape searching aircraft, but on each occasion she slid beneath the waves undetected by the flyfly boys. At dark, the *Harder* surfaced and pulled closer. Covering this period, the log reports:

"2020—Merchantman contacted by radar at range of 29,000 yards. The night was not dark enough to attempt a surface approach, particularly with the thought in mind that the destroyers probably were equipped with radar; and there was insufficient visibility for a periscope attack before moonrise. Moonrise was scheduled for 0230; so decided to make a wide run around the enemy's port flank, track from ahead while figuring out his zigzag plan, and attack from his port bow at periscope depth with the targets silhouetted against the rising moon. [Sam was a wizard at taking advantage of situations of this kind.]

"2100—Settled down to a long night of it. Stationed 'second team' of fire control party, and had 'first team' turn in for some sleep before the attack.

"2300—Targets were now abeam to starboard at range of 15,000 yards. No evidence of enemy radar and nothing to indicate that they suspected our presence."

Sam's first line fire control team got a good four hours rest while the second, made up of Levin, Brock, and Finney, with the latter on the TDC, carried on. At 0130, Buckner, Phillips, and Sampson were roused out of their sweet slumbers. Sam had called Battle Stations. But many plots and changes had to run their course before the hour of attack struck at 0335. This was mainly due to the complications set up by the two destroyers which constantly changed the picture.

Neither of the DD's were pinging. Instead, they resorted to the use of slow speed and listening for submarine propeller sounds—a trick at which the Japs were amazingly expert and accurate. To provide constant listening, one destroyer would take position about 1000 yards ahead of the AK, while the other—its engines slowed—would drop back past the AK and listen intently for the slow beat of submarine propellers and for characteristic submarine noises such as bow planes, stern planes, and pumps. This operation made it almost impossible for the *Harder* to keep track of both DD's at the same time.

The *Harder* tried to maneuver into position for attack from the port side and thus keep the targets in the moonstreak. Even though the light was feeble, because of overcasts and frequent rain squalls, it did serve to silhouette the targets.

At 0321, Sam was in a perfect position for a 3000-yard shot at the merchantman, but our Texan did not want him. He had his heart, if not his sights, set on bagging one or both of the destroyers. But how to do it? That was the question. However, Fate apparently willed it otherwise. The DD on the AK's port quarter, in the most favorable position—from Sam's viewpoint—was swallowed up in a rain squall. With this much-wanted bird hidden in a rainy bush and the other DD nowhere in sight, Sam decided to take the bird in hand, meaning the AK, now within easy reach at 1800 yards. So, before it was too late, at 0335, four bow torpedoes streaked toward the merchantman. But let us turn to Sam's own interesting word picture of what took place:

"About one minute after firing, I heard and saw one torpedo strike the cargo vessel just under its bridge. Flames and heavy black smoke shot up, covering the entire forward part of the ship. I shifted search then to the port quarter of the AK, hoping to find the destroyer. I didn't find it until one of the torpedoes did! A second explosion (nine seconds after the first) was seen and heard striking the destroyer.

"A large sheet of flame, similar to that made by the first torpedo, momentarily covered the destroyer, but the target was still in the rain squall and I could not tell where it was hit. 'Timers' in the conning tower and both torpedo rooms now clocked both of the other torpedoes exploding at the end of their runs. The periscope was now swung back to the cargo ship which was furiously ablaze. Looked around for the other destroyer but it could not be seen. Ordered full right rudder to clear the torpedo tracks and went to deep submergence.

"Reached 300 feet before the depth-charging started. Received eight depth charges over a period of the next two hours. The propellers of the destroyer were heard to pass directly overhead three separate times, but its depth charges were released on only one of these occasions. None was too close and no damage was sustained."

When the *Harder*, on 17 April, made a cautious return to periscope depth at 0620, Sam saw, in the light of the early day, the sinking AK topped by towers of intensely white, brilliant, and almost smokeless flames. There was no sign of the damaged destroyer. Still later in the morning, when conditions allowed, the *Harder* made a thorough search of the area. No signs of sinking ships. No survivors. Both vessels, it seemed, had vanished. So, having no proof, Sam claimed only one AK sunk and one Fubuki destroyer damaged.

Thus ended the long—almost round-the-clock chase of a set of targets which Sam was just too stubborn a fighter to let get away.

During the early morning hours of 20 April, while cruising some ten miles north of Woleai, Sam took inventory of his fuel and decided, after a conference with Frank Lynch, that he had just enough left to make the 3300-mile run to Freemantle, with maybe a bit to spare. It had been a long cruise from a mileage standpoint. First 3000 miles from Pearl to Woleai; next 4600 miles of cruising in the patrol area. Now a long way to down under. If he had a couple of thousand gallons left on reaching Australia, he would be lucky.

"We'll end the patrol tomorrow or the day after," said Sam, "but, before we bow out, I'd like to add my bit to the case of war nerves that the Woleai Japs must be having."

What was coming now, Frank wondered. He had great respect for the wide-ranging combat ingenuity of his Skipper.

"How about this? At the crack of dawn, we'll make a short, fast in-shore run and bombard the airstrip with high-explosive shells from our new four-inch gun. It'll raise heck among the Japs and I'm sure that all our boys are so fed up on Woleai that they'll get a big bang out of trying to blow it off the map. What say?"

Frank agreed heartily on every point. "Let's give them a real barrage," he suggested. "Not only with the four-inch but also with the 20-mm guns. Those little guns can put up a lot of noise and maybe do some real damage. At any rate, it will be good for the morale of our gunners."

Making a rough sketch of the main island with pencil on paper, after summoning Tom Buckner who was also Gunnery Officer, Sam drew a loop-shaped line that began north of Woleai, flanked the north coast for about 1000 yards, and then doubled upon itself out to the north. "We will time it so that we are within 2000 yards of the beach at about 0630. We'll allow not more than five minutes and thirty rounds of four-inch ammo for the shooting run."

"That will take an awful lot of swift handling of the stuff by the shell brigade," injected Lynch.

"I know that, Frank," replied Sam, "and I have solved that end of the problem. Just before daylight—say about 0545—we'll pass the ammo up on deck and stack those shells up like cordwood right handy to the gun. All the loaders will have to do is reach and grab."

Frank laughed as he observed, "But suppose a Betty comes snooping around and we have to dive with all that stuff on deck?"

"Well," soothed Sam genially, "that's what the War College boys call a calculated risk."

Neptune was with the *Harder* that morning as Davy Jones looked the other way. The shells were stacked on deck and the gunners—Thomason, Ryan, and Paquet—and the loaders were in their places as the submarine, at full speed on the electric motors, raced silently toward the beach. A kindly rain squall cooperated by deluging the ship as she bored in toward her target, thus hiding her from enemy lookouts until the planned radar range of 2000 yards had been reached, when the downpour suddenly ceased. The submarine swung hard left and the drenched loaders and gunners hastily dried their eyes and hands on towels passed up from the control room.

The island was nicely silhouetted in the morning twilight by the light of the rising sun and, as the ship swung onto her northwesterly course at 0627, Sam gave the command: "Commence firing!"

All hell broke loose then, with the big gun barking its hate at a rate of about ten shots to the minute, shell cases clanging onto the deck, loading crews working like mad, Tom Buckner shouting ranges and the four 20-mm cannon yapping like angry terriers. The decks quickly were littered with empty cartridge cases which, sad to relate, were swept into the briny deep when the submarine finished her run and dived—just another small item in the ledger of the costly business of war.

It seemed that the pandemonium had hardly begun when the thirtieth four-inch shell was slammed into the breech and went screaming off to join its fellows—in a Jap plane, Sam hoped. Tom's whistle shrilled for "Cease fire," the weapons were secured with lightning speed, men rushed for the hatches to the accompaniment of "Clear the bridge." At the double squawk of the diving klaxon, the submarine nosed under and no target remained for enemy gunners. So rapid had been the attack—seven swift minutes from "Commence firing" to periscope depth—that not a shot was fired in return and not an airplane left the ground.

"No actual material damage was observed," logged Sam, "and no fires were started. Hopes are entertained that some of the parked planes might have been struck, but we'll never know. However, from a psychological viewpoint, Tojo's boys must have waked with a good many headaches."

That afternoon the *Harder* set her course for the Southwest Pacific Area and, eventually, Fremantle, the seaport of Perth, where Comsubsowespac, recently changed to Comsubs Seventh Fleet, had his headquarters. From that time onward the voyage was fairly humdrum, enlivened only by frequent aircraft contacts—and avoidances. All told, the *Harder* avoided or evaded no less than 112 enemy planes in some 57 contacts—a nerve-racking gantlet to run in anybody's submarine. But the major calamity, which the crew remembers, is that the ice cream freezer broke down just north of the Equator and was out for the rest of the patrol.

Throughout this period of unproductive days the *Harder* ran submerged during most of the daylight hours. To avoid the sharp eyes of Jap fliers, she would maintain a cruising depth of 150 feet.

One noontime during this humdrum stretch, the third-string relief team had the watch at periscope and diving stations. Meanwhile Dealey and most of his officers, as well as the majority of the chief petty officers, were at mess. Orders—and they were strictly standard—were for the Watch to plane the *Harder* up to periscope depth every fifteen minutes for a routine looksee. And then glide down again to 150 feet submergence after a round-the-horizon swing with the scope.

In wardroom and dinette, all hands were stowing away big helpings of strawberry shortcake heaped with whipped cream, unaware that Death—invisible and silent—was closing in upon them. As they neared the end of noonday chow, the *Harder*—unknown to all—was nosing deeper and deeper into depths where the pressures of the sea are too enormous for all but a few denizens of the deep.

Second by potent second, the sub nosed downward from a periscope look. She was already far below the limits of her test depth—at a level so perilous that at any moment the terrific pressures of the mighty deep would close like jaws of steel and crush the *Harder* and all on board into pulp.

But no one—not a living soul—aboard the *Harder* was aware of the terrible jeopardy in which they stood.

Throughout the ship, men were eating or loafing or at their stations. In the control room, the still-inexperienced relief Diving Officer fought vigorously to force the ship down through what he thought was a layer of cold water—a dense, ping-proof stratum of low-temperature water beneath which subs like to seek sanctuary against pursuing destroyers.

The Diving Officer was annoyed and puzzled. The needle on the diving dial stood firm at 120 feet despite his every effort. He had already flooded additional ballast water in the forward trim tank to give her more down angle. She took the angle all right, but the needle still hung at 120.

"Flood auxiliary," he ordered, with more than a touch of asperity. "Damn her cranky soul, anyhow!"

Every pound of water that entered might well have been a clod dropped on the lid of the *Harder's* coffin. Deeper she went. Moment by moment the almost unendurable pressures on the sub increased. The breaking point was creeping close.

But no one aboard the *Harder* knew it. Back in the maneuvering room, Electricians Mate, 2nd class, Robert G. McNamara of Colorado Springs, one of the *Harder's* many plank owners, stood duty at main motor controls. Above his head was a depth gauge. The needle on this gauge was not at 120 feet. It had swung far over to the right—to the deep, deep depths that are out of bounds for mortal men and their puny creations.

McNamara normally paid only casual attention to his depth gauge. The depth at which the submarine was running was no concern of his. That was handled in the control room. His primary task was to be alert to increase or decrease speed on signal from the Diving Officer.

McNamara was mildly wondering what took the *Harder* so long to level off when he happened to look up at the depth gauge. His thick crop of hair almost stood on end and deadly cold chilled his bare and sweat-shining back.

"Holy mackerel," he gasped, sudden fear almost choking him as he seized the intercom and shouted: "Hey, Control Room, Control Room—what's up? My depth gauge is way over in the red—the needle is almost up against the stop!"

In control room—in torpedo rooms—in the wardroom— all over the ship—the warning cry was heard with heart-stopping effects. In the wardroom, Dealey and Lynch were on their feet and headed for the nearby control room before most of the shocked hearers realized what had been said. Sam took a running squint at the depth gauge in his cabin. What he saw almost made his blood congeal. This could be it. Big and heavy as he was, Frank had a running start on his Skipper. He reached his long-familiar diving station a moment ahead of Sam and took over.

To bring the *Harder* back to a safe level from a depth so low that it cannot even be divulged for reasons of security was a tricky job that demanded skill, coolness, and, above all, speed of decision.

"All back, emergency!" was the order McNamara received in the maneuvering room. "Blow bow buoyancy. . . . Pump auxiliary to sea" were the orders given in the control room while all hands held their breath and watched the main ballast pressure gauges—the only depth-indicating gauges which appeared to be working. The hiss of high-pressure air, the chatter of the trim pump, and the thrumming of the propellers trying desperately to pull the ship back from oblivion were the only sounds in the compartment.

None dared to speak. Everyone was listening for the first terrifying crack of steel plating which would spell their doom. Gradually the forward motion of the ship was reversed; slowly the bow came up; and with agonizing hesitancy the pressure in the ballast tanks lessened.

"Thank God!" was the audible murmur throughout the length of the ship.

What caused the near disaster? Who knows—a barnacle, a leak, a hostile gremlin—any one of them could have caused the depth gauges to stick. Now, no one remembers the casualty to the gauges, but one thing they will always remember is the name of a man—Robert G. McNamara—who, that day, saved his ship and his shipmates.

Whatever disciplinary action Sam Dealey took in the matter was meted out privately and no record remains. He did not even mention the incident in his log.

"Don't ever take a sub for granted," admonished Sam to no one in particular, as he stood with his elbow hooked over a rung of the control room ladder, "any more than you'd think of standing with your back to a longhorn bull."

In view of the fact that Zoomie Galvin became a member of the *Harder's* complement at the very start of its patrol, he had, as an outsider, a unique opportunity to observe and evaluate the sort of existence which men who lived and fought in pigboats had to conform to. His comments along those lines were frank and interesting. Here are some excerpts from his report.

Life aboard was very commonplace until the fun started. The real ordeal came when we jumped a convoy, at night. We sank another destroyer and one merchant ship. For many hours we lay at maximum depth, getting thrown around by depth charges.

The officers and men showed a coolness and courage under fire I never dreamed possible. Throughout the depth bombing, Commander Dealey never left the controls. He stripped down to his shorts and, with a towel around his neck, calmly and quietly gave orders and directions for the entire period under continuous depth charging. And later on, they admitted to me that some of them were very close.

When we finally surfaced after weathering this, he had the nerve to turn to me and ask me if I wouldn't rather do that than dive in a plane through AA fire! An emphatic *No* was the answer.

All the time the Skipper was a great kidder and always he had a happy crew. The enlisted men that I talked with all seemed to think he was a little too daring, but said as long as he was the skipper they would go anywhere with him.

The entire crew's morale was very good, but it rose and fell with their victories. After a kill, everyone in the sub would be jabbering like a house full of monkeys and all patting themselves on the back.

Lynch did the navigating and his felicitations were returned by a constant teasing by the Skipper on his method of computing position. One day the captain asked him where we were, and Frank said quite nonchalantly, "Damn if I know, Captain!"

As we pulled up to the dock of the Sub Base everyone was out to welcome us, including the band. What a live-wire outfit! Certainly no surface ship or home-coming air group was feted like this! They seemed to have something in the way of spirit and morale that all the other units of the Navy lacked. This was reflected all the way through from the top down. Even Admiral Lockwood's messages were distinctive in this manner. Maybe it was because everyone in the Submarine Service goes to sea at one time or another.

This impression of being welcome at the Seventh Fleet Submarine Base in Australia was echoed by all aboard the *Harder*.

"Well, sir," chuckled Frank as he and Sam eyed the big bunch of welcomers who filled the pier to overflowing, "the place is different, but the picture is the same even down to the ice cream, mail truck, and the band."

Sam nodded.

Submarine Combat Insignia

"Wonder if they've added our score in anticipation of our arrival?"

"Oh, that . . ." shrugged Sam. "That's not too hot. At best, including one destroyer sunk and one damaged, the count is only about 7000 tons."

"Quite true, sir. But the *Harder's* sum total for all four patrols to date is more than 100,000 and that's not to be sneezed at."

After Rear Admiral Christie, his Operations Officer Captain Tichenor, and their technical staff members had welcomed Comdr. Dealey and the *Harder* to Aussieland and to the Southwest Pacific, the first order of business was a brief conference in the submarine's wardroom. Over cups of black coffee produced by Alabama, Sam spread his charts and his reports on the table for the Admiral's inspection.

Too, he introduced his Exhibit "A," Lieut. (jg) John Galvin, to prove that the *Harder* had won her spurs in the Lifeguard League. Admiral Christie, after hearing the highlights of the skipper's report, was full of praise for Sam's summary treatment of the Jap destroyer off Woleai. He also asked to meet the members of the party who rescued Galvin and congratulated each of them on their daring and determination.

Galvin, incidentally, was not out of the war for long. In a week or so, he was on his way back to his carrier, the *Bunker Hill*. Since he had been a working member of the ship's company of the *Harder* when she inflicted important losses on the enemy, he is entitled to wear the Submarine Combat Insignia, a submarine silhouette on which is mounted a star for each successful patrol—a decoration which all submariners prize and all swivel-chair submariners, including myself, covet.

Before the war ended, he was credited with seven Jap planes and two probables—as well as a 5500 ton Jap transport sunk by skip bombing.

The gamble Dealey had taken in rescuing this zoomie really paid off.

Sooner or later we'll put them all under,
Our patrol runs will be a thing of the past,
No charges, no bombin's, no sinkin's, no nothin',
Then home for the crew of the *Harder* at last.
—*Harder Hymn*

★★★★★★★★★★★★★★★★★★★★★★★★★★★★★★★★★★★★★★★★ **15**

# All Hits—No Errors

"Commander Dealey, I want you to know Major Bill Jinkins of the Australian Imperial Forces." The Admiral glanced from one to the other as the two officers shook hands and continued, "You gentlemen are, in my book, birds of a feather. You should have many a good yarn to swap."

The speaker, Rear Admiral Ralph W. Christie, the handsome, amazingly young-looking Commander Submarines Seventh Fleet, smiled at his guests as they stood before him in the spacious living room of his flag quarters at the "Bend of the Road," Perth, Western Australia.

Comdr. Sam Dealey, recently arrived in port from his fourth war patrol, found himself shaking hands with a khaki-clad Aussie of about his own age and height. He wore one of those musical comedy cavalryman's mustaches which only a Britisher can get away with. His sandy hair was cleanly parted on one side and his blue eyes looked straight into Sam's. He bore himself with the confident air of a trained soldier, hard as nails.

As they faced each other, one could not fail to note how remarkably alike they were in features and in expression: strong faces they had, with firm chins, straight noses, and smiles that radiated personality.

"Congratulations, Commander," said Jinkins, "on a couple of jobs jolly well done. Wish I could have been with you."

"Oh, those were just good breaks, Major; just a lot of good luck—plus a topnotch team."

"Not what I'm told, Commander," he replied; "I'm told it takes a skipper with a lot of guts to put his ship's nose deliberately on a reef in enemy waters." Then glancing at Christie, he moved closer and continued quietly: "The Admiral," said Jinkins, coming straight to the point, "has given me permission to talk to you, Commander, about a small hush-hush business that needs a bit of doing—and soon. May we meet tomorrow over a spot of gin and bitters and have a look at it?"

Dealey smiled. He liked this lad, liked the way he looked you straight in the eye, liked his approach straight from the shoulder.

"Sure, Major," he replied, "any time you say."

Thus began an association and a friendship which was to take both of them into strange and dangerous situations—situations into which they probably wished they had not gone.

The 'twixt patrols set-up in the Perth-Fremantle area—the arrangements for comfort, rehabilitation, and repair of submarines and submariners, whether for minds, bodies, hulls, or equipment, were, in principle at least, identical with those in effect in Hawaii.

A beach hotel, the Seaside, near Fremantle, and the St. George in Perth had been taken over by the Navy for the accommodation of the chief petty officers and other enlisted men. Blocks of rooms were rented at the Adelphi and Esplanade hotels for the officer complement, except the commanding officers, for whom two private residences—the Old Men's Homes, as they were known—had been leased on Birdwood Parade. While not so swank as the Royal Hawaiian in Honolulu, these accommodations were clean and comfortable and not too far from the beautiful beaches which fringe the Indian Ocean north of Fremantle.

Only one other submarine commander was in residence and relaxing when Sam moved in. He was an old friend dating back to Academy days, Comdr. J. C. "Jack" Broach, who was then skipper of the *Hake*.

Since the gap between the *Harder's* fourth and fifth patrol was very brief—only three weeks—Captain Dealey's relaxing period did not produce the restlessness and desire to get back to sea which he had suffered between previous ventures into the shooting country. Being essentially a man of action in time of combat, Sam's attitude toward inaction was, for himself, one of uncompromising intolerance.

One day Skipper Dealey learned that Admiral Christie's headquarters had received the Navy Cross awarded to him for his third patrol. Learning also that the Admiral planned to present the award soon, Sam begged off until awards he had recommended for officers and men of his command had been awarded. If there was anything that Sam hated almost as much as a Jap it was the kind of ceremony that held him up as a solitary hero. His own estimate of his successes was that they were 50 per cent due to luck and the other half due to the skill and courage of that all-inclusive title: the *Harder* Gang.

One subject that gave some food for thought was the question: What would his future assignment be? From what he could gather here and there at Headquarters, he was slated for at least two more patrols. After that, he might be ordered to a shore job in the Pacific area; or, if his luck held, be sent back to the States for either new construction or to duty as an instructor in the Submarine School at New London. Of the three possibilities, the first held no appeal whatever. Most of all, Sam wanted a chance to be Stateside long enough to spend some considerable time with his family in Santa Monica and Dallas. Going home for new construction and waiting for the completion of a new submarine was a fairly decent compromise. But in Sam's opinion, the ideal job would be duty at the Submarine School. Not only because he would once more be home with his family—Wena, Joan, David and Barbara Lee—but also because he felt that he had ideas for improving the course that deserved to be tried.

The news as to the *Harder's* complement was both good and bad. On the blue side of the ledger was the promotion

of Frank Lynch to the rank of Lieutenant Commander and
the advancement of Carl Finney to Lieut. (jg) from Warrant Officer. On the red, was the loss of Keith Phillips, a
plank owner from New London days, and Ensign Clarence
C. Brock, Jr., a relative newcomer to the *Harder*. Taking
their places were Lieut. (jg) Daniel R. James and Ensign
Robert B. Roosevelt of Norfolk, Va. The loss of Phillips
was a bitter pill for Sam to swallow. He had become by far
the top man on the *Harder's* plotting table.

Dealey's meeting with Major Jinkins at Admiral Christie's quarters was not an unexpected occurrence. Several
other meetings or conversations had led up to it. After two
submarines had made unsuccessful attempts to pick up a
nine-man coast-watcher-sabotage party which Jinkins had
left in Borneo, the situation of the gallant little band
became desperate. Major Jinkins, at his Melbourne post,
therefore asked for a conference with Comsubs Seventh
Fleet. Of this meeting and subsequent actions, the Major
writes: "My conference with Admiral Christie began in
Brisbane where I was flown from Melbourne to give my
first-hand report of the situation in Borneo and to submit
my opinions for the failure of *Redfin* and *Haddo*—and also
to persuade the powers that be to let me do it. It was in
Brisbane that the door opened and Admiral R. Christie
suggested I fly to Perth to see Cy Austin and Chester
Nimitz to hear their accounts. This was done and I sub-
mitted a suggestion to Admiral Christie of the plan which
was finally successful. Loss of security at home was very
evident and several instances were actually found out."

Regarding these preliminaries, Capt. Murray Tichenor,
Admiral Christie's Operations Officer, says: "I wanted to
go out in the *Harder* and finally got Admiral Christie's
okay. So when I got the Boss's okay for that, I decided
that we in the *Harder* should do the Borneo job. The Boss
also gave that his okay. As I recall, Dealey did not particularly want to do the Borneo job but only for the reason
that he was opposed to special missions of any type. All he
wanted to do was sink ships and drown as many Japs as
possible."

"Sam's approval," writes Bill Jinkins, twelve years later, "was won over personal contact at a party given by Admiral Christie and developed at other meetings culminating in Sam taking me in to have a chat with Murray Tichenor and Ralph Christie."

What charm the Major used to persuade Dealey, just back from a most perilous venture into shoal waters, that he wanted another of the same sort, I do not know. But I venture that Sam's concurrence was due to sheer admiration for this kindred spirit, this man in whose veins ran the same cool daring and determination that flowed in Sam Dealey's—this man who looked you straight in the eye and invited you to come along on an expedition that could easily cost his life and possibly your own. . . . And so, under a cloak of strictest secrecy, preparations for the Borneo pick-up went forward—with what result we already know.

The combat highlights of the *Harder's* Fifth Patrol were given in the opening chapters of this volume. His log for that patrol laid claim to sinking five destroyers for a total of about 8500 tons. The sinkings allowed for this patrol by the post-war Joint Army-Navy Assessment Committee were three destroyers for 5500 tons. It is hard to see how JANAC, with Japanese records at its disposal, can be wrong. Nevertheless it is equally difficult to see how the very conclusive evidence presented by Comdr. Dealey can be wrong. Of course, it is always possible that additional evidence may come to light in the future.

In any event, at the outset of this, the first telling of the entire *Harder* story, it is underscored how important—from a human standpoint—was the rescue of the Australian agents from the coast of Borneo and how even more important it was—from a military standpoint—to obtain information on the movements of the Jap fleet in our Navy's old Tawi Tawi anchorage. How the *Harder* brought confusion to the enemy by virtue of its relentless attacks upon supposedly superior destroyers was also established. However, in order that the significance of this unparalleled submarine activity may be evaluated by an impartial source, the authors have obtained permission by the editors of the U.S. Naval Institute Proceedings, and from the author as well, to use part of a copyrighted article which appeared in that publication in July, 1947, from the pen of Fletcher Pratt entitled: "Two Little Ships." In introducing the author, the U.S. Naval Institute Proceedings said: "Fletcher Pratt is well known as a writer on naval affairs both in the services and to the civilian reading public. He is the author of numerous books on naval and historical subjects. 'Two Little Ships' was devoted to the analysis of the victories scored, and their overall impact, by the *England,* a destroyer escort in sinking Jap submarines and the *Harder,* a submarine, in sinking Jap destroyers."

In that part of his analysis which is devoted to the far-flung effects the *Harder's* presence had upon the collapse of the enemy's imminent battle plans, Mr. Pratt writes:

On June 12, the second day of Vice Admiral Mitscher's planes over Saipan, Admiral Ozawa put into effect the plan for the defense of the Marianas Islands. That plan had been drawn in the spring for what Tokyo then considered the unlikely event of an American attack on Saipan. It provided for a double operation. Part of it would be an attack on our forces off Saipan by all the air groups of the Bonins Sector, reinforced by those from metropolitan Japan as fast as the latter could be staged through. The pilots of these planes were still in the advanced training stage (the few experienced air groups had been shifted to meet the expected attack on Palau), but it was recognized that an American attempt on the Marianas would constitute so serious an emergency as to justify employing even inexperienced flyers in combat. Moreover, the danger from their inexperience was really less than it seemed, for they would be attacking the Americans simultaneously with the planes from the reborn Japanese carrier fleet.

The fleet was to refuel close to the Philippines, then run toward the Marianas, flying off its planes at about the 137th or 138th meridian, the planes striking the American fleet and then landing on the Marianas fields in the evening, since the carrier pilots had not yet been trained in night deck landings. They would stay overnight on fields, refuel, rearm, and attack the Americans again in the morning on their way back to the carriers, which would be forging steadily toward the scene of action. The ships would be too far away for an American counter-attack on the first day of this operation. By the second, the Americans would have twice been hit by some 500 carrier planes and at least 300 land based planes. Japanese strategists considered that a fleet which had received attention from over 1,600 plane sorties would not be in very good condition to deliver counter-attacks when counter-attacks for the first time became possible, and they were probably right.

Into this scheme, which depended upon the most exquisite timing, the *Harder's* operations now introduced a major temporal error. When Mitscher's planes first attacked Saipan, the commanders there, General Saito and Admiral Nagumo, thought they were receiving a heavy raid like that in the previous February. Indeed it took the appearance of our underwater demolition teams on the night of June 14 fully to convince the General that his island was going to be attacked, and the overall Marianas defense plan was not ordered placed in operation from Tokyo till the following morning, when the Marines were already landing.

In the meantime, of course, informative and preparatory orders had already gone out to Admiral Toyoda and Ozawa at Tawi Tawi. As we have seen, they were having with the *Harder* an amount of trouble every bit as unprecedented as that their own submarines had experienced with the *England*. (Toyoda, incidentally, gently reported his losses as "four destroyers damaged.") They had made at least 20 contacts on the *Harder* and more than one on the *Redfin*, which was working near the same area. It would seem to be about the same time that they succeeded in sinking the submarine *Rabalo* off Borneo. Toyoda made another of those deductions every commander must make on evidence. He reported that the Tawi Tawi anchorage had been "discovered" and the Americans had concentrated around it an immense force of submarines, perhaps as many as half those they had in service. He could no more conceive of a single boat producing all these manifestations than he could of a single DE eating up all his own submarines. He lacked the destroyers to handle so dangerous a concentration; the only thing he could do was clear out.

When the warning and informatory order about American plane strikes in the Marianas came through, therefore, Toyoda and Ozawa decided to construe it as a permission to put their part of the Marianas defense plan into operation, and they did so at once. Of course this had the effect of bringing Ozawa up the Sulu Sea and through San Bernardino Strait more than 24 hours early, before the planes in the Empire and from the Bonins sector could start. His presence in the Philippine Sea so far ahead of plan had two fatal results.

He had contacts on no less than three more American submarines after he ran through the straits, and it seemed to him clear that there was another force of American submarines there, screening the movements of our fleet, which would be working westward in response to the submarines' contact reports. He therefore altered the original plan without, as he thought, losing its essential feature of striking without being counter-attacked. Instead of running east of the 137th meridian, he took his fleet northward, 300 miles west of that line. The original plan had made it possible for the Japanese carriers to take their planes back aboard in an emergency; under this revised version, landing the planes in the Marianas became an absolute necessity. We know what happened; the Marines had captured the field on Saipan, that on Tinian had been shelled out, the runways on Rota and Guam were bombed out during the big battle, and of all those 400 carrier pilots whom the Japanese had spent two years training into the semblance of a service, Ozawa got not one back.

The other fatality was even more directly the result of

running away from the *Harder*. Something had to be done with those extra hours while the planes from the Empire were moving into position for the combined attack. What Ozawa did do was mill around the Philippine Sea at high speed on a sinuous track which brought him two or three times through the same spot. This proved very puzzling to Admiral Spruance when our submarines, and ultimately our air scouts, reported on it (the overall distance covered and the speeds the Japanese were using simply did not add up). But in the one direction it permitted the American leader to make his preparations for the surprise party in the air off Guam, and in the other it brought Ozawa into submarine water, into water occupied by U.S. submarines which had performed their function as news gatherers and were now free to attack.

One of these submarines was the *Cavalla;* she put three torpedoes into the big carrier *Shokaku* that had survived nearly every Pacific battle, and she went down with half her planes still on her decks.

Another of the submarines was the *Albacore;* she torpedoed the new *Taiho*, largest carrier in the world, just as she was gassing planes, and the largest carrier in the world blew up. The operations of the *Harder* have in them something truly of the antique mold, of the adventurous and valiant seamen who made our Navy great in 1812. No one can fail to be struck by the aggressiveness of that submarine's action; how time after time, when the normal thing to do would have been to run and hide, she attacked. Of course it was skill that made the attack successful; but it was the persistent aggressiveness, the willingness to attack destroyers as though the submarine were part of a large fleet acting under some kind of special orders, that sowed confusion in the counsels of Japan. It was something outside Japanese experience, and indeed outside most naval experience.

It would be too much to call the *Harder's* exploit a determining force in the development of naval warfare in the sense that afterward the relation of destroyer and submarine was changed. It is probably true that the relation has changed, but the credit belongs to the whole American submarine service. The cruise of the *Harder* lies exactly at the median point in the total list of the destruction of Japanese destroyers by American submarines, which means that this type of event was slightly more frequent in time afterward than before, though no more so than would be accounted for by the fact that the number of submarines in operation steadily increased. But it can hardly have been common practice to fire down-the-throat shots or to go deliberately hunting patrols, as the *Harder* did with the pair of destroyers off Sibutu Passage. There was probably some contribution here.

Yet the strategic contribution was the main one. Perhaps this may lead us to a new definition of strategy from an angle of approach not usually taken—that in strategy all ships are equal, that it may involve large units or very small ones, since the effect of strategy on the mind of the enemy is in the same proportion as the effect of tactics on his physical equipment.

Since it is not the purpose of this biographical history of a ship and its Commanding Officer to dissect the structure of its strategy or the fabric of its tactics, the foregoing observations by Mr. Pratt are presented because of the impressive and concise analysis and evaluation it gives of the heroic courage of Comdr. Dealey and those who served with him aboard the *Harder*.

As previously reported, Admiral Tichenor (then Captain and Operations Officer in the headquarters staff of Submarines Seventh Fleet) was an observer aboard the *Harder* during its history-making Fifth Patrol. In a letter to Admiral Lockwood he told the authors how the *Harder's* mission was conceived and executed. Since much of the contents of this letter was presented in the early chapters, we here present only those parts that are pertinent to Admiral Tichenor's personal observations and participation:

"The *Harder* was the most high-spirited boat I ever saw. She had had four wonderfully successful patrols under your operations control and was really 'raring to go' on her fifth patrol and first in SoWesPac. Dealey, as you know, was a most modest, self-effacing man with but one goal in mind—to sink Jap ships and get the war ended as soon as possible. Officers and men of his ship absolutely worshipped him, and no one even spoke or thought of him except in superlatives. They had complete confidence and faith that his ability and good judgment would bring them successfully through any situation. They tasted a lot of glory with him, and this in itself put their morale at the very highest level. Dealey was a hard taskmaster. He drove himself and his crew for perfection at all times, but his driving was always coupled with human kindness and thoughtfulness. He mingled with his crew a great deal but always maintained his dignity and their respect. He was blessed with a 'tower of strength' in his Man Mountain Exec., Lieut. Comdr. Frank Lynch. Lynch was cool, calm, intelligent, capable, and indefatigable. Dealey leaned on and depended on him heavily, with great respect for his sound judgment."

Having expended her last torpedo and accomplished a two-fold mission—first, reporting the strength and sortie of the Jap's Tawi-Tawi battle forces; second, rescuing the Aussie agents from the perils of Borneo—the *Harder* set course for Port Darwin where she arrived on 21 June. There she discharged her grateful rescuees and took aboard a new load of torpedoes for a twelve-day supplementary patrol. At Darwin, Captain Tichenor also stepped ashore. His place was taken by Rear Admiral Christie, whose willingness to make himself useful aboard the sub was demonstrated by his offer to stand his turn as Junior Officer of the Deck. The offer was accepted and watches were stood accordingly.

When the news of this supplementary Fifth Patrol project spread among the crew, there was bitter disappointment. They felt they had done a tough job and that a speedy return to the rest camps at Perth was indicated. That they had done an outstanding job was attested by the Navy Department which, later, was to call it "the most brilliant submarine patrol of the war."

As the ironies of fate would have it, this additional patrol period, from 22 June to 3 July, was completely unproductive of sinkings. Somehow Lady Luck, who had been looking over his shoulder all the way, and Sam's fabulous Irish luck must have gone ashore at Darwin and overstayed their liberty, for on this postscript patrol the only luck that the *Harder* encountered was hard luck. Perhaps her Guardian Angels felt that the patrol should have terminated there and the triumphant but badly worked-over submarine and crew should have returned to Fremantle for a bang-up hero's reception and a much needed rest.

Writing of this phase twelve years afterward, one of the *Harder's* radio technicians says: "After blowing up the last destroyer on 10 June, everyone was overjoyed, figuring on a short patrol and then back to the Rest Camp in Perth. Unfortunately we pulled into Darwin and Admiral Christie wanted to go out with us. The crew was pretty sore. However, because of the short patrol run, everyone had plenty of cigarettes, which were good for trade in beer. Consequently, before the evening was over, everyone felt much better."

Whatever the intangible reasons were for the lack of success in her two weeks' foray into the Flores Sea and the Gulf of Boni, the fact remains that not a torpedo was fired and no Japs bit the dust. The time was spent chiefly in evading planes—including one Aussie Catalina "black cat" (night flyer) in the Flores Sea, which made a nuisance of itself by dropping a magnesium flare and holding the submarine down for several hours.

Vice Admiral Christie, now retired and living in Honolulu, has this to say of his attempt to cut off a valuable cargo of strategic materials bound for the war industries of the Empire: "My decision to join *Harder* was to take advantage of the rare opportunity to make a patrol within the time I might be allowed away from the office. After Sam's expeditious near-annihilation of the Jap destroyer force, I flew to Darwin to board *Harder* for a quick foray into the Gulf of Boni to intercept and destroy the weekly

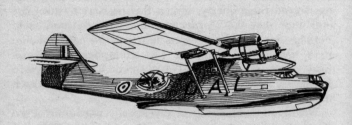

Aussie Catalina

"Nickel" ship which loaded at Pomaela. There you will find evidence of one of the very rare instances in which Sam was fooled. He was tempted to surface and examine a small vessel close inshore. I no sooner got to the bridge when almost simultaneously we spotted the "Nickel" ship and were spotted and forced down by an enemy plane.

"In the patrol report our sighting of a Jap light cruiser and two DD's at 0800 was noted. We could have made an attack if they had been sighted perhaps as little as five minutes sooner. Incidentally, I had the periscope watch at the time.

"I said to Sam something to the effect that if he exposed his conning tower, they would close and he could knock them off.

"Later Sam asked me if I had really meant that. Of course, I was neither criticizing nor directing, although the way we felt about Sam and the *Harder,* the risk was not great."

Returning to Darwin to put Admiral Christie aboard the "air train," which was that city's chief link with the outside world, Sam's conversations with the Admiral reflected the uncertainties that possessed him with respect to the subjects of future patrols and future duties. Many criss-crossing problems were involved. Not least among these was the understandable hesitancy on the part of Sam to give up the Harder. In his heart, in his head, and on the record, she was his ship. At his command, the colors of the United States of America and the commission pennant of a man-of-war had been hoisted aboard the *Harder,* thus transforming her from an inert steel structure to a moving, pulsing, sturdily defiant link in the chain of our national defense. Under his leadership she had been forged, in the intense fires of combat experience, into a marvelously effective weapon—one of the best of her kind. To Sam, as to other skippers in similar cases, the *Harder* was not a ship of chilled steel, but a living, breathing being. In all her sailing days, she had known no other master. Of course, a day of separation was inevitable. But, thought Sam, it was up to him to defer the coming of that day as long as he could.

Comsubs Seventh Fleet also had plans for shifting the commanding officer of the *Harder* and, writing on this subject a dozen years later, says: "I had planned and taken steps to send Sam home after the Fifth Patrol and give *Harder* to Frank Lynch. Sam vetoed the idea during the patrol when we discussed it. I asked him to think it over and we'd talk of it again after his rest period, which he spent at the 'Bend of the Road.' At that time, he reiterated his desire both orally and in writing to make another patrol, and gave reasons which were accepted as sound."

Certainly, with Sam living in his own Flag Mess, playing golf with him from time to time, and engaging in the favorite evening game of darts, Admiral Christie had every opportunity to study him closely and gauge his fitness for making another patrol.

Those who were closest to Sam during this pre-Sixth Patrol period felt that his most earnestly desired solution of the problem would be to take the *Harder* out on one more patrol, after which he would leave her in the capable hands of his Second in Command, Frank Lynch. After that, as he wrote to Wena, "I'll be coming home on a wing and a prayer."

The *Harder's* home coming from her history-making Fifth Patrol had been memorable and most fitting for the occasion. With all hands on deck, standing straightfaced but glowing with pride, the crew saw their Skipper receive the second Gold Star in lieu of his third Navy Cross. This time Sam did not mind the presentation as much as he did on the previous occasion. Through channels he had learned that the awards he had recommended for officers and men under his command had been awarded, including four Legion of Merit awards, five Silver Star Medals, and eleven Bronze Star Medals. If there was one thing Sam hated with all his might—it was a ribbon hunter. He disliked intensely to stand alone to receive decorations in the company of men whom, he felt, had also earned awards.

But the Gold Star presentation did not end the ceremony. Next, the Admiral handed Sam a unique trophy. It was a wooden plaque. In its center appeared a woodcut that showed a Jap destroyer, broken in half and both ends sinking. Above it, deeply cut, appeared the words: "To Comdr. Sam Dealey." And beneath the cut appeared the brand new title: "Destroyer Killer." At its bottom the plaque read: "In grateful appreciation from his fellow submarine skippers."

These were honors indeed. To be put on this pinnacle of fame by his submarine peers was not only unprecedented but, even though presented half in jest, it placed an accolade of admiration and approval on his success more precious to Sam than any official decoration that he could receive. In a letter to Wena that night in which he modestly played down the whole deal, he credited the idea to his old friend and classmate, Comdr. Jim Davis, skipper of the *Raton*.

Sam, always considerate of his officers and men, felt that before taking the step from exec. to skipper after the approaching sixth patrol, Frank Lynch should have a breathing spell. In this new job, Kansas-born, Missouri-bred, Man Mountain Lynch would have to carry all the responsibility of the ship upon his broad shoulders—and on his mind. He had been with the *Harder* since long before she was commissioned, and a short break in continuity of duty was certainly indicated and well deserved. From the very time he first heard of it, Frank was opposed to the plan to take him off the *Harder* during its forthcoming venture. Despite his pleas and cajolings, Sam ended up by telling him that it was an order—and he made it stick. Another *Harder* officer who remained behind when she shoved off on 6 August was Lieut. Levin. To take up the slack caused by the absence of these officers, Sam obtained the promotion of Hiram Hatfield, his electronic expert, to Warrant Officer. Also, by a stroke of some kind of luck, his old Chief of the Boat, "Tiger" Sloggett, now a Lieutenant (jg), came to Sam for the solution of a personal problem. Sloggett said he needed one more combat patrol to be eligible for return to the States—and could Cap'n Dealey find room for him on the *Harder*? Could he? He most certainly could! And did.

The absence of Lynch as Exec. on the Sixth made a few other changes necessary. Ramrod Logan was moved up to Exec. Sloggett, by virtue of past experience in handling the boat, was made Diving Officer; while Finney, who had forgotten more about Diesels than most experts ever know, officiated as Chief Engineer. Hatfield looked after communications and Tom Buckner remained where he was as TDC officer.

While these dispositions were being made, Sam had an unexpected but welcome visit with Comdr. Freddy Warder, his old training inspector in Pearl and wolf pack leader in the Marianas.

Warder told Sam that he had been transferred to New

London to take command of the Submarine School and, to Sam's great—and pleasant—surprise, he asked Dealey if he would like to become one of his officers. Would he? Would a duck like to swim? At that particular period in Sam Dealey's affairs—about 25 July—the prospects were that he would return to New London and the old Electric Boat Company after his Sixth Patrol, where he would wait to take command of a newly constructed submarine. Before their meeting ended, it was agreed between Freddy and Sam that the former would stop over in Washington on his way to New London and put in a plea with the Detail Officer to have Sam join his school staff—permanently, if possible; temporarily, if necessary. Sam was as near seventh heaven as he had ever been since the day Wena said yes. His problems had been solved.

This interview took place in Sam's old room at the Old Men's Home for sub skippers, where he had returned after his stay in the Flag Mess in order to dig into pre-patrol training runs and the final polishing up of the *Harder*.

# ★★★★★★★★★★★★★★★★★★★★★★★★★★★★★★★★★★★★★★★★★ 16
# Dealey—Wolf Pack Leader

Dealey's meeting with his former boss, Fearless Freddy Warder, at this time was particularly fortunate because the *Harder's* next foray, like her Third Patrol, was to be as part of a wolf pack. On the former run, Warder had been the group commander; this time Dealey was to lead one of his own. Another milestone—another stepping stone—had been reached in the career of a man who, a scant fourteen months before, had begun his first patrol as one of the junior skippers of the Submarine Force. Now he was receiving his first group command—a valuable opportunity to gain experience for future division, or higher, commands.

Sam felt deeply his responsibility for his pack mates and plied Warder with keen, well-thought-out questions to obtain his advice and experience as to communications, recognition, and spacing of units.

He assured Wena, back in Santa Monica, by letter the following night that "you can bet this next patrol is going to be one of the conservative type." Maybe he was just trying to reassure her, or perhaps Freddy Warder had poured some restraining counsel into his ear.

The other subs in the *Harder's* pack were to be: the *Haddo*, Lieut. Comdr. Chester W. Nimitz, Jr., who, like his famous dad, the Big Boss of the Pacific, had entered

early in life into the Boats; and the *Hake,* Lieut. Comdr.
F. E. Hayler, who had just relieved Comdr. Jack Broach
of her command after his Fifth Patrol. The *Ray,* Lieut.
Comdr. W. T. Kinsella, was already at sea patrolling the
Java Sea and up the west coast of Borneo and Palawan.
She was to join Sam's pack unofficially for 20–21 August off
Mindoro.

The *Harder* and *Hake* departed from Fremantle at 1300,
5 August, 1944, the *Harder* backing away first. Among the
many who watched this routine shoving off for patrol was
Lieut. Comdr. Frank C. Lynch. Now in the research
branch of the General Dynamics Corporation—of which
the Electric Boat Company of Groton, where the *Harder*
was built, is a Division—Captain Frank Lynch says: "I
never felt lower in my life as I watched that boat shove off.
She hadn't moved a foot since commissioning without me
on board. I felt like I had been marooned on a desert
isle."

The *Haddo* followed on 8 August. Two of the trio topped
off with fuel at Exmouth Gulf and one at Darwin. The
*Harder* and the *Haddo* proceeded via Lombok Strait,
while the *Hake* took a short cut from Darwin around the
east coast of Timor and northward through Molucca Strait.
All were headed for a rendezvous with the *Harder* by the
night of 19 August in an area west and north of Manila
Bay.

Timing their arrival to an exact day and hour proved to
be impossible because of the many times that each was
chased under by planes or spit-kit patrol boats. These
latter were dangerous to attack with the gun because one
lucky hit on a submarine could be fatal, and they were
terribly difficult targets for torpedoes because of their
small size and shallow draft. Hence, there was nothing to
be done but evade them and cast aspersions upon the
parentage of their honorable ancestors.

The result was that the *Harder,* with Sam Dealey pressing, as he had written to Wena, "to get back out there, so
I can hurry home when the patrol is over," was first to

arrive off Cape Calavite, the northwest point of Mindoro, some sixty miles southwest of Manila Bay.

He still was not in his proper area when, at 2036 on 20 August, he was contacted by the *Ray*, which was lying about ten miles to the westward of Cape Calavite, watching a convoy which she had run to earth in Paluan Bay. At this stage of the war, the Japs were learning that sudden and violent death awaited convoys on the high seas at night. Hence, whenever possible, they anchored in some sheltered spot before dark. In short order, a two-way identification was established, following which the *Ray*, by means of SJ radar keying, asked the *Harder* for a rendezvous as soon as possible. The *Ray* had a problem but could not talk about it on the air.

Answering that there was no time like the present, Sam Dealey told the skipper of the *Ray*—Bill Kinsella—to close in to megaphone range. Kinsella was a first-patrol Commanding Officer who had already fired forty-two torpedoes in a double-barrelled patrol of only forty-two days, with a torpedo reload at Fremantle in the middle. He now had only four shots left in the locker. These shots he wanted to use on the fat convoy which he had been harassing for the last two days. Skipper Bill was a submariner of Sam's own kidney.

When sight contact was established by the *Harder* and the *Ray* at 2200, the two subs pulled to within biscuit toss of each other and Kinsella manned his megaphone.

"Looks like I have got a tiger by the tail over there in Paluan Bay and I need a little help. For a couple of days I've been trying to whittle down a big Jap convoy—about a dozen new-looking, heavily loaded tankers and cargo ships, guarded by half a dozen destroyers or other escorts."

After modestly informing Sam that two days earlier he had nicked the convoy for one tanker and one AK, the young first-time skipper continued: "I knew your wolf pack was coming in from the south and I hoped you'd get here in time. I've only got four torps left. May I join your gang, unofficially?"

"You sure can, Bill," replied Sam with enthusiasm. "Glad to have you on the team any day."

Captain Kinsella, writing of this conference after a lapse of a dozen years, says: "He [Dealey] was just arriving in patrol area via Apo Pass and had Chester Nimitz in *Haddo* tagging along as part of his wolf pack. Sam and I worked out a plan whereby the three boats would approach to one mile off Cape Calavite for a dawn attack. *Ray* would approach from northwest, *Haddo* from west, and *Harder* from southwest. I may say that Sam appeared to be in excellent spirit and was just itching to get at that convoy. At 2210 we wished each other good luck and *Ray* headed north at slow speed. Dawn on 21 August, 1944, was bright and clear and the sea was like glass. At 0457 *Ray* submerged one mile off the Mindoro coast and three miles south of Cape Calavite Light. *Harder* was submerged about 8000 yards to the south of us. I never had contact with *Haddo*, but as events turned out, she eventually gained an attack position several miles to the north of *Ray*."

Two wild cards in the well-stacked deck of this pack were the *Guitarro*, Lieut. Comdr. E. D. H. Haskins, and the *Raton*, Lieut. Comdr. M. W. Shea. These two boats had been patrolling the area to northward of Manila, for which Dealey's pack was headed.

On the 19th, expecting Dealey to arrive, they had shifted southward to a new area and selected the now famous "Windy Corner," where 5000-foot Mount Calavite marches down to the sea at Cape Calavite, as the stand at which to await their quarry. Hence, on the night of 20–21 August, the *Raton* was close in to the north and the *Guitarro* close in to the south of the high and rugged cape.

When the *Haddo* reached the rendezvous at 0130 of 21 August, Sam, leaning over his bridge rail, was jubilant: "Looks like it should be the battle royal of the century," he shouted.

Then he laid out his battle plan for a dawn attack the next morning. *Ray* and *Guitarro* were to attack from the northwest—near the lighthouse—as the convoy sortied;

*Harder* was to attack from the west; *Haddo* to attack from the southwest. The *Hake,* according to Sam's figures, could not possibly arrive in time to get into the fracas. The plan, of course, pre-supposed that the anchored convoy would sortie at the crack of dawn and round Cape Calavite.

Five submarines were thus positioned in a space which a Texas cowboy might almost have covered with his saddle blanket. It is amazing that no near collisions occurred among our own ships, but, except for a fleeting radar contact, which the *Ray* made at 2245 on what she believed to be the *Guitarro,* they had no indication of each other's presence.

Into the midst of this embattled pack of sea wolves serenely steamed Little Red Riding Hood in the form of a Japanese hospital ship, fully lighted, headed south. There had been many charges that Japanese hospital ships, of which they had some twenty-five, did not limit their cargoes strictly to medical supplies; rescued prisoners of war swore they had, as dock laborers, unloaded ammunition from such ships. Undoubtedly dark thoughts went through the minds of our waiting, tense-nerved submariners, and some trigger fingers probably itched, but no torpedo rumbled from its tube—the sanctity of the Geneva emblem of mercy was not violated.

As the first light of dawn began to flush the eastern sky, the stillness of the undersea world was broken by sounds of enemy activity. Sam's estimate of the convoy's intentions was about to be proved correct.

"At 0545, the sonar man picked up pinging," writes Captain Kinsella, "and at 0551 I sighted the convoy standing out of Paluan Bay. I could see three DE type escorts patrolling to seaward of the leading ship in the column, which was a large transport. At 0555 we heard three explosions in the direction of the convoy that sounded like torpedo hits. Sam had apparently fired at the escorts, but none of them appeared to have been hit or damaged. Apparently the explosions were the torpedoes going off on the rocky coastline, which was only a mile away. By his attack Sam drew off two of the three escorts, who com-

menced dropping the first of thirteen depth charges on
him at 0557. This enabled *Ray* to have a beautiful shot at
the leading transport, comparatively unmolested by the
one remaining escort. At 0618 *Ray* fired her last four
torpedoes at the leading transport. The target zigged to
conform to the coastline during firing, but a quick correc-
tion resulted in the fourth torpedo hitting amidships and
sinking the transport. After observing the torpedo hit, I
ordered 350 feet, rigged for depth charges (we got them,
too), and cleared the area."

Although the *Ray's* skipper heard the crash of three
torpedoes which he believed were fired by the *Harder* at
0555, what actually exploded has never been substanti-
ated. Even so, a depth charge barrage of king-sized proportions was released by the rapidly cruising enemy escorts.
In his log, Comdr. Nimitz—whose *Haddo* was about 4800
yards south and east of the *Harder* —made this entry:

"Depth charging was started on all sides and it kept up,
almost without interruption, until 0616. I have never heard
such a din, nor would I have believed it possible for the
whole Jap fleet to unload so many charges so rapidly. I
could see two escorts on port bow and three on starboard.
They were about 3000 yards away and dropping charges.
Great geysers of water were coming up all around them.
The escorts to starboard were closing, those to port were
opening. I had to shout to make myself heard in the
*Haddo's* conning tower."

Kinsella, in the *Ray*, counted 126, forty of which were
definitely intended for his ship.

At 0619, just as the vigorous depth barrage had rolled to
a halt, Nimitz saw the leading ship—a big 7000-ton merchantman get hit. From the direction, it looked as if one of
the *Ray's* torpedoes had made a hit. . . . It had.

This triggered off another barrage of DC's that lasted
until 0625. Stealing a look, Nimitz saw three ships in
column sheer off to their left to avoid the now-burning
lead ship in the convoy. In sheering off, the vessels made
a perfect three-ship target for the *Haddo*. Bang went—in a
well-spaced spread—six of the *Haddo's* forward torpedoes.

Score: two vessels sunk for a total of almost 11,000 tons. A bit later the *Guitarro* sent a 5000-ton tanker to the bottom. As luck would have it, neither the *Raton* nor the *Harder* scored that morning. But, at least, Sam had the great satisfaction of having planned and led in the execution of a mass attack on one of the best-protected convoys our subs ever tackled in those Asiatic waters.

Soon after dark, on the evening of that same day, 21 August, the *Haddo* and the *Harder* joined up and set course toward their assigned area north of Manila. Soon after midnight, off the never-to-be-forgotten Bataan Peninsula, both subs made radar contacts on three ships at a range of 13,000 yards. It did not take extensive tracking by Dealey and Nimitz to make them realize that their zigging targets were on a base course for Manila Bay entrance at about 11.5 knots. With the *Harder* on the port quarter and *Haddo* on the starboard flank, the tracking hunter-killers stole slowly closer to their victims. When the *Haddo's* skipper sent Sam a message to the effect that he thought the targets were ships too small to bother with, Sam's reply was brief and to the point: "Not convinced!"

At 0356, 22 August, after two hours of patient and stealthy trailing, the *Harder* fired a salvo of torpedoes which cut the darkness and the silence of the night with violent explosions and flames shooting high above the masts of the target.

As he recorded later, Chester Nimitz realized that he had been taught a lesson in evaluation. Sam Dealey, with his characteristic careful and almost intuitive estimate, had been right again. These three targets were new-type frigates and indeed worthwhile. The enemy's most recently built anti-submarine vessels, which we designated as frigates, were specially equipped ships of the deadliest kind. They were, in their way, just as efficient against submarines, if not more so, than their larger sisters, the first-line destroyers.

Profitting from the example the *Harder* had set, the *Haddo* closed in swiftly and at 0424 fired a salvo of three torpedoes at an enemy frigate. One fish hit the target with a flaming explosion, while a second blasted the vessel next in line.

The *Haddo* pulled away to take stock, but the radar operator shouted up the hatch that he still had the original three pips on his scope. In view of what had happened, this was unbelievable to Nimitz—one good hit should have cooked the goose of any of those spit-kits. He reversed course and again approached the luckless hunters who had so suddenly found their roles reversed. With dawn about to break, the *Haddo* could not approach too close; so she fired three torps at long range. All missed because of an error in the speed estimate. The frigate was stopped instead of making the feeble 3 knots which the TDC solution had ground out. With a few well-chosen remarks about the proper consignment of electronic brains anyhow, Chester cleared the bridge, pulled the plug, and, at periscope depth, closed in for the kill. What he saw in the gray morning light were three paralyzed ships, two of which he identified as DD's. Actually, all were 900-ton frigates, named the *Matsuwa*, the *Sado*, and the *Hiburi*, according to post-war reports. They were in varying degrees of disarray and, even as he was examining them, a torpedo from the *Harder*, at 0549, ended the career of one.

Not to be outdone, Nimitz fired three torpedoes at the two remaining wrecks. Two at the nearest, some 2400 yards off; one at the other, some 3000 yards away and at a none too easy angle. The first vessel sank; the other target remained untouched.

A submariner's log is many things: a diary of his thoughts, a record of his actions—even a confessional for his errors. Boldly, self-critical Chester Nimitz, a chip off the old block, wrote this about the incident: "I realize now that I should have waited for a better set-up on DD #2. A wasted torpedo!"

This was at 0620. Sixteen minutes later he made the following interesting entry:

"0636—While jockeying around at periscope depth for set-up on the remaining destroyer, heard screws very close aboard—could be heard through the hull, and simultaneously heard *Harder's* call on the sound gear. She was between us and the target. Interpreted her signal to mean 'Gangway,' so went to 150 feet and cleared out.

"0655—heard *Harder* sink the third and last ship. Watched it go down with its stern sticking out. Cruised off to westward submerged."

Thus, in three swift hours, two American submarines, superbly handled, had ignominiously destroyed three of their most hated and most dangerous enemies. Under the "Hit 'Em Harder" banner of Samuel David Dealey, the mice were turning with a vengeance on the mousers. Things were getting really tough for the Mikado's "cavalry of the sea."

According to plan, the *Haddo*, *Hake*, and *Harder* were to meet shortly after sunset on 22 August sixty miles off Cape Bolinao. While en route, the *Harder* instructed the *Haddo* to rendezvous off the Luzon coast north of Subic Bay. Arriving there at 2139, the *Haddo* found the *Hake* in position, but no *Harder* as yet. While she waited, the *Haddo* got a destroyer in her sights. But the fish she shot at it failed to produce hits—only a vigorous depth charging. The following day the *Haddo* expended all of her remaining five torpedoes in an attack on a destroyer that was escorting a tanker. The DD's bow was blown off, but the target failed to sink. Nimitz had to look on helplessly as trawlers towed the stricken vessel toward the beach while planes flew protective circles overhead.

When the *Harder* and the *Hake* came up at 2220, they were too late to be of any assistance. Sam, on being informed by Chester that he had no more fish, endorsed his plan to return to Mios Woendi, New Guinea, where the tender *Orion* was located, for a fresh load. He gave Chester his well-earned blessing. Standing on no further ceremony, the *Haddo* headed south at three-engine speed for the newly established advance base—which, incidentally, rejoiced in the fitting code name of "Stinker." Nimitz wanted to get back as soon as possible to play some more high-explosive games of tag on Sam Dealey's team.

Young Chester, himself an aggressive competitor, liked the brand of water polo the Torpedo Totin' Texan played.

As Nimitz raced southward for the nearest stockpile of torpedoes, leaving his two packmates at the rendezvous, the *Harder* and *Hake* closed in for a council of war.

This was the first time the new skipper of the *Hake*, Lieut. Comdr. Frank Hayler, had had a chance to talk with his pack commander since they parted company after leaving Fremantle. Frank's spirits, as he saw the *Harder's* dark form approaching through the gloom, were not of the highest; in fact, they were on the down side. While the *Harder* and *Haddo* had been piling up nice fat bags of game, the Hake had gotten "damn all," as our Limey allies say. Because of his late arrival in the area, Hayler had missed the epic battle of Paluan-Calavite, and only last night, when he and Chester Nimitz were tracking down an Asashio class destroyer, the *Haddo* had fired first and robbed the *Hake* of her target.

"On the *Hake*, there!" came Dealey's clear hail from the oncoming black blob.

"*Hake*, aye, aye!" replied Frank.

"My course is zero zero zero; speed 3 knots. Suggest you stop engines and shift to motors so we can talk better. Besides, there might be some Jappo around who could hear our engines."

"Aye, aye, sir," agreed Frank.

As the two submarines drew within biscuit toss of each other and crept at a snail's pace on parallel courses over the starlit waters, Hayler could see Sam leaning over his starboard bridge rail.

"The *Haddo's* cripple got away, Frank," said Dealey. At this short range his megaphoned voice was calm and hardly raised above its normal level. "Chester thinks they towed it into Dasol Bay," Sam continued, "or maybe had to beach it near the north entrance. Unless we can knock him off early in the morning, the Japs might manage to tow it down to Manila."

"Right you are, Sam," answered Frank, with a note of resignation in his voice as he continued, "and since you are the official Destroyer Killer around these parts and since R.H.I.P. [Rank has its privileges], I assume you will lead the way—and I shall follow."

"Oh, no," chuckled Dealey, "after you, my dear Alphonse. You haven't had any hair yet, while I've got at least two scalps. In the morning, on the flood tide, you go in and give the tincan the works. I'll guard the entrance—just in case any Son of Heaven should try to sneak up on you."

"You—you really mean that?" gasped Hayler in surprise—surprise that registered also in the faces and soto-voce exclamations of his bridge watch. With competition for enemy ships as keen as it was among submariners, this gift of a nice chunk of sitting-duck tonnage was generous, indeed.

"You really are going to give me first crack at him, Sam?"

"I sure am, Frank. I figure you should head in about 0800. I'll ride shotgun for you, outside. Hope you blow him higher than a kite."

No one in the Pacific was a greater believer in training for himself and his subordinates than Sam Dealey. Here was a fine chance to train one of his packmates, a new skipper who might be a bit jittery in his first big command. And so it was arranged, with a typical display of Dealey leadership and unselfishness. The two captains then set the rendezvous for the succeeding night, wished each other "good hunting," and opened out for mutual SJ radar checks. With the *Harder* diverging slightly to the northward, they laid courses which, at an easy speed, would bring them close to the Dasol Bay entrance by daybreak. This bay, which lies just south of Lingayen Gulf on the west coast of the island of Luzon, was becoming more and more an overnight anchorage for jittery Japanese ships that were finding the high seas unhealthy at night. More than just a crippled DD might be found in this haven.

The *Hake* dove before dawn and took her station about four miles off Hermana Mayor Island, which divides the entrance to Dasol Bay. At 0532 her sonar operator reported pinging to southward, and immediately Hayler changed course to south. As the sound of enemy echo ranging became more distinct, it was apparent that there were two ships, and excitement grew in the *Hake's* conning tower.

"This really changes the picture," exulted Hayler with a broad grin at his Exec. "Two real targets, alive and kicking, and not a washed-up tincan."

"What about the *Harder*?" inquired the Second-in-Command, "Shall we pass the word to her?"

"No," answered the Skipper, "it's too risky. These targets are alert and they'd be sure to hear our sound transmissions. . . . Besides knowing that bunch of hotshots on Dealey's boat, it's a safe bet they have already heard those Nips."

By 0554, with dawn breaking over the blue-green hills of the Luzon coastline, the tops of two vessels peeped above the southeastern horizon and Hayler changed course to 100 degrees, true, in order to close in on the enemy. At a sign from the Captain, the quartermaster sounded the General Alarm and, to the accompaniment of the familiar bong, bonging, the loud speakers squawked, "Battle Stations, torpedo."

"Oh, boy," murmured the Exec., "this is what the doctor ordered; it's been a long, dry run."

As the range shortened, the larger target was seen to be a three-stacker—maybe a cruiser—while the other was possibly a destroyer. The escort was keeping position on the inshore bow of its consort, thus leaving her wide open to the *Hake's* attack. The conning tower crew were jubilant. However, the Naval Intelligence identification book quickly dampened their spirits when it refused to produce a cruiser similar to their target. Only the old Thai destroyer *Phra Ruang* seemed to fit the picture—250 feet long and armed with a couple of peashooters. From its looks, it might be a relic from the days when Commodore Dewey invaded Manila Bay. The other vessel was definitely a fairly modern mine sweeper whose guns, depth charges, and echo-ranging gear commanded a certain de-

gree of respect. Its foremast bore a curious rig which
might be a radar antenna. With the altering picture, Hayler's
morale drooped. The last straw of depression was added
when, suddenly, at a range of 6200 yards, the ancient DD
zigged sharply away and headed for the entrance to Dasol
Bay. The mine sweeper remained outside and swung her
bow to seaward in the direction of the waiting submarines.
Her pings began to register on the Hake.

Meanwhile, aboard the *Harder*, it is fair to assume that
orders had been given and action taken similar to those on
the *Hake*—that, when the targets hove into view, the
familiar call of "Battle Stations, torpedo" was sounded. All
over the combat-tested vessel, men slipped into their appointed places with the easy speed of veterans whose
bodies and brains are attuned to the task at hand.

Young Sam Logan, the new Exec., was already in the
conning tower. Swift-moving, fast-thinking Ramrod Logan, like Frank Lynch before him, was running the preliminary phase of the attack. Almost at the first bong of the
General Alarm, Wayne Brostrom, always at the helm in
battle, popped up the hatch from the control room and
took over his accustomed job. Sloggett, first Chief of the
Boat, now wearing lieutenant's bars, was the Diving Officer; while Tom Buckner ran the Torpedo Data Computer.
The plotting table was manned by Lieuts. James and Sampson; and, at the dials of the conning tower electronic eyes
and ears, were men of long experience supervised by that
wizard of sonar and radar, Radio Electrician Hiram Hatfield. Others in the tight little space were the yeoman,
scope jockey, talker, and quartermaster.

Captain Dealey entered the control room, en route
from his cabin to the conning tower. As usual, he looked
around the compartment with a friendly light in his warm
brown eyes. He noted the old-timers, Majuri and Paquet,
at the bow and stern plane controls; Lieut. Carl Finney,
watching intently, was learning the Diving Officer's job
from Sloggett. With a swift scrutiny of the chart spread on
the table and a glance at the depth gauges, Sam was up
the ladder and at his accustomed post beside the ladder

leading to the bridge. There, left arm hooked over the fifth rung, the Captain would stand waiting patiently, and without any kind of nervous pressure, for the moment when he would step to the periscope to close in for the kill.

Throughout the *Harder* that morning (as in any sub under similar circumstances), while the space that separated the hunter and the hunted shrank from miles to mere yards, men stood at their stations, silent, immobile, alert. . . . Waiting. . . . Waiting for the ship-wide squawk box to signal the action:

"Stand by to fire spread of three fish from the forward tubes."

And soon, on the firing order, off would go three well-aimed, torpex-loaded torpedoes.

Or, deciding that the game—for one reason or another—was not worth the cost or the candle, the Skipper would be heard to say: "Left full rudder; head out to sea; take her deep. Rig for depth charge, rig for silent running."

Quite early that August morning, Skipper Hayler of the *Hake* decided that the set-up was not to his liking. Reads his log:

"0646—Broke off attack and came left to 000 true.

"0647—Sighted *Harder* periscope dead ahead about 600–700 yards.

"0710—Came right to 180, true."

What did the *Harder's* Captain say—what did the squawk boxes repeat?

"Fire three" or "Take her deep"?

No one will ever know. For on that August morning, the Last Pilot came aboard the *Harder*—the Grim Helmsman assigned to guide Comdr. Samuel David Dealey and all his gallant fighting crew through waters beyond human ken.

That brief sighting of the *Harder's* periscope by the skipper of the *Hake* was the last time friendly eyes saw that valiant lady. At this fateful moment the *Harder* was giving her farewell salute. As before, the evading *Hake* heard echo-ranging. Coming from a distance, she was soon to hear the rumble and roar of exploding depth charges.

What were the words of the *Harder's* Hymn—the prophetic lines of the closing stanza?

> We're proud to have sailed her, and proud to have fought her;
> Our Queen of the Seas, she always will be.
> We've followed the Skipper through hell and deep water. . . .

And so they did!
To a man!
To the end!

They followed Sam Dealey
*Through Hell.* . . .
                        unleashed by exploding depth charges
*And.* . . .
                              into peacefully serene and silent
*Deep Water.* . . .

# "Home is the Sailor"

When the *Hake* went to deep submergence, in a routine evasive maneuver, followed by the thunder of depth charges at some little distance from her, there was nothing in the brief drama which had just ended to indicate that, for the *Harder*, its results had been fatal. Dealey was noted for bold and aggressive handling of his submarine. It was routine for him, on sighting an enemy, no matter what her category—if large enough to be worth a torpedo —to order Battle Stations and close in on the target. By the end of her Fifth Patrol, the *Harder* had earned the reputation of being "the Submarine Force's most terrible opponent of destroyers," as stated in the Bureau of Personnel summary of submarine losses. There can be no doubt, therefore, that when last seen, her periscope was already lined up for down-the-throat shots at the oncoming mine sweeper. If torpedoes were fired, what tragic twist of Fate caused them to miss the submarine's small, shallow-draft attacker, we shall never know.

Of this phase, Captain Hayler, last American ever to see the *Harder*, writes: "I believe at 0710 the mine sweeper actually had two targets, Sam and myself, and was probably somewhat confused, but at any rate at 0728 we heard a string of fifteen depth charge explosions. This suggested a stern drop coordinated with side or quarter thrown charges.

Mavis

This was the one and only attack made, and it must be the one that got Sam. We remained in the vicinity the rest of the day and observed a considerable amount of aircraft activity—Mavis-type planes mainly. We surfaced at 2012 and attempted to contact *Harder*, as previously arranged, with no success. During this time we searched the area carefully with negative results. The strange thing to us was the lack of any sort of debris, oil slick, or odor of Diesel fuel. Our search was continued daily, as were our attempts to effect radio contact."

Even as late as 30 August, Hayler sent a dispatch addressed to Admiral Christie's headquarters at Perth and to the *Harder*.

When Lieut. Comdr. Nimitz in the *Haddo* returned from Mios Woendi with a new load of torpedoes in early September, he knew nothing of the *Harder's* status and tried to contact her as she entered Mindoro Strait on 9

September. Failing to make contact, he headed out toward Macclefield Bank in the belief he would find Dealey in that vicinity, as indicated by a dispatch from Perth.

To those who are not familiar with submarine operations, this gap in contacts between group partners may seem strange. But wolf packs do not operate as closely knit fleet units. The thread of command that unites such subs, as well as their radio communications, is tenuous and elastic so as to leave to each commander wide latitude to make the most of every opportunity for attack and for concealment from enemy direction-finding beams. Too, there have been instances when a submarine maintained an enforced silence for days or weeks because her radio had been wrecked by enemy action.

On the night of 10 September, the *Haddo* established contact with an American submarine. At first, her captain believed he had the *Harder* in sight. The vessel turned out to be the *Hake*. Then it was, as the two vessels lay within hailing distance in the velvety darkness of a tropical night, that the two skippers compared notes. Then it was that Hayler gave Nimitz the disturbing information that Sam Dealey had not been heard from since the morning of 24 August, and the tragic possibilities of the *Harder's* fate were discussed openly. Knowing that the *Haddo* would be coming up from an advanced base, Hayler had hoped against dispairing hope that Dealey had been forced, for some sudden and imperative reason, to head for such a base and that the *Haddo* would bring news of him.

No words can describe the feelings of those aboard the *Haddo* and the *Hake* as, with the former as pack leader, they set out to complete their patrols.

Hope as they might—and did—they could not escape the numbing realization that, if Dealey were still in the land of the living, someone would have heard from him. The Philippine area was patrolled by many American submarines. Even with wrecked compasses and radio equipment, the *Harder* should have stumbled on one of them. If the ship had been abandoned and survivors had reached shore, radio-equipped guerrillas should have reported. The inescapable conclusion was that the *Harder* and her gallant band were lost. . . . Both skippers, in their hearts, swore vengeance for the *Harder,* but only Nimitz was able to send another Jap to the bottom before the patrols ended—the *Katsuriki,* a 1540-ton surveying vessel.

When the news reached Perth, it was received with shock and disbelief. It was incredible that the *Harder,* with her almost fabulous record, could meet a fate similar to that which she had meted out to a score of enemy ships—including seven destroyers. To their hundreds of friends, old shipmates, and messmates, it did not seem possible that the *Harder,* Sam Dealey and his men, "one of the greatest fighting teams of the Pacific War," could perish. . . . Nor will they perish. That ship—those men and their deeds—will live forever in the memories of American submariners and in the annals of the United States Navy.

One question as to the cause of the loss of the *Harder* that sprang from many lips was this: Fatigue? But that was ruled out by senior officers who knew submariners well and watched them closely. On that score, Captain Tichenor said: "I believe that, when he came in from his Fifth Patrol, Sam was quite tired, and Admiral Christie seriously considered taking him off. However, Dealey had marvelous recuperative powers and bounced back to real health and fighting spirit in a very few days. Dealey himself suspected that he might be pulled and stepped into the breach. He was terribly proud of the *Harder* and didn't want anyone to get command of her except his Exec., Lynch. But Lynch had had five patrols, too; so Dealey insisted that Lynch stay for a rest and he (Dealey) would take the *Harder* out for her sixth patrol and Lynch could then relieve him when he came in. He got his way."

As for Frank Lynch, who was to have taken command of the *Harder,* he eventually relieved Comdr. Chester Nimitz, Jr., in command of the *Haddo* and had an outstanding fighting career in that vessel with a record of four enemy ships sunk.

Sam was never jauntier nor was he ever shining with

bolder purpose than when the *Harder* backed away from her pier at Fremantle on 5 August, 1944. As Sam Logan, the new Executive Officer who had replaced Frank Lynch, maneuvered the sub and pointed her bow seaward, Sam Dealey stood on the bridge, his dry pipe in his mouth. On his head, instead of his regulation cap, Sam wore the cock-feather-adorned, ten-gallon hat of the Aussie soldier. This particular hat had been given Sam at a party staged for him by a group of Major Jinkins' officers in appreciation of his rescue of their comrades on the coast of Borneo. The hat's wide brim had been autographed by every person present, and Sam treasured it highly. As the *Harder* pulled away, he lifted it from his head, waved it in broad sweeps, and replaced it at a rakish angle. Yes, indeed, as all on the pier could see, the Torpedo Totin' Texan was in high good humor on that memorable day.

Further proof that the slowing grip of fatigue had no hold on Sam, the Submariner's Submariner, was given in the swift and masterful manner in which he arranged for the mass attack on the big Jap convoy on the morning of 21 August at Paluan Bay. Also, his swift and decisive action in the attack and sinking of three deadly coast defense vessels through the morning of 22 August was not the work of a skipper or, for that matter, of a ship slowed down by battle weariness.

What then could have happened?

To venture but one answer, it is my belief that the more powerful depth charges, which three submarines reported that they had heard and felt the effects of in the Paluan-Cape Calavite battle on 21 August, not only were heavier but were capable of being set for greater depths than those previously used.—This action—the improvement of their depth charges—the enemy undoubtedly took as the result of information given to the press by an headline-seeking American official, as mentioned in a previous chapter. It is probable that the *Harder* did not get down fast enough or deep enough to evade those 440-pound cans of death-dealing explosive.

Search of Japanese records following the end of the war

revealed that on the morning of 24 August a battle had been fought by Jap patrol craft against American submarines off Caiman Point. The records claimed that, as a result of an attack with 440-pound depth charges, a large amount of oil, wooden chips, and scraps of cork had appeared on the surface of the sea.

On 29 September—after several weeks of search and waiting that proved equally unproductive—Sam Dealey's wife in Santa Monica, Calif., and his mother in Dallas, Texas, were notified by the Navy Department that the *Harder* "must be considered overdue and presumed lost due to enemy action." In answer to a letter for fullest possible information on behalf of Mrs. Virgie Dealey by Sam's uncle, George B. Dealey, publisher of the *Dallas News*, Admiral Christie wrote Sam's uncle as follows under date of 26 October:

Dear Mr. Dealey:

It was my very painful duty to report on the 29th of September that the *Harder* under the command of Commander Samuel D. Dealey must be considered overdue and presumed lost due to enemy action. In that report I stated in effect that the *Harder* had sunk in her brief career 20 vessels, including 7 Japanese destroyers. Her magnificent career under the inspiring leadership of Commander Dealey has added a glorious page to naval history.

The *Harder* throughout her career was led into combat with the enemy with complete disregard of the hazards involved. Her successes in six patrols were timely and important and have considerably advanced victory to the Allies over the Japanese. The *Harder* has been the pride of this force where the competition for first place has been very keen.

I have mailed to Mrs. S. D. Dealey in Santa Monica a book of photographs and mementoes. I am enclosing a very fine photograph of Sam and a photostat copy of a glorious tribute by General Douglas MacArthur to the *Harder* and her gallant Captain. Sam was a great friend of ours, and we had the pleasure of having him live with us at my quarters during his leave period between his fifth and sixth patrols. You will note that the photostat copy of General MacArthur's letter is marked "Secret." While the subject matter is no longer secret, I must ask that its contents be reserved for the members of the family and is not for publication.

The *Harder* has been recommended for two Presidential Unit Citations. I have recommended Sam for the Congressional Medal of Honor for his performance of duty as Commanding Officer of the *Harder* in his fifth war patrol. Whatever the outcome of these recommendations, I assure you that I can speak for the officers of Submarines, Seventh Fleet, and say that he deserves every reward and recommendation that a grateful country could give.

I would appreciate it if you would convey this information to Sam's mother with my utmost sympathy.

Very sincerely yours,
R. W. Christie
Rear Admiral, U.S. Navy

Despite this seemingly final news, hopes that some sort of a miracle might have saved a few of the *Harder's* personnel still existed. Such a brief and slender hope appeared on the horizon in a letter Admiral Christie wrote to Sam's brother, Jerome, on 27 October. It read:

I cannot honestly give you but the barest suspicion of hope that Sam may possibly have got ashore on one of the islands of the Philippines. There is an unconfirmed rumor that some submariners did get ashore. I leave it to your judgment as to whether or not that information, which I have given no one else, should be passed to his mother, and I will certainly give you any further information that may come to me.

The loss of Sam Dealey and the *Harder* was a very bitter blow to all of us in the submarine service who admired him as a Captain and loved him as a friend. His magnificent performance of duty will remain always an inspiration to the officers and men of the United States Navy.

* * *

When the *Harder* vanished she had, for a submarine with five patrols to her credit, a rather unusually large number of old hands or plank owners aboard—men who had put her in commission—a wonderful tribute to the kind of leadership exercised by Sam Dealey. Bear in mind that after every patrol he was required to furnish a quota for new construction. Including the skipper and Sam Logan, the number of men who had made all six patrols ran to a round baker's dozen. Tom Buckner would have been in that category had he not been hospitalized with a broken leg during the first patrol. Following is a list of the *Harder* men who made up her complement when this combat champion among submarines stood out to seas beyond human horizons. The number behind each man's name indicates the total of his *Harder* patrols.

Comdr. Samuel Dealey, Dallas, Texas—6
Lt. Samuel Logan, Owensboro, Ken.—6
Lt. (jg) Thomas Buckner, Nashville, Tenn.—5
Lt. (jg) Vernard Sloggett, San Diego, Calif.—3
Lt. (jg) Daniel James, Philadelphia, Penn.—2
Lt. (jg) Philip Sampson, Mound, Minn.—3
Lt. (jg) Carl Finney, Philadelphia, Penn.—6
Lt. (jg) Hiram Hatfield, Lemoore, Calif.—6
Ens. Walter Haloupek, Belle Plaine, Iowa—1
Ens. Robert Roosevelt, Norfolk, Va.—2
Charles Altherr, MoMM2c, Flat Rock, Mich.—4
Robert Baber, MoMM2c, St. Paul, Minn.—2
Walter Beutelspacher, Sc3c, Baltimore, Md.—2
Robert Blum, MoMM3c, Joliet, Ill.—5
Sumter Bourg, GM3c, Los Angeles, Calif.—2
Wayne Brostrom, SM1c, Staples, Minn.—6
Calvin Bull, RM2c, Springfield, Neb.—5
Vivian Cash, MoMM1c, St. Louis, Mo.—2
Roland Chenard, F1c, Fall River, Mass.—1
Harold Crask, S1c, Trinidad, Col.—3
Wilbur Clark, RT2c, New Hampton, Mo.—3
John Conley, MoMM1c, Watsonville, Calif.—5

James Cromwell, StM2c, Richmond, Va.—2
Donald Dahlheimer, MoMM2c, Osseo, Minn.—5
Vincent Dallessandro, TM1c, Buffalo, N.Y.—6
Edwin De Voe, F1c, Bristol, Penn.—1
William Diamond, RM1c, Pensacola, Fla.—2
James Edgar, Fc2c, Monroe, La.—3
George Fisher, Jr., MoMM3c, Ironton, Ohio—3
Robert Gifford, TM3c, St. Louis, Mo.—5
Joseph Glueckert, MoMM2c, Chicago, Ill.—6
Daniel Gully, Y1c, Fayetteville, Texas—3
Earl Hood, TM1c, Parma, Mo.—2
Vard Hutcherson, CMoMM, Elmhurst, N.Y.—6
Roy Jones, MoMM3c, Pittsburgh, Penn.—1
Roland Keckler, CEM, Waynesboro, Penn.—3
James Kellogg, EM2c, Chicago, Ill.—1
George Lakey, S1c, Winston Salem, N.C.—1
Joseph Lane, EM1c, Binghamton, N.Y.—2
Henry Lawson, MoMM3c, Providence, R.I.—1
George Levin, RT2c, Chicago, Ill.—1
Sylvester Lilley, S1c, Camp Ruby, Texas—5
Angelo Lo Cascio, PhM1c, Los Angeles, Calif.—3
John Lonas, CMoMM, Veto, Ala.—6
Harvey Lynn, Jr., TM3c, Arlington, Calif.—2
Frank Majuri, Jr., EM1c, Jamaica, N.Y.—6
Ralph Manning, EM2c, Sacramento, Calif.—5
Frank McGrevy, EM2c, West Springfield, Mass.—3
Gordon McWilliams, Bkr3c, Pacific Grove, Calif.—3
Benjamin Medley, RM2c, Marfa, Texas—3
Chester Miller, CTM, New York, N.Y.—2
Robert Mills, EM3c, Show Low, Ariz.—2
Charles Moffett, Jr., MoMM2c, Woodside, N.Y.—5
Otto Moore, SM2c, Chicago, Ill.—3
Robert Moore, Ck2c, Hattiesburg, Miss.—6
Arthur Morgan, EM2c, Kalispell, Mont.—5
Roy Moss, S1c, Burlington, Okla.—3
Myles Murray, TM2c, Portland, Ore.—5
Thomas Ogilvie, S1c, Monks Corner, S.C.—1
Larry Opisso, MoMM2c, Long Island, N.Y.—4
Freeman Paquet, Jr., GM1c, Vallejo, Calif.—3

Elroy Peck, S1c, Muskegon Heights, Mich.—3
Richard Pick, S1c, Centralia, Ill.—2
Ralph Pratt, S1c, Weymouth, Mass.—1
Robert Przybilla, EM2c, Minneapolis, Minn.—5
Max Rogers, TM3c, North Manchester, Ind.—5
Marvin Rogers, S1c, Central, Ariz.—4
Francis Scheibelhut, MoMM2c, Mishawaka, Ind.—1
Melvin Schwartz, MoMM3c, New York, N.Y.—1
Donald Simon, RM3c, Syracuse, N.Y.—1
Austin Smith, TM2c, Anderson, Calif.—1
John Snipes, Jr., MoMM1c, Asheville, N.C.—6
Walker Snyder, TM3c, Salt Lake City, Utah—4
Lloyd Sommerschield, Cox, Melbourne, Fla.—6
Nelson Spice, MoMM3c, Fort Wayne, Ind.—5
John Swagerty, MoMM3c, Bowie, Texas—5
Leonard White, TM3c, Chicago, Ill.—3
Buford Young, So2c, Dozier, Texas—3
William Zander, MoMM2c, Hankinson, N.D.—1

With the *Harder*, as, indeed, with practically every submarine engaged in the Pacific Theater of War, discrepancies were found to exist between sinkings officially credited by Force Commanders and those allowed in the post-war report of the Joint Army-Navy Assessment Committee. As to damage inflicted, it was clearly impossible for JANAC even to attempt an assessment.

By her two Force Commanders—Comsubpac and Comsubs Seventh Fleet—the *Harder* was credited with having sunk twenty ships, including eight destroyers, for a total of 82,500 tons. Credit for damaging seven ships for 29,000 tons was also given.

By JANAC she is credited with having sunk sixteen ships, including six DD's or DE's, for a total of 54,002 tons. Some of this discrepancy stems from the difference between the estimated tonnage of a ship as seen through a periscope and as listed on Japanese shipping records.

However, other discrepancies arise from disallowed credit for sinkings. Cases in point are:

On 12 November, 1943, the *Harder* got two hits on a

freighter. According to Sam's periscope observations, the after half of the ship sank, tail-high, in ten seconds; the forward part disintegrated.

Later that day—at dusk—he surfaced and, at the range of 100 yards, gunned the waterline of an armed trawler which had evidently blown her own stern off with a depth charge.

Neither of these ships was credited to the *Harder* by JANAC.

As a result of several battles in Sibutu Passage, during the period June 6–10, 1944, the *Harder* claimed to have sunk five destroyers; three were allowed by JANAC.

Regarding these disputed claims, Captain Murray J. Tichenor—now Rear Admiral (Ret.)—who was an observer aboard the *Harder* at the time, says: "The first four DD's sinking was actually witnessed by Sam, Lynch, and Tichenor, as well as some others. My only explanation for being credited with only one DD in Sibutu Passage is that the trailing vessel may have been a much smaller patrol vessel. When we surfaced right after the attack, I went on the bridge and thoroughly concurred with Dealey (and, I believe, Lynch) that we saw two vessels go down from very close range.

"My only explanation for not getting credit for the fifth DD is that we possibly could have erred in our analysis of what occurred. Everyone of us believed that we hit and that the DD blew up right over our heads at a depth of around 100 feet. Later, on surfacing and return to the area, we sighted a ring life buoy in the water. Maybe what blew up over our heads was a depth charge, but I doubt it. We had taken too many of them in the previous four days not to know what they are like."

But that, as we say in submarines, is water over the bridge. Even without these disallowed four ships, the *Harder's* record is splendid.

Sam, by virtue of his personal heroism in combat and, as he insisted, because of the skill and valor of his teammates, became one of the most decorated submariners in the United States Navy. In addition to such major decorations as the Presidential Unit Citation, with one star; the Navy Cross, with three stars; Comdr. Dealey held that most coveted award of all—the Congressional Medal of Honor. At the time this highest honor was recommended by Admiral Christie, Sam was still in the world of living men and had already been presented with the DSC by General MacArthur. Since two decorations cannot be given for the same act of heroism, the General courteously withdrew his DSC to make way for the Medal of Honor. Many months later this decoration was presented to his widow. At that time, in 1945, Wena lacked the strength, so hard had the blow of Sam's death struck her, to go to Washington to receive the award from the President at the White House. Instead, with simple formality, she received it at Santa Monica City Hall from the hand of Comdr. F. S. Gillette, USNR, a former Mayor of the city and a long-time family friend.

Scores of letters poured in to the Dealey family and to Edwina, his wife, from men who had served with Sam—men who admired, respected, worshipped the rugged Texan. Regrettably, space does not permit quoting these. To many who fought beside him, he was a god—no less.

What Australian Colonel Bill Jinkins, who went ashore from the *Harder* to Japanese-held Borneo, has to say undoubtedly expresses the thoughts of hundreds. He wrote:

"I have traveled around the world, crossed the equator three ways, 'under, over and on' in many ships, sea and air. I have never met a more respected and idolized skipper than Sam Dealey. As a fighting commander I have not met his equal. His coolness in the tight spots and his initiative and determination in attack were the best I had the pleasure to witness. His aggression when being hunted saved us time and again.

"I was fortunate to be able to witness the sinking of the destroyer prior to the pickup, the two in the Sibutu Channel, and the last one of the hunter-killer group (as I think you called them) when his pal took off over the hill. I did not see the second last one—the one that blew up on top of us and put everything out including the gyro and nearly us.

"The experience will live with me for all times.

"Right now my son, two years, is not old enough to be told—but I have a story for him when he is.

"I was on the U.S. Submarine *Harder* that sank five destroyers, picked up my pals in Borneo, sat outside Bongao Harbor and observed the Jap fleet being assembled for the Battle of the Philippine Sea, and later reported the composition of the fleet as it sailed. All on the one cruise. I also met the bravest man I have had the pleasure to know."

To Sam's home folks, probably the most valued tribute came from the Commander-in-Chief, Pacific, Texas-born and bred Fleet Admiral Chester W. Nimitz. During an ovation given him by the city of Dallas in October, 1945, Admiral Nimitz, before tens of thousands of fellow Texans, praised Dealey's heroism in the highest terms. For inclusion in this epilogue, the Fleet Admiral generously has written:

"Samuel D. Dealey is a worthy successor to a great sea fighter—John Paul Jones—who, in Revolutionary Days, established for our infant Navy such high standards of skill, devotion to duty, intrepidity, and indomitable will to win. Dealey's record in U.S.S. *Harder* shines brightly in a company of illustrious submarine captains where distinguished performance is the average. His fighting career will live forever as an example to Navy men—particularly submariners."

Tributes to Dealey and his gallant kind were voiced by two of their bitterest enemies.

After the war had ended, Admiral Soemu Toyoda, Commander-in-Chief of the Japanese Combined Fleet, made this statement: "Early in the war I think the submarines were the part of the United States Navy which I considered the greatest threat."

Sam Dealey was one of the brave submarine skippers who made it impossible for Toyoda to change his mind.

The other Japanese comment was intercepted on being sent from a Jap shore station in the Philippine area shortly after the three brand-new coast defense vessels had been sunk by the *Harder* and the *Haddo* on 22 August, 1944. Translated, it read: "We dislike American submariner. He treats us with contempt."

Fully a dozen years have passed since the *Harder* made her final fatal dive. As has been the case in nearly every one of her sister ships which failed to return from combat patrol, she vanished without trace. But during the years that have passed, neither the *Harder* nor those who went down with her have been forgotten by the Navy, by our submariners, or by the Sea Mother on the banks of the Severn. In memory of Sam, a Destroyer Escort, the *Samuel D. Dealey*, was launched in 1953. It was christened by his wife, Edwina Dealey; to honor a gallant name, a new *Harder* has joined the submarine fleet; and at New London's Submarine Base, the magnificent Dealey Welfare and Recreation Center was established in 1945.

Sam Dealey, devoted son and loving husband and father, was a product of peace.

Sam Dealey, deadly torpedo marksman and destroyer killer, was a product of war.

In retrospect one might pause to wonder what might have been the plight of our nation if the small hard core of professional career officers, that stood the gaff of reductions and disarmaments, had yielded to human temptations to quit the service.

Sam exploded into the Torpedo Totin' Texan, boldly unafraid of his enemies because his sense of justice and fair play had been outraged, and because his country's foes were a threat to human freedoms. He symbolizes, in a way, the capacity of *Everyman* to rise far above himself to meet situations that demand strength, skill, and determination.

One of the most interesting analyses ever made of Sam Dealey was worded by Captain Roy S. Benson, USN, a lifetime friend and contemporary of Sam Dealey and, like Sam, a brilliant combat submariner in World War II.

"Frankly," he said, "I was surprised to learn during the war that Sam was doing so well. I don't mean by that, that I thought he would do badly. I expected him to do about as well as the rest of us submariners.

"A study of the records will indicate that most of the damage done to Jap shipping was done, not by a few, but by an everyday good job by many.

"I would have added Sam to that great number. I definitely would not have chosen him as likely to do anything much different from what the great number did—devoted, intelligent, and competent people.

"It is not my purpose to detract from him; on the contrary, he stands as eternal proof of the fact that no one can predict who will do what in a war."

Yes, if only we had ways of knowing the true stature of a man when the voice of emergency calls. Sam Dealey—half-Irish, half-Texan, half-Johnny Reb, and All-American—had that stature in heroic proportions.

On the seaward wall of beautiful Memorial Hall at the United States Naval Academy at Annapolis and outside Sam's old room in Bancroft Hall—the room where he learned the deathless tales of fighting ships and the men who fought them—two simple bronze tablets perpetuate, for all time, the sublime, unassuming heroism and inspired leadership that were the spiritual armor of Samuel David Dealey.

"Blessed are the pure in heart," say the Beatitudes, "for they shall see God."

No one who knew Sam Dealey can doubt that in death he went to stand before his Maker as he had stood before Him all his life—

Pure in heart and unafraid.

★★★★★★★★★★★★★★★★★★★★★★★★★★★★★★★★★★★★★★★★★★★★★★★

# Appendix

## Complete Complement of *U.S.S. Harder* from Commissioning to the Sixth Patrol

| NAME with RANK or RATE | HOME TOWN | PATROLS |
|---|---|---|
| Altherr, Charles Raymond, MoMM2c | Wellston, Ohio | 2-3-4-5-6 |
| Archbald, John Joseph, Jr., RM2c | | 4 |
| | | |
| Balevicz, Adolph Michael, TM1c | North Arlington, Mass. | 1-2-3 |
| Barber, Robert O., MoMM3c | St. Paul, Minn. | 5-6 |
| Beebe, William F., Ensign | | 2 |
| Benson, Ernest Louis, S1c | Poquonock, Conn. | 1 |
| Berg, Richard Munger, RT1c | Houston, Texas | 1-2-3 |
| Bishop, Thomas Rosey, EM2 | | 2 |
| Beutelspacher, Walter F., SC3c | Baltimore, Md. | 5-6 |
| Blanton, Osie Wheeler, TM1c | Houston, Texas | 1 |
| Blum, Robert Aloysious, F3c | Joliet, Illinois | 2-3-4-5-6 |
| Bodnar, Daniel, F2 | Groton, Conn. | 1 |
| Boshart, James Isaac, S1c | Wayland, Iowa | 1 |
| Bourg, Sumter, GM3c | Los Angeles, Calif. | 5-6 |
| Bradshaw, Everett Burnett, CPAM(PA) | Turlock, Calif. | 1-2-3 |
| Brock, Clarence C., Jr., Ensign | Washington, D.C. | 4 |
| Brostrom, Wayne Allen, SM3 | Staples, Minn. | 1-2-3-4-5-6 |
| Bryson, William Jackson, S1c | Berrysville, Ark. | 1-2-3 |
| Buczek, Frank Michael, EM1 | Gonic, N.H. | First Sailing |
| Buckner, Thomas W., Ensign | Nashville, Tenn. | 3-4-5-6 |
| Bull, Calvin Arthur, RM3c | Springfield, Neb. | 2-3-4-5-6 |
| | | |
| Callaway, Richard Hubert, MoMM1c | | 1 |
| Carver, Audley Methen, CSC | Joliet, Montana | First Sailing |
| Cash, Vivian J., MoMM1c | | 5-6 |
| Chenard, Roland Raymond, F1c | Fall River, Mass. | 6 |
| Clark, Clarence Cleo, MoMM1c | Chehalis, Wash. | 1-2-3 |
| Clark, Wilbur Lee, RT3c | New Hampton, Miss. | 4-5-6 |

325

| NAME with RANK or RATE | HOME TOWN | PATROLS |
|---|---|---|
| Conley, John Chester, MoMM2c | Watsonville, Calif. | 2-3-4-5-6 |
| Crask, Harold Frederick, S2c | Trinidad, Colo. | 4-5-6 |
| Cromwell, James Edward, StM2c | Richmond, Va. | 6 |
| Czegledy, Alex, TM3c | | 1 |
| | | |
| Dahlheimer, Donald Bernard, F1c | | 2-3-4-5-6 |
| Dallessandro, Vincent Louis, TM2c | Buffalo, N.Y. | 1-2-3-4-5-6 |
| Dawson, Wesle Edward, CS1 | Providence, R.I. | First Sailing |
| Dealey, Samuel David, LCDR | Dallas, Texas | 1-2-3-4-5-6 |
| Del Signore, Carl, TM3c | Coketon, W.Va. | 1-2-3-4 |
| De Voe, Edwin Warren, F1c | Bristol, Pa. | 6 |
| Diamond, William V., RM1c | Pensacola, Fla. | 5-6 |
| Dubord, Robert Vernon, EM3c | | 2-3-4 |
| Dugan, John Vincent, SC2c | | 2-3 |
| Dunn, Martin Peter, S2c | | 2-3-4-5 |
| Dvorak, Frank Charles, MoMM1c | Montville, Conn. | 1 |
| | | |
| Easler, Bernard Lee, SM3c | | 4-5 |
| Edgar, James McKinley, FC2c | Monroe, La. | 2-3-4-6 |
| Eletto, Richard Joseph, S2c | | 2-3-4-5 |
| | | |
| Finney, Carl Edwin, CMoM(AA) | Philadelphia, Pa. | 1-2-3-4-5-6 |
| Fischer, William Ira, Jr., S1c | Atlantic City, N.J. | 1 |
| Fisher, George Eugene, MoMM3c | | 4-5-6 |
| Formalo, Santo Hubert, TM2c | Key West, Fla. | 1 |
| | | |
| Garbati, Edward Peter, Jr., GM2c | Groton, Conn. | First Sailing |
| Geletka, Michael Christopher, MoMM1c | Stoneham, Mass. | 1-2-3-4-5 |
| Gifford, Robert Lee, S2c | | 2-3-4-5-6 |
| Givens, Aubrey Willis, RM3 | Evansville, Ind. | 1-2-3 |
| Glave, John Robert, QM3c | Bayonne, N.J. | 1-2-3-4-5 |
| Glueckert, Joseph Lewis, F3 | Chicago, Ill. | 1-2-3-4-5-6 |
| Goode, William O., MoMM1c | Benham, Ky. | First Sailing |
| Guiang, Rufino, CST | Province Zamboango, P.I. | 1-2-3 |
| Gully, Daniel John, Y1c | | 4-5-6 |
| | | |
| Haddock, Ronal Thurman, S2c | | 4-5 |
| Haloupek, Walter Orville, Ensign | Belle Plaine, Iowa | 6 |
| Hatfield, Hiram Delbert, CRM(PA) | Groton, Conn. | 1-2-3-4 |
| Hettinger, Thomas Charles, F3c | Philadelphia, Pa. | First Sailing & 2-3-4-5 |
| Hinton, Earl V., TM2c | | 5 |
| Holden, William Frazee, EN1(SS) | Jacksonville, Fla. | First Sailing |
| Holt, Francis James, S1c | | 2-3 |
| Hood, Earl Verner, TM1c | Parma, Mo. | 6 |
| Horst, Donald Earle, LTjg | Lebanon, Pa. | 1 |
| Hoschke, Edwin Herbert, S1 | Annadale on Hudson, N.Y. | 1 |

| NAME with RANK or RATE | HOME TOWN | PATROLS |
|---|---|---|
| Hubert, Joseph Rowe, DEM(PA) | Port Orchard, Wash. | 1 |
| Hudson, J. N., GM2 | Amarillo, Texas | 1-2-3 |
| Hutcherson, Vard William, MoMM2c | Jackson Heights, L.I., N.Y. | 1-2-3-4-5-6 |
| Imrie, David Gibson, S1c | Washington, Maine | First Sailing |
| James, Daniel Richard, LTjg | | 5-6 |
| Jeske, Otto Albert, EM2 | Boston, Mass. | 1 |
| Johnson, Ralph B., CMoMM(PA) | | 1 |
| Jones, Roy Edward, MoMM3c | Greenfield, Pa. | 6 |
| Keckler, Roland Wilbur, EM1c | | 4-5-6 |
| Kellogg, James Hubbell, EM2c | Chicago, Ill. | 6 |
| Keough, James Charles, TM3 | Seattle, Wash. | 1-2-3-4-5 |
| Kernan, Howard Albert, MoMM2c | | 2-3-4-5 |
| Kerns, Eugene Max, LT | Melrose, Mass. | 1-2-3 |
| King, Henry, Jr., TM3 | San Diego, Calif. | 1 |
| Kurczakowski, Edward Thomas, EM3c | | 4-5 |
| Lakey, George William, S1c | Winston Salem, N.C. | 6 |
| Lane, Joseph M., F1c | | 5-6 |
| Larimore, Billie Eugene, TM2c | Altamont, Ill. | 1 |
| Lawson, Henry Wilfred, MoMM3c | Providence, R.I. | 6 |
| Levin, Evert J., LTjg | Mt. Iron, Minn. | 3-4-5-6 |
| Lilley, Sylvester Benjamin, S1c | | 2-3-4-5-6 |
| Lo Cascio, Angelo, PhM1c | | 4-5-6 |
| Logan, Samuel Moore, LTjg | Owensboro, Ky. | 1-2-3-4-5-6 |
| Lonas, John Payton, CMoMM(PA) | Veto, Alabama | 1-2-3-4-5-6 |
| Lynch, Frank Curtis, Jr., LT | Davon, Pa. | 1-2-3-4-5 |
| Lynn, Harvey A., Jr., TM3c | | 5-6 |
| Majuri, Frank Paul, Jr., EM3c | Jamaica, N.Y. | 1-2-3-4-5-6 |
| Manning, Ralph Erskine, EM3c | Sacramento, Calif. | 2-3-4-5-6 |
| Maurer, John Howard, LCDR | Washington, D.C. | 1-2-3 |
| Mays, Elmo Bruce, CTM(AA) | Paris, Ky. | 1-2-3-4-5 |
| McCutcheon, Donald Frederick, EM3 | Holden, Mass. | 1-2-3-4-5 |
| McGrevy, Frank Bartlett, EM3c | | 4-5-6 |
| McMasters, James Arthur, Y1 | Brooklyn, N.Y. | 1 |
| McNamara, Robert George, Jr., EM3 | Colorado Springs, Colo. | 1-2-3-4-5 |
| McWilliams, Gordon Keith, BKR3c | | 4-5-6 |
| Medley, Benjamin Ralph, RM2c | | 4-5-6 |
| Melton, Robert Hamilton, MoMM2c | Louisville, Ky. | First Sailing |
| Miller, Chester, CTM(PA) | | 5-6 |
| Mills, Robert R., EM3 | | 5-6 |
| Moffett, Charles Allen, Jr., F1c | | 2-3-4-5-6 |
| Moore, Robert, CK3 | Hattiesburg, Miss. | 1-2-3-4-5-6 |
| Moore, Otto, Jr., SM3c | | 4-5-6 |

| NAME with RANK or RATE | HOME TOWN | PATROLS |
|---|---|---|
| Morgan, Arthur Bernard, EM3c | | 2–3–4–5–6 |
| Morrison, Harold William, F1c | | 2–3–4–5 |
| Moss, Roy Benjamin, S2c | | 4–5–6 |
| Mount, Victor Leon, MoMM2c | Dallas, Texas | 1–2–3–4 |
| Murray, Myles Harlan, TM3c | | 2–4–5–6 |
| | | |
| Nichols, Ray Hamby, MoMM1c | Boise, Idaho | 1 |
| | | |
| Offner, Milton, CMoMM(AA) | Brooklyn, N.Y. | 1 |
| Ogilvie, Thomas Daggett, S1c | Monks Corner, S.C. | 6 |
| Olender, John, TM3c | Brooklyn, N.Y. | First Sailing |
| Opisso, Larry Anzo, F1c | | 2–3–4–5–6 |
| | | |
| Padilla, Johnnie, S2c | | 2–3 |
| Paquet, Freeman, Jr., GM1c | | 4–5–6 |
| Patberg, Kent Henry, F2c | Huntingberg, Ind. | First Sailing |
| Peck, Elroy Rufus, S2c | | 4–5–6 |
| Peck, Richard S., S1c | | 5 |
| Penzes, Louis Joseph, GM2 | | 1 |
| Phillips, Keith Rufus, LT | W. Los Angeles, Calif. | 1–2–3–4 |
| Pick, Richard Sample, S1c | Centralia, Ill. | 6 |
| Platt, Joseph Jesse, EM2 | Olathe, Colo. | 1–2–3–4 |
| Plume, George Gustave, Jr., SM1c | | 2–3 |
| Polk, James Charles, EM1 | Philadelphia, Pa. | 1–2–3 |
| Pratt, Ralph Edson, S1c | Weymouth, Mass. | 6 |
| Provencher, Rolland Sylvio, Jr., QM2 | Suncook, N.H. | 1–2–3 |
| Przybilla, Robert Peter, EM3c | | 2–3–4–5–6 |
| | | |
| Rainstrick, Richard A., EM3c | | 5 |
| Rak, Mike, CY(AA) | | 2–3 |
| Rhodes, Leinster Gerald, RM2c | San Mateo, Calif. | First Sailing |
| Roche, Thomas Edward, TM2 | | 1 |
| Rogers, Max Myrval, S1c | | 2–3–4 |
| Rogers, Mervin M., S1c | Central, Ariz. | 6 |
| Roosevelt, Robert Barnwell, Ensign | Norfolk, Va. | 5–6 |
| Ryan, Francis Xavier, F2 | Brooklyn, N.Y. | 1–2–3–4 |
| Ryback, Walter, F1 | Clifton, N.J. | 1–2–3 |
| | | |
| Sadowski, Frank, MoMM3c | | 5 |
| Sammut, Andrew Patrick, SC3 | Charlesville, N.Y. | 1 |
| Sampson, Philip T., Ensign | Mound, Minn. | 4–5–6 |
| Sauvageau, Joseph Gordon, MoMM2c | Poquonnock Bridge, Conn. | 1–2–3–4 |
| Savicki, Joseph, TM2 | | 1 |
| Schelling, Arthur Leonard, RT2c | | 4–5 |
| Scheibelhut, Francis Xavier, MoMM2c | Mishawaka, Ind. | 6 |
| Scheutzow, Elmer George, F2 | | 1 |
| Schwartz, Melvin, MoMM3c | | 5–6 |

| NAME with RANK or RATE | HOME TOWN | PATROLS |
|---|---|---|
| Simon, Donald John, RM3c | Syracuse, N.Y. | 6 |
| Skidmore, Charles Garner, EM3c | | 2–3–4–5 |
| Skiles, Nornan Fearing, RM3 | Wilmington, N.C. | 1–2–3–4–5 |
| Sloggett, Vernard Leslie, CTM(PA) | Fremont, Neb. | 1–2–6 |
| Smith, Austin, TM2c | Anderson, Colo. | 6 |
| Smith, Paul Leslie, TM1 | Belhaven, N.C. | First Sailing |
| Snipes, John William, Jr., F1 | Asheville, N.C. | 1–2–3–4–5–6 |
| Snyder, Walker Ncal, S1c | Salt Lake City, Utah | 2–3–4–6 |
| Sommerschield, Lloyd Hammond, S1c | Melbourne, Fla. | 1–2–3–4–5–6 |
| Spice, Nelson, F2c | | 2–3–4–5 |
| Spoonhour, Alfred Earl, StM2c | | 4–5–6 |
| Staley, Joseph J., Jr., LTCDR | | 2 |
| Strebig, Richard Willlam, RM3 | | 1 |
| Studstill, Edward Lee, GM3 | Ft. Meyers, Fla. | 1–2–3–4 |
| Swagerty, John T., F2c | | 2–3–4–5–6 |
| Talerico, Samuel Peter, F2 | Enterprise, W.Va. | 1 |
| Thomason, J. W., SC1 | Los Angeles, Calif. | 1–2–3–4 |
| Vance, Ward, S2c | | 3 |
| Way, Raymond Gaither, CSM(AA) | New London, Conn. | 1 |
| Weidenback, Rudolph Fred, FC3 | San Francisco, Calif. | 1 |
| Weidman, Lloyd Irwin, DEM(AA) | Vallejo, Calif. | 1–2–3–5 |
| White, Leonard M., S1c | | 4–5–6 |
| Willibey, Phillips Edwin, F3 | | 1 |
| Wittenborn, Charles Gene, FCS3c | | 4–5 |
| Yandell, Leon Tower, CMoMM(AA) | Portland, Ore. | 1–2–3–4 |
| Young, Buford John, SC3c | | 4–5–6 |
| Young, William Franklin, TM3 | Silver Spring, Md. | 1–2–3–4–5 |
| Zander, William Gordon, MoMM2c(T) | Hankinson, N.D. | 6 |

# Join the Allies on the Road to Victory
# BANTAM WAR BOOKS

☐ 26350-1 **BAA, BAA BLACK SHEEP** P. Boyington     $4.95

☐ 26777-9 **DAY OF INFAMY** W. Lord     $4.95

☐ 28640-4 **THE LAST 100 DAYS** J. Toland     $6.95

☐ 26721-3 **CLEAR THE BRIDGE** R. O'Kane     $4.95

☐ 28784-2 **THE NIGHT HAMBURG DIED** M. Caidin     $4.95

☐ 24487-6 **STUKA PILOT** H. Rudel     $4.95

☐ 22897-8 **THE BATTLE FOR GUADALCANAL** S. Griffith II     $4.95

☐ 26729-9 **BLACK THURSDAY** M. Caidin     $4.50

☐ 27489-9 **BAT 21** Anderson     $4.95

☐ 27055-9 **COMPANY COMMANDER** MacDonald     $4.95

☐ 28603-X **THUNDERBOLT: THE FABULOUS U.S. 56th FIGHTER GROUP** Cardin     $4.95

☐ 26316-1 **WITH THE OLD BREED** Sledge     $4.95

Buy them at your local bookstore or use this page to order.

**Bantam Books, Dept. WW2, 414 East Golf Road, Des Plaines, IL 60016**

Please send me the items I have checked above. I am enclosing $\_\_\_\_
(please add $2.50 to cover postage and handling). Send check or money
order, no cash or C.O.D.s please.

Mr/Ms _____

Address _____

City/State _____ Zip _____

WW2–9/91

Please allow four to six weeks for delivery
Prices and availability subject to change without notice.

# THE STORY OF AN AMERICAN HERO

☐ YEAGER: An Autobiography       25674-2/$5.95

The story of Chuck Yeager who rose from rural boyhood to become the one man who, more than any other, led America into space. From his humble West Virginia roots to his adventures as a World War II fighter pilot; from the man who escaped from German-occupied France to the test pilot who first broke the sound barrier: this is the real story of the man with the RIGHT STUFF.

☐ YEAGER: AN AUTOBIOGRAPHY is now on
     audiocassette!       45012-3/$7.95

This exclusive 60-minute audio adaptation of the bestselling autobiography, YEAGER: AN AUTOBIOGRAPHY, features General Chuck Yeager telling in his own words the amazing story of his life and exploits.

☐ PRESS ON! Further Adventures in the Good Life
     by Chuck Yeager       28216-6/$4.95

PRESS ON! is a remarkable portrait of a remarkable individual—it completely captures Yeager's head-on approach to living the good life. Using extensive examples and stories from all the times of his life, Chuck Yeager makes it clear that he always did—and always will—live the way he wants to.

**Look for both these books at your bookstore or use this page to order:**

Bantam Books, Dept. YE2, 414 East Golf Road, Des Plaines, IL 60016

Please send me the items I have checked above. I am enclosing $_____
(please add $2.00 to cover postage and handling). Send check or money
order, no cash or C.O.D.s please. (Tape offer good in USA only.)

Mr/Ms _____

Address _____

City/State _____ Zip _____

Please allow four to six weeks for deliver
Prices and availability subject to change without notice.

YE2–11/90

# *William L. Shirer*

## A Memoir of a Life and the Times Vol. 1 & 2

☐ 34204-5   TWENTIETH CENTURY JOURNEY,
             The Start 1904-1930                     $12.95

☐ 34179-0   THE NIGHTMARE YEARS,
             1930-1940                          $14.95

In Volume 1, Shirer recounts American/European history as seen through his eyes.  In Volume 2, he provides an intensely personal vision of the crucible out of which the Nazi monster appeared.

---

# *Charles B. MacDonald*

☐ 34226-6   A TIME FOR TRUMPETS         $14.95
The untold story of the Battle of the Bulge.

---

**Bantam Books, Dept. WW3, 414 East Golf Road, Des Plaines, IL 60016**

Please send me the items I have checked above.  I am enclosing $_____
(please add $2.50 to cover postage and handling).  Send check or money
order, no cash or C.O.D.s please.

Mr/Ms _____

Address _____

City/State _____ Zip _____

WW3–7/91

Please allow four to six weeks for delivery
Prices and availability subject to change without notice.